D1232879

Leading through the Troubles

A life in the GAA
PADDY MacFLYNN
with Alan Rodgers

Published in September 2013 by
Lumen Publishing, Main Street, Beragh, Co Tyrone.

All Rights Reserved
Alan Rodgers

This book is sold subject to the condition that it shall not, by way of trade or otherwise, be lend, sold, hired out or otherwise circulated without the publisher's prior consent in any form of binding or cover other than that in which it is published and without a similar condition including this condition being imposed on the subsequent purchaser. No part of this book may be copied, stored in a retrieval system or transmitted in any form or by any means without the permission of the publisher.

A CIP record for this book is available from the British Library.

ISBN – 978-1-869919-20-7

Dedicated to
Denny and Margaret McInnes

CONTENTS

Foreword

Introduction

Epilogue

Bibliography

FOREWORD

Is cúis mhór áthais dom no focail seo a leanas a scríobh don leabhar tabhachtach seo agus muid ag ceiliúradh saol CLG Pádraig MacFloinn.

It gives me great pleasure to pen these words to acknowledge the publication of this most welcome addition to the GAA library, one that outlines the wide and highly valued contribution to the GAA of Paddy McFlynn.

Paddy is a man known the length and breadth of Ireland, a person held in the highest of regard and someone whose expertise, experience and wisdom is sought and given on a regular basis. He had the distinction of serving as Uachtarán between the years of 1979 and 1982 and he made an impression on all of those who were fortunate enough to work alongside him during his term and indeed both before and afterwards too in various different roles and capacities.

It goes without saying that the years in question brought with them their own challenges as the Troubles raged and the Association had to carefully navigate its way through what is commonly regarded as one of most testing times of modern Irish history. The insight, leadership and fortitude provided by people like Paddy was hugely instrumental in ensuring that the GAA succeeded in coming through this phase with its focus on the promotion of our games and culture intact.

To focus on Paddy's role as Uachtarán alone would be to do a disservice to a lifetime of involvement in the GAA. For that reason it is fitting and proper that an attempt has been made to bring the full story between two covers in a publication such as this.

Not only will such an exercise preserve and place on record details that will form a valuable addition to the GAA library, they will also rekindle memories of those who were alongside Paddy when the various different events and passages of time were unfolding.

They will also inform younger readers and members of the GAA of the great lengths and commitment that so many of our people go to, to better the Association and to leave it on a better footing for those who follow. To that end there is no doubt that we are indebted to Paddy McFlynn and I am delighted to share in the celebration of his lifelong involvement in the GAA through the publication of this book.

Rath Dé ar an obair,

Liam Ó Néill

Liam Ó Néill
Uachtarán Chumann Lúthchleas Gael

FOREWORD

Pádraig MacFloinn

It is a great honour for me to write these few words in recognition of the outstanding contribution of Pádraig MacFloinn to the GAA and to the Country as a whole. I first knew Pádraig due to his involvement with the South Down Board and the Down County Board but it has been in the last thirty five years that I have really got to know the man who has worked so diligently for our Association over most of his life.

He is meticulous in everything that he is involved in and he gave the same consideration and support to everything that required his attention. The early days in his beloved Derry and his pride in the O'Donovan Rossa GAC, Magherafelt, his role as Secretary of the Derry County Board or his many roles within Down. His outstanding service to the Ulster Council as a County Delegate for both Derry and Down, Treasurer from 1947 until 1954, Vice President from 1958 until 1960 and President of the Ulster Council from 1961 until 1963. During this time he saw Derry and Down make their breakthrough in winning their first senior championships.

Pádraig Mac Floinn, however made his greatest contribution in the leadership of the GAA as President from 1979 until 1982. He was there at a time when the days were difficult but like all other aspects of his life he dealt with the issues of the day with courage and courtesy. The views of the GAA people were important to him and in a quiet and efficient manner ensured that the Association was strengthened by adversity and united by its ideals.

The inadequacy of these few words in encapsulating a lifetime generously given to our great Association are clear but I had the privilege of travelling with Pádraig on many occasions to wakes and funerals and even in recent times was astounded at his interest in the affairs of the GAA. He read the minutes, followed the stories and he knew what was the way forward. It was great to listen to his enthusiasm. While he spent most of his life in Down, where he met and married his late wife Kathleen, he became active in Down's affairs, was a respected part of Tullylish, where he made friends in great numbers including the late Billy Byrne but the genes of Pádraig MacFloinn are in Derry and the O'Donovan Rossa Club. We, regardless of place are all the better for the contribution to Ireland and the GAA throughout a long and significant life of a great man. Well done Pádraig.

Dónall Ó Murchú,
Rúnaí, Comhairle Uladh

INTRODUCTION

IF for some reason, you thought that this book might be the usual account of the goings-on in GAA meeting rooms from Magherafelt to Croke Park and many places in between – then think again.

The former President, Paddy MacFlynn, through his biographer, Alan Rodgers, tells a far more colourfully eventful story than that of the ninety odd years of his action-packed life.

So, you will marvel at his memory and his power of recall as you read about his days as a lively inquisitive youngster in the town of Magherafelt and its surrounds. Those days in the 1920s when the train still called, when butchers killed their own pork, publicans bottled their own stout and teachers still used canes to encourage learning.

You will progress through his exploits on the rugby fields of Rainey through to his 'breaking of the GAA's ban' at Twickenham Internationals, as a student at St Mary's Teacher Training College in leafy Strawberry Hill. And his observation of the preparations in London for World War Two just before the completion of his studies.

The founding of the O'Donovan Rossas in Magherafelt and his subsequent rise through the GAA ranks which led to the Ulster Presidency and eventually to his election as the GAA's 27th President at the time of the Troubles.

So, 'Leading through the Troubles' definitely is much more than a 'A Life in the GAA' – much more.

Thanks in particular are extended to Donal McAnallen, Connla Young, Ciaran Woods, Bertie Leckey, Sean Og McAteer, Anne Murphy, Mick Millar and Rory MacFlynn for advice, proof-reading and other assistance provided.

Thanks are also extended to Frank Rodgers for his guidance and proof-reading throughout this project.

Last, but by no means least, the unfailing friendship and dedication of Noel Foster, Bellaghy, Co Derry and Margaret and Denny McInnes, Co Down has been absolutely vital in ensuring that 'Leading through the Troubles' has reached fruition.

Finally, to Paddy MacFlynn for his support, co-operation and kindness throughout the research, writing and completion of the book. May it be a fitting acknowledgement of his loyalty, friendship work and service to the GAA and all aspects of life.

Alan Rodgers
Beragh, August 26th, 2013.

GAA PRESIDENTS 1884-2013

Maurice Davin (Tipperary) 1884-1887

EM Bennett (Clare) - 1887-1887

Peter J Kelly (Galway) - 1889-1889

Frank B Dineen (Limerick) - 1895-1898

Michael Deering (Cork) 1898-1901

James Nowlan (Kilkenny) 1901-1921

Daniel McCarthy (Dublin) - 1921-1924

Patrick Breen (Wexford) 1924-1926

Liam Clifford (Limerick) 1926-1928

Sean Ryan (Dublin) 1928-1932

Sean McCarthy (Cork) 1932-1935

Robert O'Keefe (Laois) 1935-1938

Padraig McNamee (Antrim) 1938-1943

Seamus Gardiner (Tipperary) 1943-1946

Dan O'Rourke (Roscommon) 1946-1949

MV O'Donoghue (Waterford) 1952-1955

Seamus McFerran (Antrim) 1955-1958

Dr JJ Stuart (Dublin) 1958-1961

Hugh Byrne (Wicklow) 1961-1964

Alf Murray (Armagh) 1964-1967

Seamus ORiain (Tipperary) 1967-1970

Pat Fanning (Waterford) 1970-1973

Dr Donal Keenan (Roscommon) 1973-1976

Con Murphy (Cork) 1976-1979

PADDY MacFLYNN (DOWN) 1979-1982

Paddy Buggy (Kilkenny) - 1982-1984

Dr Mick Loftus (Mayo) 1985-1987

John Dowling (Offaly) 1988-1991

Peter Quinn (Fermanagh) 1991-1994

Jack Boothman (Wicklow) 1994-1997

Joe McDonagh (Galway) 1997-2000

Sean McCague (Monaghan) 2000-2003

Sean Kelly (Kerry) 2003-2006

Nickey Brennan (Kilkenny) 2006-2009

Christy Cooney (Cork)2009-2012

Liam O'Neill (Laois) 2012-2015

Over 20,000 GAA members from throughout the north pictured marching from the Falls Road to Dunville Park to Casement Park in December 1980.
Picture courtesy of Belfast Media Group.

LEADING THROUGH THE TROUBLES

Pádraig Mac Flainn
President of the G.A.A.   Thursday 25/2/82

Finally President I must start of this note by apologising for not being able to write to you in our own language, (which I am in the process of learning at the minute) But dispite this tradgey I beg you to have patience with me and kindly help me with my request if you please.

I am here in the H-Blocks of Long Kesh and I would dearly love to Promote the G.A.A. sport. Now to go about this properly I believe I would need to start of finally by doing a lecture or lectures on the entire history of the sport and then progeed from there, But unfortunately I do not have this information to do lecture or lectures of this kind, so that is the reason why I am writing to you President, and I beg you President Please do not let me down, Please forward a good lecture or lectures on to me as soon as possible, Below are a few points which might let you know the kind of lecture or lectures that I am looking for, though I dont say you know exactly what I need for such a lecture.

1. I would like to know the very first existence of Gaelic football, Hurling, Handball, that was ever played, on Irish soil, How many took part in a game, what way the scoring was done, How long the game lasted, The type of ball +, Sticks which were used in those days, How the games Gaelic football, Hurling, and Hand-Ball, come into being. Were there many people interested in the games at that time, was it promoted in any way, plus everything in general about Gaelic football, Hurling, Handball, and any other sport that at that time, was played in Ireland at that time.

2. When the G.A.A. was first Founded and by whom, the rules that were laid down at that time, and how they have changed over, the years right up to this present day, When was Gaelic football + Hurling first played on a propers pitch, was club football and Hurling played before they were played at county level, and for how long did clubs represent the county.

3. at what times did the differents grades of G.A.A. come into being example Senior, Junior, Intermediate, U-21, Minor, and other grades, example school football, this for both football and Hurling, as well as camogie and girls football, and at what time did the National football and Hurling Leagues come into being, as well as other things in general.

4. what is the present standard size of Gaelic football pitches, and Hurling pitches, and camogie pitches, as well as the present day rules, for these sports.

5. I would like a list of the county which has won the all Ireland most times at all grades in football, and Hurling, and camogie, and girls football, as well as the National football, and Hurling Leagues.

6. also when was Gaelic

LEADING THROUGH THE TROUBLES

Perhaps it was appropriate that a President from the north led the GAA through one of the most difficult periods of the whole 'Troubles' between 1979 and 1981. My northern background and residence in Laurencetown, right in the middle of the north, provided me with a deeper understanding of the issues and people involved than might otherwise have been the case.

It was clear to me as a member of the Management Committee and later as GAA President that a lot of the people down south simply didn't understand what was happening. There was the potential that the GAA could have been split and there was absolutely no doubt in my mind about the seriousness of the situation which we faced.

This was brought home to during the Hunger Strikes when I decided to attend an Ulster Council meeting. Liam Mulvihill expressed concern afterwards that the visit was made alone. But there was severe criticism from the counties in attendance. This anger centred on what they felt were the policies being adopted by the GAA. The toughest time which I experienced was at an Ulster Council meeting when the delegates were displeased, accusing me of sitting on the fence, doing nothing. I thought I was handling the situation well.

Nevertheless, it was clear that something needed to be done to raise awareness of the issues involved and their impact. There was a meeting of the national Management Committee subsequently, to which each of the nine Ulster chairmen were invited. On my prompting, each one of them related exactly what was happening in their respective counties.

Many of the members of the Management committee were shocked to hear what was going on and what was being faced by the GAA members within them. Each county brought a different story; Derry, Tyrone and Armagh which were very troublesome.

There was terrible tension and uncertainty about what was going to happen next. Yet many people down south simply had not appreciated the extent of the pressure. It wasn't until the nine Ulster chairmen attended that meeting in Croke Park that the level of awareness began to improve. They gave a very clear view of what was going on and the number of clubs involved.

The central issue was whether or not the GAA should openly lend support to the campaign of the H-Block committee. In the later part of 1980, I think it was late October or early November, myself, Liam Mulvihill, my good friend, Alf Murray, and a number of other GAA officials met with this group. Their delegation included Bernadette McAliskey.

The National H-Block committee wanted to harness public support for an end to certain conditions being imposed on the prisoners. Their demands were that they had the right prisoners, the right to organise educational and recreational facilities, to have one weekly visit and send out one letter and receive one parcel weekly.

This presented a challenging situation for the GAA. The strength of feeling in Derry, Armagh, Antrim and Tyrone was very clear. But the chairman in Down at that time never allowed any discussion on the H-blocks. The view, which I supported, was that the GAA was a non-political organisation which existed merely to promote Gaelic games and culture.

The H-Block committee applied a lot of pressure for the GAA to officially back them. This would have meant them having a presence in every parish. To get the GAA behind them would represent a major boost.

What the H-Block committee did was send an invitation to clubs to take part in a black flag parade, which usually prompted a debate at club level that could be extremely bitter. I was afraid of all these clubs coming out in favour of the H-Blocks rather than following the official GAA line. If this had happened, then the danger was there for them to start up on their own outside the GAA, and this would have spilt the Association straight down the middle.

I had been elected to run the Association as President rather than presiding over its demise. It was a time of great stress and worry and the people of the south didn't understand.

The tension in the north was palpable and heightened by the propaganda war. But our policy was to stay clear of political issues such as the H-Blocks. As President, I had every sympathy with the prisoners, their demands were reasonable and should have been granted on humanitarian grounds. This was always made clear and the GAA never at any stage came out to support the very strong campaign launched by the H-Block committees.

That was a very difficult stance to adhere to. There were members of the GAA's Management Committee who held very strong views on both sides of the issue. Two in particular were Donal 'Duck' Whelan, a former hurler from Waterford and one of the two national Trustees of the GAA. He was caught helping to import arms on the Claudia in the early 1970s. Another was Aidan McGowan from Sligo, whose whole family were very strongly republican.

I knew that some disagreed vehemently with what I was doing as GAA President in staying clear of direct support for the H-Blocks. However, there was still full support from them simply because their loyalty to the association came first. The H-Blocks arose at any and every function which I attended in the north.

In 1980, there were also concerns about the potential threat of violence through holding the annual congress in Newcastle. The event went well and I was pleased that it was held

Bernadette Devlin McAliskey, Fergus O'Hare, Maura McCrory, Dick Gregory (American comic and hunger strike protestor), Jim Gibney at a press conference in May 1981 in the Glen Inn with members of the H-Block committee. Picture courtesy of Belfast Media Group.

there. But at the same time, it was vitally important that the GAA was not complacent when it came to issues of violence. It would have been reckless to assume that there was not a risk attached to holding the congress in Newcastle.

Correspondence from various people around the country also heightened this pressure. In October 1980, the decision was taken to ban a H-block protest on GAA grounds in Co Down. A few days later a Kildare man wrote to me saying that the support for the move from a Unionist MP speaks for itself. He went on to relate how our move meant that the GAA was now following the British government on the H-blocks and that he was withdrawing his membership.

In January 1980, a letter-writer from Enniscorthy in Co Wexford stressed that the GAA should simply tell the British soldiers to 'get the hell out of our country.' He pointed out that the games were the most important thing in Irish life, but that the language and culture had fallen to the 'English way' and that Croke Park could be 'held mainly responsible.' Other letters accused me of threatening the future of the association through my actions in relation to the north. There was certainly a steady flow of correspondence during this period, and it offers a fascinating glimpse into the strongly held views of ordinary GAA people who took the trouble to write to me as president.

In April 1981, the situation was further heightened by a newspaper advertisement from five Tyrone clubs supporting one of the hunger strikers, Bobby Sands, in the Fermanagh and South Tyrone by-election. Once again, this was used as an opportunity to criticise the so-called 'ambivalence' of the GAA towards the violence and political issues which were going on. It was said that this advert was a 'blatant breach' of Rule 7 that the GAA is non-party-political.

The allegations that the GAA supported violence and were ambivalent towards it were regularly made. However, nobody produced any proof. The simple fact of the matter was that the Association condemned violence, I spoke to many people involved and they were quite satisfied with this attitude.

Tom Woulfe from Dublin wrote to me on a number of occasions about this and other issues. In 1981 he proposed a motion to Congress which sought to introduce an 'anti-violence' clause into the GAA constitution. He felt that this would remove any implication of support for violence, despite the fact that we had held a consistent line on this issue.

There were times during this period when I simply didn't know what way to turn. It was a very worrying time indeed and several people stood by my shoulder at the time. Two of them were Liam Mulvihill and Alf Murray. Their help to me during that period was invaluable.

Seamus Clarke from Ballycastle and Sean Stinson lambasted me for not supporting the cause despite the fact that I was great friends with them. Seamus, who has since died, wrote a draft history of the GAA in Antrim, but its rather polemical tone prevented it from being published'.

The situation at grassroots level

One of the most important areas of concerns was the situation among clubs who were at the coalface of what was happening. The difficulties which many of them faced should not be underestimated.

On a number of occasions I visited clubs who were experiencing difficulties. Usually what happened was that a couple of activists pushed the need for support for the H-Blocks. My strong line was that if this policy was pushed through then the club and ultimately the GAA would be split.

The people with whom I had most sympathy with were the families with teenagers and I spoke to many at that time. They did not want the GAA becoming involved. Their great fear was that their young children – young lads and girls - would be sucked into the armed struggle if they were out on parade with black flags. They told me that the GAA should be concentrating on playing the games and promoting Irish culture, but nothing more. Teenagers can be a law onto themselves at times and we had to try and do the right thing.

My native South Derry was experienced very great problems at that time. I was extremely aware of this due to regular trips back to Magherafelt. There were often occasions when

Advertisement for the official opening of the Loup grounds. It was there that a number of the GAA officials were verbally criticised for participating in refreshments afterwards. But it was only the traditional GAA tea.

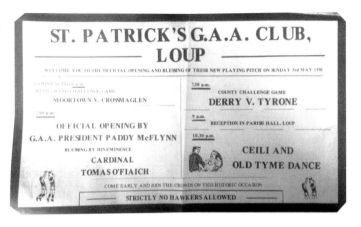

I had debates with people. A particular occasion which stands out in my memory was the opening of the new grounds at Loup. There was a black flag parade around the field and then, when we went into the parochial hall, we were barracked by people who accused us of going for a big feed when there were hunger strikers dying. We were merely taking the traditional GAA 'meat tea.' I had been a founder member of the Bellaghy and Slaughtneil clubs, but didn't have occasion to visit either during that period. The strength of feeling was emphasised when Slaughtneil withdrew from Derry competitions at this time. As President, I was obviously aware of their decision. But, perhaps strangely, nobody from the Derry County Board asked me to intervene. In any case, I knew the Slaughtneil people well, had great respect for them and felt sure that they would return.

By stressing the non-political nature of the GAA and its condemnation of violence, I felt that a stand had to be and was taken. It was important to stick to that decision. On both sides people became very emotional about what was happening and it was very difficult to defend the situation in the areas where these young lads came from, particularly if they had been involved in the GAA.

Clubs were under immense pressure and some people left clubs in south Armagh at that time and never came back.

Phone-calls were made to my home in Laurencetown calling me a 'west Brit' and other such names. The ironic thing is that a lot of the people down south thought I was a 'provo'. Their ignorance was amazing, worrying and even shocking.

The murder of Garda Morley and Byrne

The shooting of Garda John Morley and Garda Henry Byrne in July 1980 caused understandable problems and led to increased difficulty between the GAA and the Gardaí subsequently.

The association sent a delegation to the funeral of Garda Morley and Byrne, which included myself. But the Garda believed that we were ambivalent towards the whole issue of the H-Blocks and supported the armed struggle. They were also extremely angered by adverts supporting the H-Blocks which were included in some northern newspapers. This was further increased when Detective Garda Seamus Quaid was killed in Wexford in October 1980.

My chief contact at government level at that time was the Garda Commissioner, Paddy McLaughlin. He was also very helpful in providing me with advice and had a special insight from holding regular meetings with the RUC Chief, John Hermon. Paddy kept me informed of the thinking and what was going on. Our meetings usually took place at the Garda headquarters. But we never had any contact with the British government, with the police or anyone in the north at government level.

However, during 1980 a delegation from the GAA which included myself as President travelled to London to meet the Minister of State for the north, Michael Alison in the House of Commons over the continued occupation of St Oliver Plunket Park in Crossmaglen. At this time some had criticised me as President for not attending a rally which was held to oppose the occupation. What they failed to realise was that I was simply unable to go due to a previous engagement to open new grounds for St Paul's club in Belfast.

Those who were due to accompany me included Liam Mulvihill and the past-president, Con Murphy. Among our points was that a wall being proposed between the grounds and the army barracks should not be built because it was on the property of Crossmaglen Rangers GAA Club. The army should never have been permitted to occupy the grounds as they did for so long a period.

There was regular correspondence in the newspapers regarding, but our viewpoint within the GAA remained unchanged. We were by no means ambivalent towards violence and, as I have stressed, condemned what was going on in the north.

There was also a tricky situation when Liam Mulvihill and I attended the funeral of that great Kerry footballer, John Joe Sheehy. "This is going to be one of those days," I said to Liam after arriving in Tralee and seeing a platform erected at the graveside for a republican funeral.

Dáithí Ó Conaill, Officer Commanding of the IRA, got up at the graveside and said there was someone in attendance who would be able to tell of John Joe Sheehy's contribution to the GAA. Two men in leather coats came around to me asking me to speak about this, but I refused to become involved. All of this had been done on the wishes of John Joe, but the tragic thing was that his family had no say.

Later I was attacked during a television interview for attending the funeral. However, I said in response that John Joe Sheehy was a chairman of the Munster Council and a

Owen Carron speaking to the crowd who participated in the H-Block march to Casement Park on March 14, 1981. Picture courtesy of Belfast Media Group.

Vice-President of the Association. As a result, it was my duty as President to respect that contribution.

The chief problem was that shots were fired and the funeral generated a whole furore with me in the middle representing the GAA. But I felt we acted with decorum by attending, and then quietly made our way home.

In the summer of 1980 a demonstration was organised by Sinn Fein and took place at Casement Park in Belfast. It was one of a number of similar demonstrations held there during the H-Block crisis. Each one led to much coverage in the newspapers and media.

Among the most significant was in August 1979 when arms were brought into the ground as part of a demonstration to mark the 10 year anniversary of the deployment of British troops.

During a television interview, the interviewer then brought up the issue of the IRA showing new weapons which they had obtained at Casement Park. I responded by saying that any number of soldiers and police weren't able to stop what happened, so what chance had the GAA. My instructions to the chairman of the Antrim County Board was to open the gates and let them in because we weren't going to stop them.

On this occasion, I issued a very direct and clear statement which reiterated the GAA's condemnation of violence from whatever source and re-affirmed our policy of promoting the national games and creating better community spirit and involvement among all the people of Ireland.

We regularly had to make statements when something happened at a GAA ground. Every word had to be very carefully weighted and analysed because there were people waiting around to attack us. This was the same when I was interviewed on radio or television.

But what I soon realised was that it wasn't the holder of the office who mattered, but rather the office itself. The office of President of the GAA was very highly regarded.While I was critised verbally in person and through letters, the clubs which I visited as President respected the position and its significance.That was something which became very clear to me and still holds true today.

There were a number of background aspects to the whole situation. Firstly, there were those who felt that the GAA was solely a sporting organisation and should not become involved. In the middle were the members who didn't mind one way or the other.Then, there was the other group who felt that we should officially join this broad coalition of organisations against the H-blocks. For them, this would have entailed us actively supporting clubs in taking out advertisements and attending rallies as a unit under their own banner.

The GAA could have been spilt

THE deputation from the newly formed Gaels Against the H-Blocks committee arrived in my house at dusk on an August evening in 1981. Their demands were clear – they wanted black flags to be flown at the All-Ireland Final in Croke Park and for me as President to make a speech at half-time on behalf of the Hunger Strikers.

At that time, the H-Block committee extremely anxious to gain official GAA support for their cause. For this to have happened could have given them a significant boost, as well as a crucial foothold at local level in all parts of the country. An indication of how delicate affairs were is evident from the establishment of this group called 'Gaels Against the Block' which aimed to recruit all the GAA clubs. A certain number did join from around Belfast, but the idea didn't catch on.

It was to this background that the delegation arrived here in Laurencetown.What they might not have known was that I had known about their demands three days beforehand and had been able to prepare my response accordingly. Hugh McPoland was the Antrim chairman at the time and a great friend of mine. He knew a couple of people on the group, with the result that any decisions made were immediately relayed to me.

I told the deputation clear and simply that their demands weren't going to be met. It was something which would have offended many people at the game. But they were extremely annoyed by my refusal to do this and their logic was simply that if we as the GAA weren't with them, then we were against them.

My great fear during this period was that the GAA would be split. Marcus de Búrca, the eminent historian, wrote an article in which he stated that the Association might have spilt on three occasions. The first was over Parnell, the second at the time of the Civil War in the 1920s and the third was over the hunger strikes. He saw that the seeds were there.

There were several low points when I believed we were in real trouble. This was especially the case when clubs and particularly large clubs broke away and came out strongly in favour of the H-Blocks by putting adverts in the newspapers and urging members to attend parades.

Protests were held at half-time in the 1981 Ulster final and again at a match in Newcastle when T. P. Murphy contacted me telling me that he had been intimidated into permitting a parade. I told him to let them go because there was no point in him becoming annoyed. These parades were a big feature and there's no doubt that the public relations exercise was paramount and effective.

No area was strong enough within the GAA in the north to ensure a split. There were pockets of support for the H-Blocks in the counties, but they never got together. At the same time the danger was always there, particularly if things had gone on any longer.

I thought it was a very big advantage for the GAA at that time to have had myself, as a northerner, in the role of President. For example, my predecessor, Con Murphy, would have been much further removed geographically, and would thus have had less direct contact with the minute details and the undercurrents of the whole situation.

It was fortunate for the Association to have my understanding and the two people who stood by me were Alf Murray and Liam Mulvihill. Liam was only 34 at the time and saw the difficulties which were being faced. We were both starting from scratch almost and he understood precisely my position. On one occasion I appeared on television with Tom Woulfe and I felt the interview had not gone well. A little while later, Liam rang to reassure me that it had in fact gone well.

I also held a number of secret meetings with the Dublin headquarters of the H-Block Committee. Alf Murray accompanied me and he was very tough and good in pointing out that the GAA would be split if the H-Blocks continued to pressurise the Association and this split organisation would be no good to anyone.

It was an extremely difficult period to have been President. While the other aspects of the association were something which proved immensely enjoyable and rewarding, the situation in the north and the issues which become important were not easily dealt with. All this was taking place in a very tense environment where people from all parts of the community were losing their lives in tragic circumstances. But I never felt really afraid and fortunately never got any direct threats. I had a great feeling for the home clubs of the hunger strikers. Ultimately, whether you agreed or disagreed with what they were doing, these young men were still the children of neighbours.

G.A.A. AGAINST 'H' BLOCK
G.A.A. MARCH
On MONDAY 24th AUGUST,
Assemble CASEMENT PARK 6.15 p.m. Sharp
To March to SHAWS ROAD
for Hurling Match:—

NORTH ANTRIM SELECT
V
SOUTH ANTRIM SELECT
All G.A.A. in Antrim are asked to attend with Club Banners and Colours
SUPPORT THE PRISONERS 5 DEMANDS
Remember, Monday 24th August, 6.15

An advertisement for a GAA match in support of the H-Blocks.

The telegram sent to myself as President following the death of Kevin Lynch from Dungiven.

Newspaper article highlighting my defence of the GAA.

Evidence against us 'flimsy' says president

THE G.A.A. president, Mr. Paddy McFlynn, last night described as "a bit flimsey" the blame being levelled at the G.A.A. for the playing of The Men Behind The Wire during a recent hurling match in Wexford shortly after the murder of Detective Seamus Quaid. It would be too much like censorship to ban certain songs from being played or sung at intervals of matches, he said.

Mr. McFlynn said he wouldn't like the idea suggested by Sergeant Phil Callanan, President of the Garda Sergeants and Inspectors Association for the expulsion of G.A.A. members who support subversive organisations.

"That would create a terrible situation. It would mean the carrying out of a witch hunt and even political parties don't do that."

Mr. McFlynn said that he is very concerned about the accusations being made by Gardai around the country regarding ambivalence among the G.A.A. members towards violence.

"There has been a very close association between the Garda Siochana and the G.A.A. for many years and I wouldn't like it to be damaged in any way," he said.

Mr. McFlynn said that the matter would be idscussed

Paddy McFlynn

next weekend at a management committee meeting of the G.A.A. and also at the All-Ireland national committee meeting early next month.

Mr. McFlynn said that the G.A.A. had agreed to support the HpBlock prisoners on humanitarian grounds.

"We are in good company here. We have the Cardinal expressing the same concern," he said.

Sergeant Phil Callanan, a Scott Medal winner for bravery, said that now is the time to expel members of the G.A.A. who support subversive organisations and thevvvgwfcce.

"The G.A.A. is really a social service and not a political association. It is about time they came out and showed their sincerith regarding their support for the Gardai.

"There is no way that I can go along to games and sing songs that in effect are showing support for subversives.

Z"There is a by-election in Donegal this week and I haven't heard one word about the Garda Siochana, their efforts or their problems from any member of any political party. Is this what the Garda Siochana means to ghe politicians of this country?

"I must say that I am worried about the sincerity and goodwill of the Government in relation to the Garda Siochana," he said.

Sergeant Callanan predicted that the row between the G.A.A. and the Gardai would become a major national issue in the coming months.

Mr. John O'Grady, a member of the Thurles branch of the G.A.A., who has frequently called for G.A.A. condemnation of subversive organisations in the organisation at national level, said last night that the G.A.A. had been led into a false position "shirking open debate at Congress so as to avoid clashes."

Mr. McFlynn said that Mr. O'Grady was a man who liked being in the public eye.

Members of Sean McDermott GAC, Rossa GAC were among South Antrim clubs who took part in a H-Block hunger strike seven-day vigil outside Casement Park terminating with a march to St Paul's ground in August 1981. Picture courtesy of Belfast Media Group.

There were occasions, too, when I benefitted from good fortune. One time the television people arrived at Croke Park to interview me. The interviewer was getting ready to ask a difficult question, but he fumbled something. There was work going on closeby and a hammer fell before he got to ask the question. As a result, I had that extra bit of time to formulate my answer.

Thankfully, in more recent years, a form of solution has been found and the 'Troubles' of that 1969-1994 period are now fading into the memory. Nevertheless, there have been tragedies and I think particularly of those GAA members who have been killed since 1994. The murder of Sean Brown was one such tragedy. He was the chairman of the Bellaghy club at the time, a club which I had been involved with right at its formation. I attended his funeral with Liam Mulvihill and the then GAA President, Joe McDonagh. Even in the most trying of circumstances imaginable, the club and community spirit was clear. Let us hope that the pain of those days is now behind us for good.

THE EARLY YEARS

Castledawson Road, Magherafelt

The MacFlynn jaunting car on the Castledawson Road

Family at the Loup. Approx. early 1930's – Millie, Eddie, Pat and Charlie.

NINE decades on my mother's voice is still clear as she calls me to lunch.

I had locked myself in the bathroom, firmly refusing to return to school. My reluctance was prompted by a fear of doing knitting at the infants' class in the Holy Family Convent School because I was all fingers and thumbs, so I decided to take action. My mother knocked on the door well aware of the MacFlynn fondness of all food. I innocently walked out, was duly caught by the ear and delivered to school.

Magherafelt was still a small market town when I was born on May 5th 1918, at what is now number 38 Church Street beside Keenan's butchers. My mother was Bridget McNicholl from an old Magherafelt family, while my father was William J MacFlynn, a native of the Loup.

My father was from a family of seven and most remained in and around the South Derry area with the exception of his brother Edward who went to New Zealand as a farrier, an occupation he had shared with his father and brother Barney.

My mother was born in Church Street. Her father was Roddy McNicholl, whom I just about remember. Her brother Dick, sold furniture and other items and subsequently operated the mart and seed business in Rainey Street.

Where my parents met, I am not sure. There were plenty of opportunities at the frequent dances held at The Battery at Lough Neagh or the O'Neill Arms in Toomebridge. There were even boat trips and dances on the Lough Neagh Queen.

They married in 1912. A photograph in my sitting room shows them seated at the foot of the waterfall in Powerscourt, Co. Wicklow on their honeymoon. They settled in Church Street and had four children. Eddie was followed by Charlie, then Millie and I was the baby of the family.

William and his brother Sam, a farmer, who was married to a sister of Sean Larkin, specialised in the preparation of pork for local farmers

William J and Brigid on their wedding day.

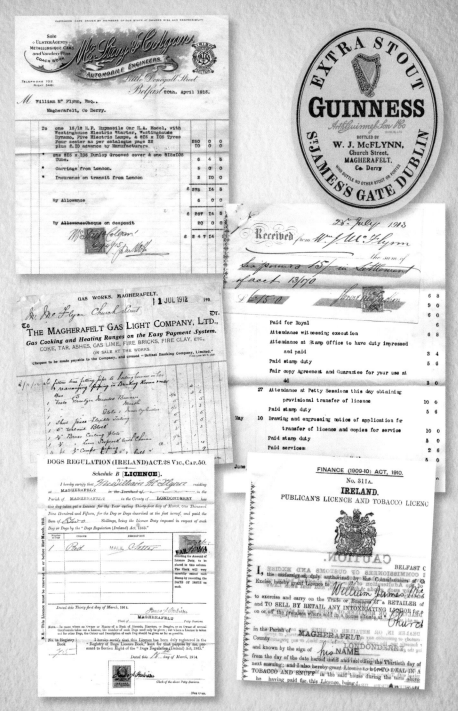

Receipts and other memorabilia from the Railway Hotel at Church Street in Magherafelt which was purchased by William J and Brigid MacFlynn in the 1920s.

who would hang the carcases and salt them for the winter. He later travelled the local marts carrying out inspections on behalf of pork buyers.

He also had particular expertise as a water douser, on one occasion being highly annoyed to find that his brother Barney had sought a second opinion from someone in Queens University before calling him in to source a well on his property

However, by the time of his marriage, he had taken out a licence as a wine and spirit merchant and signed a lease on Keenan's Public House adjacent to the family home.

In 1915, he made the very considerable purchase of a Huppmobile motor car. This was possibly the second car only in Magherafelt in those days, the other belonging to Dr Keithley. He used this for family outings and offered taxi services in the town.

A big move for the family came in 1926 when my parents bought the Railway Hotel further down Church Street. It had been leased to a McBride but was owned by the famous solicitor and politician, Louis J Walsh. In the family archives there's a letter from him to my mother agreeing to sell the premises for £1000, a good price which he said reflected the fact that he and my mother were somehow related.

My father then utilised his considerable skills as an amateur carpenter and handyman to extend and refurbish the property. Although it retained its title as Hotel, it was operated as a Public House and private residence.

My memories of those years growing up in Magherafelt in and around the pub are still very vivid. Among other things I remember was the bottling of stout which was done from kegs delivered on a regular basis. The proximity to the Railway Station meant that the pub was always busy with a great cross section of local commercial life coming and going from Belfast. There was also a connection to the Derry Central Line which passed through Maghera, Kilrea, Garvagh and into Coleraine and Portrush. There was also a connection which went through Moneymore, Cookstown, Dungannon and Coalisland and Portadown, which joined the Dublin train.

The railway station itself held endless fascinations for a small boy. It was mindboggling to see a large engine going around the turntable with one man pushing it. It was was also a great place to be in the winter time because there was always a large open fire in the waiting room. We would have gone there to play cards.

As he prospered, my father never forgot his farming roots, purchasing 20 acres of land mostly along the Castledawson Road. This gave us a taste of the farming and rural life, despite the fact that we were living in the town. One of the tasks was to make the hay and Charlie was the one who built the cocks of hay. Then the hay was brought to Church Street where it was put in the loft the stables. My job during this process was to 'tramp' it. The hay was thrown-up and I'd have to walk around the loft tramping this hay to make sure as much as possible could be fitted in. This was no easy task and I was always

Hay making on the Castledawson Road, left to right, Charlie, Eddie, William J., two McGuckins, Pat and Millie.

hoping that the horses would take their time coming back with the next load so that I could get a breath.

We kept some livestock and also a donkey and cart. I used to be a bit embarrassed on occasions with some of my fellow-students at the Rainey who'd see me leading this donkey down the street. With all these various interests my father was always a busy man.

I don't remember family birthdays being celebrated as such, however I have great memories of First Communions and Christmas. We were joined at Christmas in particular by Nurse Maquire who operated from the Dispensary across the road on the Corner of King Street. She was a devout lady and a very close friend of my mother. Frequently, a notice displayed in the window of the Dispensary would read "Gone to the Chapel, won't be long". She had a tough life covering the area on her bicycle and looking after the needs of the people of Magherafelt. She had two children, Dennis a Christian Brother and Sister Imelda, the first nun to qualify as a medical doctor who spent long years in Nigeria and lived to be a great age. My nephew, I am pleased to say, was able to attend her funeral in Dublin a few years ago.

I had a very happy upbringing in Magherafelt and we, as children generally had a relatively free hand. Our parents allowed us to stay out fairly late at night playing. One of the games we played was Handball at the flax stores just beside us in King Street. The ball was liable to go anywhere and we were keeping up the tradition because I remember my father telling us that there used to be a great handball league in South Derry based at Gausen's in Ballyronan.

Ballyronan at that time was like a seaport town where all the coal, flour and other materials came in on barges from across Lough Neagh and up the canal. That's was where the Ballyronan Marina is now and back then it was all big warehouses with big gable walls which were used for handball. As a player, I was able to pass myself and I suppose the thing that stood to me was that I was a trier.

Before the move to the Railway Hotel, living next door to Keenan's Butcher Shop in Church Street provided lots of entertainment as the butchers went about their daily routine. In the days before abattoirs this was a fairly rudimentary operation with the daily slaughter of cows (using methods which would not be considered humane nowadays). Even the pigs waiting in the "Long Shed" next door kicked up a fuss as they sensed their impending fate. Nothing was wasted as the innards were used for sausage skins and entrails being washed in vats with the resultant "soup" mixed with feed to fatten the cattle.

Paddy Keenan lived to a great age and I remember him well. At this time, his son, Roddy was the butcher and he had land at Ballyheifer just outside the town and also at Castledawson. He would regularly go in the car to look at the stock and that was always a chance for us young boys to get a trip. I became a lifelong friend of his son Pat. Among other things, the Keenans had the contract for providing meat to the workhouse. So, one Saturday, I remember heading up there and seeing the old men with big white enamel mugs and this huge boiler making the soup.

I also remember on one occasion a man who worked in the Keenan's fell down the loft and was injured He was brought into the Infirmary which was then part of the Workhouse complex which later became the Mid Ulster Hospital

Paddy Keenan, grandfather of my good friend, Pat, is among this group of dealers at the Fair in Magherafelt.

Magherafelt at that time and was a flourishing market town. Markets for cattle, pigs and flax brought great colour and excitement to our young lives. The flax market was held in King Street, just around the corner. We would watch as people came with their flax and lay it out for inspection by the buyers. Once sold, another Paddy Keenan had the job of conveying the flax in long bodied carts to the railway station for onward dispatch to the mills.

There was no general interest in politics despite my father's membership of the Irish National Foresters. Aged seven, I remember large black limousines passing the house.

St Joseph's National School in Magherafelt gathered for this picture in 1927. I am pictured on the extreme left standing in the front row.

A famous photograph of Church Street in Magherafelt which hung in Keenan's butchers for many years.

My father told me that it was the funeral of Dennis Henry, the first Chief Justice of Northern Ireland who despite being a Catholic became part of the new government at Stormont. His remains had arrived in his native Magherafelt by train.[2]

Another early memory for me was the 1926 General Strike which affected the delivery of coal. I remember they developed a fuel which was made of compressed coal dust. It was like the heel of a shoe and for some reason was called the 'Kaiser's Heel.' But for some reason this made-up substitute wasn't much good, because there was very little coal in it and as a result it didn't provide much heat. But in Magherafelt we didn't have worry too much about the lack of coal because there was no shortage of sticks and turf for the fire.

I was very close to my father. He couldn't be described as severe, but at the same time he didn't take any nonsense and any of us who stepped out of line could expect to be disciplined. While not exactly well off, he and my mother provided a comfortable, happy childhood and a good education for us all.

One of my earliest memories is of how my father used to use us children as decoys to attend cockfights in other parts of South Derry. So, the family would be put into the car as if we were going out in the car, and he knew rightly that the police were watching. I attended a couple of cockfights in the 1920s which was amazing because the men there argued so long about weighing the birds 'or giving and taking an ounce'.

These cockfights took place down around the Loughshore and at a location called great 'Long Nancy's' close to the Monaghan border. It was situated down a long lane and was kind of suited for those coming from near the border. You see, this activity was based around areas, South Derry was one, then around Larne where there was a man called Beggs. The betting was the big thing and there were very big crowds. I remember an occasion when the police came along and the men were running to get away with the game-cock in bags.

School Days

After moving on from the Holy Family Convent Infants School, I attended St Joseph's National School, where my teacher at that time was Bob Barton from Anahorish who was to become a good friend of mine over the years. At that time the subjects studied by the scholars were certainly varied.

We progressed after a few years to the "Master's" class where each morning he would inspect the troops. My job was to light the fire with bog oak which had been chopped up by others. The "Master" was a man called Edward Carville from Co Down and was a formidable disciplinarian. On one occasion he decided that the school should aim to win an award for excellence in primary schools. Needless to say, we were successful. When

2 – Dennis Henry was taken from Magherafelt Station to Draperstown following his death. He was among the first Catholic civil servants at Stormont following partition.

he left he was replaced by a man called Ned O'Brien from Co Monaghan who had a more relaxed approach to his vocation.

When I was became a senior pupil I became an Altar Boy. As an Altar Boy, you learned Latin responses, but these were really just sounds to us, but I can still remember some of them. One of my memories from my time as an Altar Boy is of Cardinal McRory going from the Parochial House to the chapel and the Eccleastical Inspection where strange questions like, "If you swallowed a pin, could you receive Communion?" were asked. However standard questions like this passed from school to school so we were ready for him.

Eddie and Charlie went on to board at St Patrick's College in Armagh. We visited them one Sunday and I remember thinking that the whole place was very grey and not very exciting and I just thought what a terrible way to spend Sundays. So, when the time came, I told my father that I didn't want to follow them and would rather attend Rainey Endowed School in Magherafelt.

I was one of about only 20 catholics at the school from a total enrolment of about 200. But the Rainey was very progressive and there was absolutely no sectarianism. We were all together, all faiths and none. Among my great friends then was a chap called Evans, who later became a Presbyterian Minister in Limavady and Ian Sinnerton from Castledawson who became a Church of Ireland Minister.

This was true integrated education. The principal was John A Calvin, a great old character who, however, taught Latin badly. He made a special point on Holy Days of making sure the Catholics got to Mass.

It was at the Rainey that I first played a bit of rugby. Every year the school played in the Schools Cup, but were always beaten in the first round. One year I remember us losing to Foyle College. Most of the team were GAA lads from around South Derry. I was a reasonable rugby player, possibly because I was big and strong. While I had no great ability as a footballer, I was able to catch and kick and played wing forward. We also played five a side soccer. The GAA didn't feature in my life in my early days at the Rainey.

On Carntogher's Braes

Our car was also used every summer in the late 1920s and early 1930s to take us to Portstewart and Mrs Kelly's boarding house on the Promenade. But after a few years I tired of Portstewart. "I'm not going back," I said and instead headed to Slaughtneill for the whole summer. I stayed with people called McKenna (Conn) who lived at a place called Backpark. Barney McKenna and my father went shooting together and were close friends. At that time the rights to shooting were owned by the Clarks of Upperlands, so it was more or less poaching. It was a very strong nationalist area and, after spending the long days wandering up Carntogher's Braes, I got my first inkling of the nationalist awaking in me.

I have a very clear recollection of my first day in Slaughtneill as I joined with the members of the family who were making hay in the upper field and later had my first meal of strong tea and griddle scones with home-made butter. I soon felt part of the Con family and became particularly friendly with the youngest son, Francis, who was slightly older than me. During the day, when he was away at work as a joiner, I was a constant companion to his father, Barney, whose knowledge of the folklore and traditions of the area was very extensive indeed. He was a great teller of tales and we would go up the turf bank on the mountain to 'rickle turf.' It's amazing now when I think back the enjoyment which I got from those days and Barney could name every height and hollow and each had a special name, Irish in origin. The last field before the heather was called Gort na gCapall and further up was Lough Muck. When we arrived at the bog, we would do a little work and then Barney would light his pipe and regale me with stories and memories. He told me how Shane Crossagh, on his way to prison on Derry, escaped from the Redcoats at the snout of the Carn. He challenged the soldiers to a long-jump competition and Shane – with three tremendous leaps ran off down the mountain. Barney also told stories of 1798, mostly concerning the Maghera area and the patriot, Watty Graham. He also recalled caman being played at the beginning of the 20th century and kept his hand-made hurling stick.

He often spoke as well of the Monster meeting in 1915 on the snout of the Carn, which was addressed by Bulmer Hobson, who was deputising for Patrick Pearse who was unable to travel. Barney told me, too, of the troubles in the twenties and his spell in Derry gaol.

Farm mechanisation was unknown at the time, so there were many young people engaged in farming operations. Crops had to be planted and harvested, turf and hay to be saved. But on those long summer evenings, there was still time for recreation, Soccer was prevalent in South Derry in those days and was played in a field of Paddy McEldowney's (Faitche) and later in Doherty's field. On Sunday afternoons, we went on rabbit shooting expeditions and Barney Conn taught me to shoot.

Another activity which was popular was tug o' war and Slaughtneill were heavily involved. I remember large poles with pulleys being erected for training purposes. After sessions of training, we went to Mary Doherty's, sat around the floor and talked into the small hours. I remember seeing Slaughtneill winning tug o' war competitions at sports meetings and the members of the team whose names I recall were Francis Conn, McEldowney's, Doherty's and a McGuigan as anchor. Tommy Doogan acted as coach and urged the team onto greater efforts.

As the years went on, I occasionally spent my Christmas and Easter holidays as well in the Backpark. I attended traditional wakes, where drink and tobacco were on offer. And, one winter I attended a dance in Corlecky school and had my first brush with romance when I left a girl home. On another occasion I broke my confirmation pledge when I took some hot poteen to cure a cold. It was an excellent and efficient remedy as well.

I owe a lot to Slaughtneill and my experiences there aroused my interest in the countryside, its people and folklore. The survival of the Irish way of life and older traditions made me aware of the culture of our country and led me to become involved in the GAA and to learn the Irish language. Had I never known Slaughtneill, I would have been poorer in mind and spirit and deprived of an understanding of an older way of Irish life. My abiding memory of Slaughtneill is of the kindness of the Con family who welcomed me and treated me with great hospitality. In that family, I came to appreciate their standards of behaviour, their commitment to the family and to the community. I have an attachment to their area, and its age-old traditions.[3]

It was around this time, too, that I almost became a member of the IRA. One of the pig dealers in Magherafelt was a man called Joe Quinn. He was originally from Ardboe, was aged in his 60s and living in Magherafelt. One night he asked me to join the IRA. So, here I was going down to Joe's house to get sworn in, but the officers didn't arrive. He was so disgusted that the whole thing was never mentioned again and I was denied a military career as a result!

---

3 – Today Carntogher and the surrounding Slaughtneill area is a hotbed of Irish cultural activity, with many native speakers and a strong gaelic games tradition.

Church Street, Magherafelt

THE HAWK
OF THE HILL

An old photograph showing what was then the **Rainey Charity** school prior to the developments of the past few decades.

A busy **Church Street** with MacFlynn's on the far left. What a difference to the scene of today.

First steps in the GAA

It's amazing to think back now how little part that the GAA had in my life during those early years. But there was a team in Magherafelt called St Joseph's which existed for a brief period in the 1920s. I remember being at one of their matches which was played out at Bellevue. The opposition was Ballinderry who were also very tough at that time as well. Anyway, a terrible row brewed up and they fought the whole evening. One of the Magherafelt players I remember was called Tom Agnew.

Football largely died away in my mind until about 1933 when my interest was aroused by that year's All-Ireland semi-final and final involving the great Cavan team which was the first from Ulster to win the Sam Maguire Cup. Around that time independent buses used to operate around the country, including in Magherafelt. At weekends they didn't have the same level of business as during the week with the result that there were always a few spare on a Saturday and Sunday. These could then be hired for a very small payment to the driver for fuel.

So, my father took me to Breffni Park to see Cavan versus Kerry in the All-Ireland semi-final and I can well remember several of the players and incidents. The three big names were Smallhorn, Blessington and Magee. M.J. Magee scored the goal in what was a very low-scoring match won by Cavan. [1] After that we followed them to Dublin and my first visit to Croke Park was for the All-Ireland final between Cavan and Galway. I was standing on the Canal End just behind the goals. The Cavan full-back, Patsy Lynch, got

My vivid memories remain of the Cavan team of 1933 and 1934 which made the breakthrough by bringing the Sam Maguire Cup to Ulster for the first time.

1 – Cavan won their first All-Ireland senior title in 1933 captained by Jim Smyth and followed that success in 1934. They remained Ulster's dominant force throughout this period.

injured, but they still won. Many years later, I remember going to a match in Dublin and meeting Lynch at the Cistercian Monastery in Collon where his brother-in-law was a monk. We had a great chat about old times and he was a great character. Cavan had one of the best players ever in Jim Smith and my reckoning is that both him and Jim McCullagh were to the two best ever produced in the province.

The whole experience of going to Dublin was amazing and a few of us decided to stay in an hotel. I had never been in an hotel before, and was mesmerised by the way things were done, and the number of knives and forks on the table. That was a big day out. But the funny thing is that my father never showed any real interest in attending matches. Going to the hotel to eat was a big occasion.

The following year, 1934, Roddy Keenan took myself and Pat to Annagher Park in Coalisland to watch Armagh playing Fermanagh. Jim McCullagh was playing for Fermanagh, but every time he went near the ball the Armagh supporters booed him. You see he was working with the Electricity Board at that time and was eligible to play for Fermanagh as a result.

Setting up the Rossas

I don't recall how I came to be in attendance at that match in the late 1920s. Curiosity was the likely reason. After that, Gaelic football died away completely until 1932 when a meeting was held in our local school, St Joseph's, to reconstruct the Derry GAA Board. Among those in attendance was a man from Cavan called B. C. Fay [2] and when that meeting was taking place I was in the club adjacent to the school which was used for billiards, snooker and cards. We used to go there regularly and some of those in attendance at the meeting came in and reported what was going on. Paddy Larkin was appointed as the chairman and a few weeks after that a match was arranged in Ballinascreen between Lavey, who played in the South West Antrim League and Ballinderry, who had been playing in Tyrone. This was done to help raise funds for the new County Board.

The Rossa's were always looking ahead. Here's their membership card from 1937.

---

2 – BC Fay from Cavan served the GAA in Ulster from 1917 until 1934. He served as Secretary from 1925 until 1934 and was replaced by Gerry Arthurs, who remained in the post until 1976.

It was events such as that which inspired us young lads around Magherafelt. So, the following year a few of us got together and decided to set up a minor club for the town.

On 15 April 1934, all the players attended a meeting which was held in the house in Church Street where my family had previously lived, but by then was vacant. One of the first points up for discussion was what to name the club. At that time, my party piece was the oration given by Padraig Pearse at the grave of O'Donovan Rossa. This was given to me by Hugh Gribbin of Anahorish, the father of the Gribbins of Newbridge[3], and I had learned it off by heart. I proposed that the club be called O'Donovan Rossas which was agreed. That was how the Rossa's came into being.

St John's Hall, Magherafelt, where the Rossa club was formed in 1934.

One of the first tasks for us was to go around and collect money for jerseys. Our first call was to the parish priest, Monsignor Ward from Carrickmore. Each donation was maybe six pence or thrupence and once this finance was gathered up we were able to purchase a football. At that time, the club jerseys were red and black and we had some great players on that initial team, many of whom went on to become household names in Derry, Ulster and All-Ireland matches. Pat Keenan, Patsy 'Sticky' Maguire, Basil and Rory McGuckian, Gerry Gallagher was centre half-back who was like Kevin Mussen in his ability to read a game well. My brother, Charlie, kept goals and I played in various positions, including centre forward. There was no such thing as a manager. Instead, we would hold a meeting, pick the team and raise the finance. Everything was done within our own group. Everybody had equal involvement, it was all about the Rossas and I think that's why it became so successful. For us, this was personal.

All of these things were in place and we needed to have a match. Around the same time, there was a sports day being held in Magherafelt and I persuaded the organisers to hold a seven-a-side minor match. A number of teams took part and we ended up winning it. That was the first trophy won by the club and the team was John Kearns, M. Quinn, myself, G. Gallagher, Pat Keenan, P. Collins and John Walls.

3 – The Gribbens of Newbridge have been Derry GAA stalwarts throughout the past 80 years and several sons of Hugh senior featured for the county in the 1958 All-Ireland Final.

Thinking back now, I was only 16 years of age, so I was definitely still very young. But then this GAA organisation and matches was a very new idea. It's amazing when I think about the early days of the Rossa's, there was just the one team. William John Halferty was our secretary for years[4], and each of us took turns as chairman.

The matches were played at various pitches locally, one at Bellevue and then at another ground on the Pound Road, situated down past the petrol station which my brother, Charlie, used to own. Eventually, after a couple of seasons, the minor club developed into a senior one. There was only a kick-about and no real training initially and that continued until about 1936, when it was decided to enter a Derry team in the Ulster Minor Championship for the first time. We played Tyrone at the Christian Brothers Park in Omagh and they won by 0-10 to 0-7. The seven Rossas players on the team were Rory McGuckian, Pat McFlynn, Joey Taylor, John Kearns, John Walls, Pat Keenan and Paul Toner. We always claimed that there should have been more of the Rossa's on that team. But then Fr Collins got a few players from St Columb's College in Derry and we didn't believe that they were up to our standard, even though there were six players from the Rossas.

It wasn't until that minor campaign that we started to train and the sessions were very straightforward compared to what would be the case now. These runs usually took place very early in the morning at about 6 a.m. Each time we would run the roads around Magherafelt and then we'd come along to a farmer who had the milk churn out. The churn duly provided us with much-needed refreshment and we used the lid as a vessel for drinking the milk which was great.

Some time later, the current county grounds on the Castledawson Road were bought for £600. Raising that money took an awful lot of collecting. The big problem with that ground was its condition; it was always wet and we had to spend a lot of time getting it drained.[5]

The funny and strange thing was that, despite being only young teenagers, the twenty of us involved were the players, the administrators and fundraisers. A great source of pride for us was in the organisation of various activities and all our events were marketed as 'Rossa Productions.' From those humble beginnings, the club thankfully flourished into the future.

How I helped found the Bellaghy and Slaughtneill clubs

The meeting to reorganise the GAA in Derry was held in 1932, but of course I was still only 14 years of age and didn't attend. Nevertheless, our efforts to get things going in Magherafelt were followed by similar attempts in other areas of South Derry especially.

---

4 – WJ Halferty served as Secretary of Magherafelt O'Donovan Rossa from 1944 until 1964.

5 – The County Grounds venue on the Castledawson Road was a popular venue for Derry county matches until the 1970s.

By the time the Rossas were finding their feet, minor football was only starting up in Derry at that time. So I attended meetings of this new county board to push for a league. Anyway, the decision was taken and wasn't I appointed secretary of the Minor Board after a man called Devlin from the Loup stepped down about halfway through the year. I couldn't even spell secretary! But I got notepaper for correspondence and managed fine.

Like any secretary, I had to make the fixtures and notify the clubs of when they were due to play. In those days, of course, there were no telephones and it was all done by post. I was also playing and helping to run the Rossas, so it was a very busy period.

The South Derry Divisional Board at that time was basically running the whole county because most of the clubs were in our area. Like any job I kind of grew into the role, and we generally held our meetings in hotels.

Our chief rivals in the parish during this period were Newbridge. Barney Murphy was one of their main players. He played for Derry and other teams who provided strong opposition were Castledawson and Bellaghy. One of those involved in the Wolfe Tones of Bellaghy was Edward Scullion. He had a pub in the village and every time they scored he blew the horn of the car to let people know that they were going well. Cars weren't widely available in those years, but we could hire a car for two or three shillings from people who did a bit of private taxing to take us to the games.

In my role as South Derry secretary, I also had a part in helping to set up a number of clubs, and among them were Bellaghy and Slaughtneil. Bellaghy had good people working for the GAA in the Diamonds and a man called Brian Toner. At that time in the mid-1930s, they had a small wooden hut situated on the Castledawson Road. I remember going down to officially open for them. In Slaughtneil, they obtained a Nissen hut which became their first headquarters.

Rainey Street from The Diamond, Magherafelt

Those were their first meetings and things spread fairly quickly after that, a bit like how Michael Cusack described the initial months after the GAA was founded in 1884. Castledawson were set up in the early 1940s and among those deeply involved was the present county chairman's father, Pearse Keenan, carried the club along with a man called Heaney who was originally from Scotland. At that time clubs like Castledawson and the Loup were quite small, so it's amazing to see how things have progressed to where they are at present.

One of the important advantages was that players in particular areas were already lining out for other clubs. So, the fact that a few from Castledawson were already lining out with Bellaghy gave them a nucleus, the same between Slaughtneill and Glen.

South Derry was very much the mainstay of the GAA in the whole county at that time, although as time went on the other parts of the county gradually became more organised. Meetings of the county board in the late 1930s didn't take place all that often, and then usually in hotels or after big club or county matches.

The representatives from the North and South divisions and the Derry City division were in attendance and I was involved in the setting up of the City division. Paddy Larkin, myself, Owen McErlain from Greenlough and Phonsie Dean met with Eddie McAteer. He was chairman of the City Board and another of those involved in doing great work was Frank Pimley from Belfast.

Becoming County Secretary

My life in the late 1930s was beginning to take shape, including on the GAA front. After returning home following the completion of my teacher-training at Strawberry Hill, Twickenham, I became secretary of the Derry County Board.

What happened was Fr Michael Collins came to me about the Derry County Board. The Chairman had just retired, while Sean Dolan had been interned which meant that there was a shortage of personnel. During that conversation, Fr Collins, who was in Ballinacreen at the time, asked me to become County Secretary. There was very little paperwork left by Sean Dolan, which resulted in me virtually having to start off from scratch. [6]

There was very little going on in the north, accept maybe Glenullin who had a team and they had the famous Harry Owens who was originally from Beragh in Co Tyrone. He was a real character, white-haired and a great man to kick a dead ball. He must have played into his forties at least. Barney Murphy from Newbridge was also a very good footballer. Bellaghy had the Cassidys and Diamonds.

A big event during my time involved in the county board was the purchase of Celtic Park in Derry by the GAA. One corner of the pitch was where the gasworks came in and then there was a small brown painted and zinc hut which served as the dressing-rooms.

An important thing during those years was to ensure that the club kept moving forward. One of those who kept us on our toes was Fr Malachy Toner, a Columban Father. He arrived in Magherafelt every summer, encouraging us to make progress and it was him who pushed us on towards purchasing the County Grounds at Polepatrick. He said "you have to move on and progress," and had some great ideas.

---

6 – Born in 1913, Sean Dolan was interned in 1939 until July 1941 when he was released unconditionally due to ill-health. He died in October 1941 at the age of just 28.

The breakthrough Magherafelt team which won the county title for the first time in 1939. I am in the centre of the back row to the left of the goalie.

But getting that ground was certainly easier said than done and understandably took an awful lot of work. John Joe McNally was a solicitor in the town and he was very helpful to the club in negotiating the deal. There was seven acres on the site which we bought for £600. Of course, reaching that stage was only part of the story and the next stage was making the ground fit for football. Some of us had great craic going down to the woods in the dead of night to cut wood for the trees. The club never had any money, and in those days the full extent of the club finances was a biscuit tin which the treasurer kept under the bed! He kept all the receipts and money there and it reminds me of Paddy Kavanagh writing about taking the price for five woodbine from the tin. In those days money was scarce and I well remember us putting in a shilling apiece to pay some debt or other.

Fortunately, the ground at Polepatrick was fairly level and the biggest thing was drainage because it was always very damp. We did a lot of the draining ourselves, going to the ground every Saturday to dig the drains and put in the stones. The dividends of our efforts paid off a few years later when the South Derry Board took an interest in the grounds. A man called James Malone from Loup, who was very much involved in the committee running the ground, wanted to secure it for inter-club matches.

It was always known as the County Grounds simply due to the involvement of the county board in the purchase and development of the pitch. An interesting aside to this which I didn't realise happened a few years ago when the Rossas were seeking grants to develop the magnificent new clubrooms and second pitch which they have today. The county board officers were still the trustees and this meant that the Magherafelt club had difficult in obtaining grants because they didn't fully own the ground. So, I helped them to get this sorted out legally.

Of course, the ground immediately became and indeed remained a popular venue for inter-county matches.

First County title in 1939

That summer of 1939 was a very important one for me. Not only did I become county secretary, but Magherafelt also became county champions for the very first time which was obviously a massive achievement for all of us. Winning that title meant that us young lads who had helped set up the club and keep it going in the earlier part of the decade had now reached maturity by becoming county champions.

There were some very tough matches in South Derry because Newbridge were extremely strong, and Lavey too. I played centre half-forward during those years and, while I had not great skill, I could catch and kick and was also fairly strong.

The names, faces and personalities of the players on that time are still very fresh in my memory. We had Pat Keenan and Patsy 'Sticky' Maguire who were the main players. Pat was a very good forward, while Sticky subsequently played for Ulster and went to live in Belfast. Tom Crilly was a latecomer to the ranks, while Paudge Toner eventually married a Moy girl and moved there. Fr Malachy Toner was great craic. Every year he would return home and at a meeting always had an idea to push us on to new heights. It was him who prompted and encouraged us to purchase the grounds. "You have to move on and progress," he would tell us, before regaling us with the story of how Polepatrick – close to where the pitch is located – was named because St Patrick's had travelled through Magherafelt on his way from Slemish Mountain to get the boat back to England! It was said by him that when he heard the children of the western sea calling, it was the children of Magherafelt beside Lough Neagh. He was very passionate about all of this and wrote a pamphlet explaining the story. Needless to say, it went down very well with the people of the town, just as that famous line from John Hewitt which states, "There's Carrickmacross and Crossmaglen and Magherafelt beats the best of men. I cannot deny it." That sentiment was very appropriate for us in 1939.

My brother Charlie was a fairly good goalkeeper on those first teams. I remember us playing in Derry on one occasion when he was losing his hair. He wrote reports for the Derry Journal and a photograph was taken by them of Charlie showing the bald patch. But Charlie wasn't having this and asked the photographer to alter the picture, which was duly done and he was shown in the paper with this healthy-looking mop of black hair.

What was remarkable about that team was the bond which developed between that team due to the fact that all of us had gone to school and grew up together. We had a sort-off family feeling within that squad, and it's interesting to note that many of the same names are still cropping up in Rossa teams.

We travelled to the 1939 county final by car and taxi. The game was played in what was the old Celtic Park and our success was a brilliant achievement for the club, only five or six years after we had started out. [7] It was probably no wonder that we celebrated in fine fashion in Derry City that night and didn't return home until the early hours. While Magherafelt wasn't considered a 'Gaelic town', people still felt very proud of our win. The families of the players all attended. During this period, too, the club used to publish a broadsheet publication every month called The Hawk. It got its name because O'Donovan Rossa was called 'the Hawk of the Hill'. I used to have all the copies. One of the regular contributors was Patsy 'Sticky' Maguire, who was very good at writing ballads. At that time, myself and Charlie would arrive home still in our rig-out. Now our mother was of the impression that all football matches were just about fighting and her first words always to us when we got back and before she would let us in were, "any fighting?" But she was very relaxed about the whole thing and in her own way was very proud of us taking part. The funny thing also was that my father never came to any of the matches, but he still had a mild interest and they were both happy that Magherafelt were winning.

My short inter-county career

Much is made nowadays about those who represent their county. It's an honour which is still held in high esteem, just as it was in my time as a player. I represented the county minors in that historic first-ever game for Derry in that grade against Tyrone in 1936. That same year, Derry defeated Tyrone in the National League at Newbridge. That team included players from Lavey, Derry City, Limavady, Newbridge and Ballinascreen, but nobody from Magherafelt. However, that was all to change as us young minors from that year began to gain in experience and I was fortunate enough to be selected on the team in 1937, just prior to beginning my teacher-training.

That match against Donegal was to take place in Ardara. The bus began in North Derry, picked me and the other Magherafelt and South Derry lads up before heading to the match. We arrived at the ground at 3 p.m and were on the field half an hour later. There was no such thing as pre-match meals or extensive warm-ups. There was a man from midfield called John from Dungloe, and he caught the ball from the throw-in and made space for himself before belting it over the bar. There's another story about that match in Ardara worth mentioning. The Derry team togged out in the Nesbitt Arms Hotel and I was looking forward to the game because I'd just bought a new pair of football boots costing me 30 shillings – a lot of money at that time. On my return home to Magherafelt, I put the boots at the bottom of the stairs so as not to destroy the carpet. But when I came down, they'd disappeared never to be seen again.

---

7 – Magherafelt won their first county title in 1939. The club won its most recent senior title in 1978.

It was a big thing for me, but then maybe I had a special advantage in being county secretary as back then it was the county board officials who picked the team. So yours truly always had a good chance of being picked.

By then, life was moving on for me and new horizons were opening up. The sense of fun, achievement and satisfaction which us young lads had enjoyed around Magherafelt during the 1920s and 1930s provided each of us with memories which have endured. Those early days roaming around the town, playing football and all the other activities also gave both me and others a solid grounding which served us well as we embarked on the challenges and opportunities which awaited.

FOREVER IN MY MEMORY

Memories of time spent in London. From left are my acceptance letter, the St Mary's College sportsday programme and a letter home recounting the difficult wartime conditions.

ST. MARY'S COLLEGE,
STRAWBERRY HILL,
MIDDLESEX.

September, 1937.

Dear Sir,

I have received notification from the Ministry of Education for Northern Ireland that you have been selected for admission to the above-named College for the Session 1937-38, according to the results of the King's Scholarship Examination and the further tests in General Suitability and Medical Fitness. The College Authorities will, accordingly, reserve a place for you for the coming Session, subject to your testimonials being adjudged satisfactory.

Kindly notify me, immediately, by postcard, if you are prepared to accept the place offered to you.

I enclose herewith the following:-

(a) List of College Requisites;

(b) Copy of the College Prospectus;

(c) Form relating to the Two Years' Course leading to the Teacher's Certificate.

(d) Form of application for admission.

(e) Copy of Questionnaire, which should be filled in by your Guarantor, and returned to the Secretary, Ministry of Education for Northern Ireland, Tyrone House, Ormeau Avenue, Belfast.

Kindly forward to me, by return of post, if possible:-

(a) Your Certificate of Registration of Birth;
(b) Your Certificate of Baptism;
(c) A testimonial from your Parish Priest;
(d) The form of application for admission, completed by you;
(e) The Form relating to the Two Years' Course leading to the Teacher's Certificate, completed by you.

The College Fees, amounting to £46, for the Session 1937-38, should be paid either before, or immediately after, entry to Col...

The Teacher's Certificate Examination, 1939, will be conduct... by the University of London, and an Examination Fee not exceeding £2.10.0. will be required to be paid by each Recognised Student before he is admitted to the Examination.

A list of text-books for class use will not be supplied to incoming Students.

The College will open for First Year Students on Friday, 17... September. Students are required to be in the College before 9 p.m., and should report to the Dean on arrival.

Luggage, if sent in advance, should be addressed to St. Ma... College, Strawberry Hill, Middlesex.

Yours faithfully,

V. MacCARTHY, ...
Princi...

35th INTER-COLLEGE ANNUAL
ATHLETIC SPORTS MEETING

Of the METROPOLITAN TRAINING COLLEGES
(Under A.A.A. Laws, by permission of the A.A.A.)

UNIVERSITY OF LONDON ATHLETIC GROUND
MOTSPUR PARK

Saturday, 21st May, 1938, at 2.45 p.m.

The Challenge Shield will be presented by the Principal of Westminster College.

Competing Colleges:

WESTMINSTER.	GOLDSMITHS'.
S. MARK & S. JOHN.	SHOREDITCH.
ST. MARY'S.	BOROUGH ROAD.

COMMITTEE OF MANAGEMENT:

PRESIDENT : Dr. A. W. HARRISON.

making London a very dark and gloomy City. With the black-out.

I wish it was over. I am sure, you do not notice it in the Country.

I am on Night duty, but. I will send you a Gift in the New Year.

We have not, very much time off. as, we can only go out certain hours.

I hope you are keeping well.

Sincerely wishing you, a bright and Prosperous New Year. With every kind wish.

Your Loving Sister,
Margaret.

Playing football with the Rossas and the social activities attached to the club had taken up most of my leisure time during the middle to late 1930s. But an increasing role in the administrative side of things with Magherafelt and also the County Board meant that life was moving on and changing.

The decision as to what career to pursue was an extremely important one. While at the Rainey Endowed school in Magherafelt,[1] I completed the senior certificate. The marks from that were added up, with the result that in 1937 I was called to Strawberry Hill teacher-training college in Twickenham, London.[2] The initial spell there was helped by the fact that Basil McGuckian, a friend from Magherafelt, had already begun his training at Strawberry Hill. As a result, he was able to tell me exactly what to expect during those early weeks and months away from home for the first time.

There were only eleven Irish at Strawberry Hill in the autumn of 1937. But there was no shortage of activities and enjoyment. We were very good at organising a variety of different clubs and committees which became part and parcel of college life. For instance, there was the geography club or the history club. Each had perks, because the members were often taken to various places of interest. Elections took place to the various clubs. Before they were held, the Irish students and indeed those from Liverpool or around Newcastle got together to negotiate and swap votes. This ensured that each group of students had a representation. It was my fortune to become involved in the geography club. One trip was to the North and South Downs.

It was at this time, too, that I began to learn Irish for the first time under the tutelage of a man called John Bell from Omeath. Lessons took place twice a week and in 1939 I had my first visit to Rannafast. My grasp of the language was still fairly basic, necessitating my initial placing among the children in the bunrang. It was always something of a great puzzle to me why I wasn't a great linguist, even though I did achieve a pass in French at the Rainey.

There was no particular reason for the decision to become a teacher, although it was after investigating other possible occupations. One of the big advantages was that someone could qualify within two years. Eddie was a doctor and had spent seven years qualifying, so following in his footsteps wasn't exactly attractive.

Bob Barton, a teacher at the Rainey, provided some useful advice. The bright lights and strange surroundings of Twickenham and London beckoned in that autumn of 1937. It was certainly a massive change anything experienced up to then in Magherafelt.

The first trip back to Twickenham after Christmas was certainly an experience. The little boats at that time bounced about in a terrible fashion and this wasn't helped by a rough

---

1 – Rainey Endowed school in Magherafelt drew pupils from both Catholic and Protestant backgrounds. In 2013 it celebrates its Tir-Centenary.

2 – St Mary's College, Strawberry Hill, was the chief teacher-training base for men from Northern Ireland from the mid-1920s until the opening of St Joseph's College in Belfast in the late 1940s.

Irish sea. Many on board were sick, and I joined them when one man accidentally kicked my heels in the bottom bunk.

Then, two or three days after arriving in Strawberry Hill, I collapsed suddenly at Mass. They probably had to dismantle the church to get me out. The next three months from Christmas until the following Easter were spent in the Royal Free Hospital in London. Fortunately or unfortunately, they never discovered what was wrong and said that it was a problem which had been there for years.

Nevertheless, the stay in hospital was interesting. The nurses worked very hard, scrubbing the floors, looking after the patients and doing any number of tasks. One of them was from Dublin and I asked her why she felt the need to come to London to scrub floors when she could just as easily get a similar job at home. After that she did indeed decide to return to Ireland!

Of course, this stay in hospital for those months at the start of 1938 also affected my studies at Strawberry Hill. The Vincentians ran the college and the Principal, a Fr McCarthy, came to tell me that I would lose the whole year of study if the final two terms weren't completed. My recovery from the mystery illness was complete within a very short time and the immediate return to Strawberry Hill came just in time to avoid having to repeat the whole year of study, something which simply would not have suited at all.

Among the teachers at Strawberry Hill at the time was a Fr Leonard who had a great knowledge, love and ability for English and was greatly involved in literary circles. An English classmate of ours asked him a silly question one day and he responded by saying that it was all a matter of taste. "Mr MacFlynn," he address me, "you know what people would say. 'It's all a matter of taste,' is what the old lady said when she kissed her donkey." He was a very funny and wonderful man.

The resident ballroom combined as the reading area and had very soft seats. It was always a welcome break to go into a nice quiet corner there and sit reading for a couple of hours. There were only eleven in the class and some of the names are still fresh. Frank Monaghan was from Tyrone, Joe Sally from Derry, W. J. McAllister from Portstewart, Jimmy Pollock from Belfast and Eddie McKavanagh who finished up teaching in Dromore.

There was also a good social side to student life, including the regular céilithe. A man called Gus O'Donnell was the Fear an Tí. In 1939 for some reason – perhaps it was the imminent onset of war or the IRA bombing campaign – there were regular visits for whatever reason from the Special Branch. This was due to the increased IRA activity, although we as students were not really affected due to the fact that most of our time was spent in the college. The Special Branch usually asked for the names of everyone present. Now Gus told us to write any name and when it came to my turn I duly signed the book "Joe Keohane, Tralee, Co Kerry." The only one who deviated from this was an Englishman who signed himself as attending Strawberry Hill. There was a subsequent investigation and the Principal couldn't understand how a solitary Englishman came to be attending this céilí. But that wasn't the only way in which attendance at these céilithe could lead to trouble.

There was also the other occasion when I was dancing happily, not noticing that all my friends had long since gone back to the halls of residence. A curfew was in place which required students to be in at a certain time and my escape from trouble came courtesy of help from Joe Kane.

Strawberry Hill is a very historic building having been once owned by Horace Walpole and later by a Lady Waldergrave. Many of the rooms still contained some of the old furnishings from that period in the eighteenth and nineteenth centuries, including tapestries on the walls. The lawns were also very old, not having been disturbed for many years. It's also interesting to recollect how the college came to be at Strawberry Hill in the first place. Prior to moving there, the teacher-training college was located in Cadby Hall, which was located beside the factory of J. Lyons and Company. They wanted to extend and needed the college, so the Corkman in charge of Strawberry Hill College made a deal for the purchase of Strawberry Hill. A road was constructed, many of the trees were sold off and students began attending the new college site in 1925. [3]

A few years ago I returned to Strawberry Hill for the first time in many years. The archivist told me that I ranked about third in the list of oldest former students. The college has become very extensive now as part of the University of Surrey.

Seeing the sights of London

It's said that 'all work and no play makes Jack a dull boy.' There was certainly time and plenty of opportunities for recreation around London during that period just before the start of World War Two. Every weekend we visited nearby Hampton Court, home to King Henry VIII. There was free entry, amazing compared to now when entry charge is about £15. It was a short and relaxing walk from Strawberry Hill and then, as now, was a very popular destination, especially with the wild deer in Bushy Park which is adjacent to Hampton Court.

There were also visits into the City of London. This trip began by getting the train from Strawberry Hill Station, a little train stop which cost sixpence in old money. The return was always timed for an hour before lights-out time at the college. We also got egg, chips, tea and a ham roll for eight new pence in a small cafe frequented mostly by the bus and train drivers.

---

3 – The original St Mary's College, Strawberry Hill was located close to the factory of the caterers, J Lyon and Company. Their expansion plans and also those of St Mary's resulted in a sale of land to the firm which enabled the purchase of Strawberry Hill, where the first pupils began attending in 1925.

The St Mary's College Rugby 1st XV from 1938-39 season. Pictured in the back row are Paddy Cullen, R Rice, GK Hickman, John Barrow, J O'Connell, CP Collins, M Quinlan, P Monaghan. Sitting in the middle row are W Wood, JJ B Ward, JJ Chamberlain, FM Donan (captain), Pat MacFlynn (vice-captain), Gerald McCormack, WJ Fanem. At front are JG Cunningham, PJ Power, FJ Breen and F Barnes.

I got to know London fairly as a student in the city. It was and still is lovely around Strawberry Hill. Among the attractions was a very scenic towpath along the River Thames which allowed people the chance to walk up as far as Windsor Castle. Alternatively, there was the chance to get Joe Mier's Steamers, who travelled along the river to Hampton Court and Windsor and had a stop at Strawberry Hill. Little has changed in Twickenham and when I last visited the little café was still there, although the Ricksaw Cinema has been turned into a large furniture store.

Of course, no visit to Twickenham would be complete without going to the famous rugby stadium. Some of the Irish students, including myself, paraded to the ground with a tricolour on the occasions when Ireland were playing there during the late 1930s. However, that tradition was stopped in 1939 on the advice of the principal after a number of bombings in London and he felt it wasn't appropriate.

One of the biggest events was the rugby sevens which at that time drew the best players from clubs throughout Europe and was of a very high standard. Jim Houston from Castledawson worked in the civil service and was a steward at the stadium. He was able to provide me with free tickets, which was very important because money was very tight and nobody wanted to be spending too freely.

Just like students nowadays, there were always ways to save. We discovered for instance that, rather than sending our socks to the laundry, it was better to buy a new pair at six pence, wash them every night and then replace them again when they were worn out!

I had ten shillings each time I left Magherafelt for Twickenham to cover my expenses for the term. God rest my mother, she'd have sent an envelope with a pound enclosed. While my father never wrote, she did correspond regularly and always signed her letters "Your POM" or "Poor Old Mother."

Playing rugby with other future GAA stalwarts

It was during this period at Twickenham that I also first played rugby and there's still a photograph of the team to prove my involvement! I was on the first team at the university and was quite good without being spectacular. Our standard was probably around the same as the third teams at London Irish or London Welsh.

Matches took place every Wednesday and Saturday and one of the big advantages and attractions was that the players got special food rations. The other members of the team included Basil McGuckian from Magherafelt, the future Tyrone chairman, Paddy Cullen who was originally from Leitrim and Paddy Donnelly, who in 1942 captained Tyrone to their first Lagan Cup title. I played in both 1937-38 and 1938-39 and was vice-captain. We never got caught for playing foreign games and the players felt that they were exempt by being in England. There was no vigilance committee around either to observe us. [4]

---

4 – So-called vigilance committees enforced the ban on foreign games which was enshrined in the GAA rule book until 1971. They were often controversial in their approach.

A cold and windy day in Twickenham didn't deter this rugby team from St Mary's Strawberry Hill which was pictured in 1937.

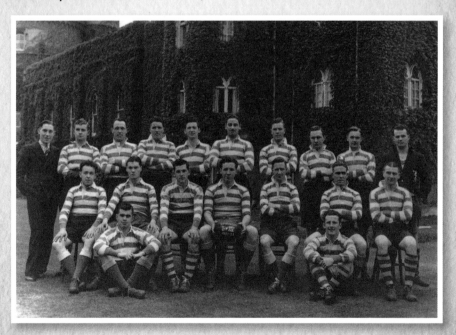

My first year at St Mary's College also saw me delve into the world of rugby. Here I am pictured fifth from left in the back row on the 1st XV team of 1937-1938.

It was the summer of 1939 when I eventually graduated with my Certificate in Education. They had a good system where those who had misbehaved were failed on what we called 'scum English.' That basically meant some pressure writing which really could have been done by a primary school pupil. Then, the following year they sent on the exam for the failed student to complete at home. They obviously passed comfortably the second time around.

Students also had the opportunity to spend another year to obtain a degree through the University of Surrey. But this wasn't for me and there was no doubting my delight at having finally qualified as a teacher. It's important to acknowledge, though, that the Irish students did have a good standard of education before embarking on their university careers.

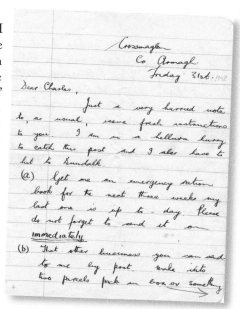

Letters home to Charlie helped keep the GAA wheels moving from Crossmaglen to Magherafelt.

This ultimately ensured that completing the course was reasonably straightforward.

Part of the qualification included a requirement to take a class in religion. It was amusing because the Northern Ireland Education sent over an inspector who would also complete an assessment with the student on teaching practice. Later on I completed a Dip-Ed or Diploma in Education and it was while completing this that I met my future wife, Kathleen.

My time in Twickenham finished just before the outbreak of war in 1939. There was a lot of panic in the city around the time of the Munich Agreement in 1938. People were out on the streets digging trenches and all of us had to go and get fitted with gasmasks. A week's holiday at home was granted due to the danger of war. One student from the Glens of Antrim didn't come back for another week because, as he said, the communications where he lived were bad and the postman only delivered once a week.

On the day after the war started, 3 September 1939, I began my teaching career in Cookstown.

My early teaching career

That momentous Sunday, 3 September 1939, was a very wet day which saw myself and the rest of the Rossa players head to Dungannon for a tournament. One of the teams we played was from Dundalk and they had a big midfielder who duly put manners on me. I thought I was tough, but he was tougher.

The next morning saw me travel the fairly short distance from Magherafelt to Cookstown to begin as a substitute teacher, receiving £3 per week. Andy McLarnon, who was the father of the late Dean Francis McLarnon was the station-master in Magherafelt and used to be wagging me down in the afternoon to catch the train.

The railway station in Magherafelt, a familiar scene for me in the 1940s.

A lot of time was spent travelling to different schools around the country while waiting for a full-time post to come along. One of these posting was to Dromard, a little country school near Draperstown. There were a number of Protestant pupils who also attended. But they went outside when religion was being taught.

On a Friday evening all the desks were pulled back for dancing. I was a reasonable dancer, so it wasn't too difficult to teach. Dean McGlinchey ensured that all the documents which came into the school were carefully altered by replacing the words Londonderry with Derry, and Draperstown with Ballinascreen. [5]

In Coalisland, the master was sick and I remember there was a small field beside the school. This allowed me the chance to run a football competition which was extremely good for both morale and discipline because any young lad who misbehaved wasn't allowed to play. This was the worst thing that could happen them and obviously did the trick.

During the early 1940s, I also spent time teaching in that great footballing stronghold of Crossmaglen which was very interesting. I stayed in a pub called Miss Harvey's and regularly bought a couple of bottles of brandy to send back to my brother Charlie at home. Each morning I'd cycle there past Hackballscross and towards Dundalk.

It was a great run to school, but not so pleasant heading home when the downhills of the forward journey became more strenuous uphill challenges on the return!

The time spent in each of the schools, of course, varied, but generally lasted a couple of months. My whole summer was spent in Crossmaglen where the big job was getting coupons for petrol and filling in the forms for the smugglers to obtain the coupons. Each coupon had to be completed with a reason for why the fuel was required. A popular reason was for the applicant to 'attend divine worship three times today.'

I also played football illegally with Culloville and in the championship no less. Joe Watters was a great friend of mine there and duly recruited me. "Master, is that ball hard

I also played football illegally with Culloville and in the championship no less. Joe Watters was a great friend of mine there and duly recruited me. "Master, is that ball hard enough?," Joe said to me before the start, and my job was to check that it was properly pumped up. I had trained with them so maybe it was a natural progression to play.

It was in this period, too, that Gerry Arthurs first became an acquaintance of mine. At weekends he would join myself, Eddie McMahon and a man called McManus on trips to Armagh matches. We would get a car to Armagh matches.

My time as a pioneer was about to end as the group regularly stopped for a drink and the lemonade started causing a sore stomach.

It was slightly easier working in both Cookstown and Dromard because I was able to remain at home in Magherafelt and then get the train and bus respectively to and from the school. In Dromard, there was a small country lane leading to the school. Then, in the evening I would go into a house for a cup of tea while waiting for the bus to go home again.

However, getting home from Crossmaglen was a lot more difficult. Newry was the first halt, and then onto to Belfast before completing the last leg of the journey from Belfast to Magherafelt on the train. Sometimes I'd leave Magherafelt on a Sunday night and have to stay in Belfast or Newry overnight because the arrangements were so awkward.

That was during the war when there was double-summertime. However, Crossmaglen kept with the old time. This meant that instead of school starting at 9.30 am it really didn't start until 11.30 am by everyone else's watches. An inspector arrived one morning at 10am and found the school empty. He eventually located me still at home in bed and asked what was going on. Nevertheless, the school still finished at 4.30pm rather than an hour later as required by the inspector and the authorities.

Many fond evenings were spent touring the beautiful countryside around Slieve Gullion by bicycle. Among the places visited was Creggan, the famous Creggan of the O'Neill's and a very historic location. It was a short trip into Monaghan from there.

Jobs were very hard to come by and around this time, too, I taught for a while in Anahorish, a small town land just outside Castledawson.

Here Seamus Heaney may have been an accidental student of mine. Most of my time there was spent teaching the young refugees and evacuees from Belfast during World War Two.[6] They were eventually subsumed into the main classes. Master Murphy was the principal and invited me down. After about three weeks a Monsignor Ward came with the bad news that the Ministry weren't going to recognise my time spent in Anahorish and that there would be no payment. Fortunately, Mrs Murphy, a decent woman, gave me three pots of homemade jam as payment. Ballymaguigan was another posting for a short period while the teacher there, Master Young, was off.

---

6 – Refugees from Belfast were evacuated to rural areas of the north in the early years of the war. Anahorish, a townland close to Castledawson and located around 30 miles from the city, was one such location.

Just like today, it was a case of going to where the work was. The time spent might only have been a day or week here and there, but the pay was £3 per week. As a result every opportunity for work was relished.

My first full-time teaching post

Finally, after a couple of years my first full-time teaching post was back at home in Magherafelt. This sojourn lasted until the move to Ballynahinch in 1948. It was just by chance that the job in Magherafelt became available. A teacher in Ballinascreen took the strange notion of joining the airforce. This created a vacancy and Felix McElhone who was the assistant in Magherafelt applied and was successful. It suited him to move because his wife was from Ballinascreen.

Canon Ward then sent for me and gave me the job which paid £162 per annum. That was a great sum considering that the previous few years had been spent living hand to mouth and substituting in a variety of schools. After a couple of years there was also an £80 war-bonus, an absolute fortune at that time. I remember rushing to the bank to open my first account.

The experience in Magherafelt was very enjoyable and there was very little trouble with the students who were invariably well behaved. Some of them still remember my time teaching them. It's wasn't a problem either teaching the sisters or brothers of my friends and neighbours.

In any case, I wasn't a great person for corporal punishment which was so prevalent at that time. The principal in one former school of mine spent a whole week with the cane out punishing the children. He asked on the Friday evening whether he would come back. Maybe he was surprised when I said no. All the canes were burnt on the Monday morning. "If that's the only way you can teach, then you shouldn't be in the job," I said to him. He was the one who made me realise how stupid it is to rely on corporal punishment. Ultimately, if a child doesn't know something, using the cane isn't going to help.

My approach to children and teaching was always very clear. There has to be respect and great care must be taken not to say anything which might be hurtful to them.

While caning was bad, the bitter tongue is even worse and to say anything, for instance if they had a physical disability, was totally unacceptable. I always used to control my tongue, even when that might have been difficult. It could be so easy and consequently hurtful to take that anger out on the children.

There were about thirty children in the class in Magherafelt at that time. One of the other teachers was Master Ned O'Brien, a famous character who was originally from Monaghan and who took a great interest in the horses and dogs. One day he was heading to a race-meeting in Omagh when suddenly who arrived only the inspector. "My father's not well," he said, waving goodbye to the inspector without a care.

Our routine generally began in the morning with Maths, followed by English. It was important to get the children interested in reading. We then did geography, but one subject that I didn't bother much about was singing, mostly because of my own limitations in this regard. However, in Gilford I taught the pupils 'Baidin Fheidhlimidh'.

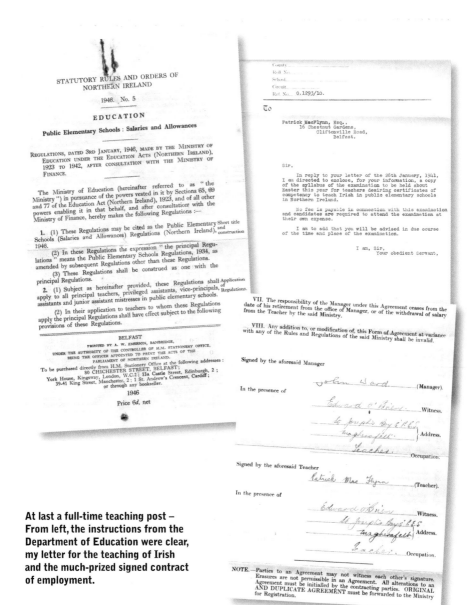

At last a full-time teaching post – From left, the instructions from the Department of Education were clear, my letter for the teaching of Irish and the much-prized signed contract of employment.

TEACHER'S CERTIFICATE EXAMINATION—PASS LIST, 1939.

ST. MARY'S COLLEGE—continued.

1321. Davies, Reginald Paul	ED	hy	—	E	e	H	—	—	—	—	F	—	—	HK
1322. Deegan, John	**ED**	**hy**	**pt**	E	—	H	—	—	—	—	—	mu	A	**HK**
1323. Diggle, Thomas	ED	hy	PT	E	—	H	—	—	—	—	—	**mu**	a	hk
1324. Doran, Francis Maurice	ED	hy	pt	E	—	—	M	—	**P**	—	—	—	a	HK
1325. Dowling, Edmund	ED	hy	PT	E	—	H	—	—	—	—	—	—	a	HK
1326. Duffy, Bernard Dennis	ED	hy	pt	E	e	H	—	—	—	—	—	—	—	hk
1327. Duffy, Thomas	ED	hy	pt	E	e	—	G	—	—	—	—	—	—	hk
1328. Dusting, James Edward Bernard	ED	hy	pt	E	e	—	G	—	—	—	—	mu	—	hk
1329. Eccles, John	ED	hy	pt	E	e	—	—	m	—	—	—	—	a	HK
1330. Egan, Gerald	ED	hy	PT	E	—	H	g	—	—	—	—	—	a	—
1331. Farren, William John	ED	hy	PT	E	e	H	—	—	—	—	L	—	—	hk
1333. Ferguson, George	**ED**	hy	pt	—	—	**H**	—	—	—	—	—	mu	a	hk
1334. Flower, Francis Bernard	ED	hy	pt	E	—	H	G	m	—	—	—	—	—	HK
1335. Ford, James	ED	**hy**	pt	E	e	**H**	—	—	—	—	—	mu	—	**hk**
1336. Fowles, Bernard John	ED	hy	pt	E	—	H	g	—	—	—	—	mu	—	HK
1337. Gallagher, Edmund	ED	hy	—	E	e	H	—	—	—	—	F	—	—	hk
1338. Guilfoyle, Herbert	ED	hy	—	E	—	H	g	—	—	—	—	—	a	hk
1339. Hackett, Henry Francis	ED	hy	pt	E	e	—	—	m	—	—	F	mu	—	—
1340. Harrison, Edmund	ED	hy	pt	E	e	—	g	m	—	—	—	—	—	hk
1342. Hodgson, James	ED	hy	**PT**	E	—	—	G	—	—	—	—	—	a	HK
1343. Hulme, Thomas Joseph	ED	hy	pt	E	—	—	g	m	—	—	—	—	a	HK
1344. Hunt, Kenneth Wreford	ED	**hy**	PT	E	—	—	g	m	—	—	—	—	**a**	**HK**
1345. Kelly, Ernest Joseph	ED	hy	pt	E	e	—	—	—	—	F	—	mu	—	hk
1346. Kilgallon, Patrick	ED	hy	—	E	e	H	—	—	—	—	—	—	a	hk
1347. Kirrane, Michael Joseph	ED	hy	pt	E	e	H	g	—	—	—	—	—	—	hk
1348. Larrissey, Joseph	ED	hy	pt	E	e	H	—	—	—	—	F	—	—	hk
1349. Lewis, James Stanley	ED	—	pt	E	e	H	—	—	—	—	—	mu	—	hk
1350. Loughran, Lawrence	ED	hy	pt	E	e	—	g	m	—	—	—	mu	—	hk
1351. McAllister, Hugh Alphonsus	ED	hy	pt	E	—	**H**	—	m	—	—	—	mu	—	hk
1352. McAndrews, John Robert Little	ED	hy	pt	E	e	H	—	m	—	—	—	—	—	HK
1353. McCarthy, Vincent Benedict	ED	hy	PT	E	—	h	G	—	—	—	—	mu	—	HK
1354. McCaughan, Hugh Albert	ED	hy	PT	E	e	—	—	M	—	—	—	mu	—	hk
1355. McCavana, Edward Francis	ED	hy	pt	E	e	—	g	—	—	—	—	mu	—	**HK**
1356. McCormack, Gerald James	ED	hy	pt	E	—	H	—	—	—	—	—	—	a	HK
1357. McFarland, Patrick Pearse	ED	**hy**	pt	E	**e**	—	G	—	**C**	—	—	mu	—	—
1358. McFlynn, Patrick Joseph	ED	hy		E		—	H	—	m	—	—	—	—	hk
1359. McGlynn, James Patrick	ED	hy										—	a	hk
1360. McGuiggan, John Anthony	ED	hy												
1361. McGuinness, James Joseph	ED	hy												
1362. McHugh, Francis	ED	hy												
1363. McKay, Alexander Patrick	ED	hy												
1364. Mahoney, Diarmudd McCarthy	ED	hy												
1365. Marsh, Francis William	ED	hy												
1366. Mayland, Cyril Frederick	ED	hy												
1367. Molloy, Thomas	ED	hy												
1368. Monaghan, Francis Joseph	ED	hy												
1369. Morgan, John	ED	hy												
1370. Mullany, John	ED	hy												
1371. Murphy, John	ED	hy												
1372. Murray, Wilfred Gerrard	ED	h												
1373. O'Brien, Martin John	ED	h												
1374. O'Brien, Thomas Edward	ED													
1375. O'Byrne, John Leonard	ED													
1377. Power, Richard	ED													
1378. Pozzi, John Clement Charles	ED													

Year of Service	Scale I		Scale II		Scale III		Scale IV	
	Men	Women	Men	Women	Men	Women	Men	Women
	£	£	£	£	£	£	£	£
1	280	250	295	260	315	275	315	275
2	280	250	295	260	315	275	315	275
3	295	260	310	270	330	285	315	275
4	310	270	325	280	345	295	330	285
5	325	280	340	290	360	305	345	295
6	340	290	355	300	375	315	360	305
7	355	300	370	310	390	325	375	315
8	370	310	385	320	405	335	390	325
9	385	320	400	330	420	345	405	335
10	400	330	415	340	435	355	420	345
11	415	340	430	350	450	365	435	355
12	430	350	445	360	465	375	450	365
13	445	360	460	370	480	385	465	375
14	460	370	475	380	495	395	480	385
15	475	380	490	390	510	405	495	395
16	490	390	505	400	525	415	510	405
17	505	400	520	410	540	425	525	415
18	520	410	535	420	555	435	540	425
19	535	420	550	430	570	445	555	435
20	550		565	440	585	455	570	445
21		440		450		465	585	455
22		450		460		475	600	465
23								475
24								485

My name is listed here with all my fellow graduates. It was a welcome boost to finally have my own money.

A Life in Colour

Relaxing with my father during a visit to Magherafelt in the late 1950s.

Church Street, Magherafelt

Church Street many years ago. Little had changed when I first remember my home street in the 1920s. The characters and people of that time are still fresh in my memory.

The Church of the Assumption on King Street, where I was baptised, received my First Holy Communion and was confirmed.

Magherafelt was a bustling market town during my youth. This is Market Street.

The MacFlynn jaunting car on the Castledawson Road.

My parents pictured on their wedding day in 1912.

Millie, Charlie and myself enjoying blowing up balloons.

RAINEY SCH. INC FORME
HEAD MASTERS' HOUSE

The Rainey Endowed School, which in 2013 celebrated its Tir-Centenary. I am one of the oldest surviving pupils.

35th INTER-COLLEGE ANNUAL

ATHLETIC SPORTS MEETING

Of the METROPOLITAN TRAINING COLLEGES

(Under A.A.A. Laws, by permission of the A.A.A.)

UNIVERSITY OF LONDON ATHLETIC GROUND
MOTSPUR PARK

Saturday, 21st May, 1938, at 2.45 p.m.

The Challenge Shield will be presented by the Principal of Westminster College.

Competing Colleges :

WESTMINSTER.	GOLDSMITHS'.
S. MARK & S. JOHN.	SHOREDITCH.
ST. MARY'S.	BOROUGH ROAD.

COMMITTEE OF MANAGEMENT:

PRESIDENT : Dr. A. W. HARRISON.

WESTMINSTER.
Dr. A. W. Harrison.
Mr. T. B. Shepherd.
Mr. W. E. Scott.

S. MARK & S. JOHN.
Mr. J. H. Simpson.
Mr. W. A. Moulton.
Mr. D. Harris.

ST. MARY'S.
Rev. V. MacCarthy, C.M.
Mr. A. D. Calvert.
Mr. J. E. Cunningham.

GOLDSMITHS'.
Dr. E. S. F. Ridout.
Mr. F. H. Woollaston.
Mr. J. E. Kett.

SHOREDITCH.
Mr. A. G. Scrivens.
Mr. J. E. Daniel.
Mr. E. W. F. Polley.

BOROUGH ROAD.
Mr. E. R. Hamilton.
Mr. J. H. S. Terry.
Mr. C. R. Gladwin.

Officials :

REFEREE : Mr. Arthur E. Wotton, Mx.C.A.A.A.

STARTER : Mr. E. F. Vowles, Sy.C.A.A.A.

JUDGES : Messrs. M. E. Dowdall, Mx.C.A.A.A.; W. G. Elwood, Mx.C.A.A.A.; G. D. Innes, Sy.C.A.A.A.;
H. C. Lomax, Mx.C.A.A.A.; A. Ovenden, Mx.C.A.A.A.; W. D. Willison, Sy.C.A.A.A.

TIME-KEEPERS : Mr. A. L. Kent, Mx.C.A.A.A.; Mr. H. J. Rothery, Sy.C.A.A.A.

ANNOUNCER : Mr. E. H. Neville, Sy.C.A.A.A.

RECORDER : Mr. J. G. Freeman.   COMPETITORS' STEWARD : Mr. P. C. Walton.

Only Officials and Competitors allowed within the Enclosure.

PRICE   -   FOURPENCE.

I played rugby while at Strawberry Hill. We were in London, so the ban on foreign games rule didn't seem to apply.

Laverty's Bar, a happy home for myself and Kathleen.

With Kathleen in France on holiday.

Our holidays away were always very enjoyable, especially driving on the continent.

Over many years, myself and Kathleen were fortunate to travel throughout Europe and particularly France and Spain. Here we are relaxing by the roadside, enjoying the scenery and at home with the dog.

TOP – The distinctive red of our Rossa membership card – a much sought after item.

BOTTOM – Luckily, my stay in Alcatraz was a short one and purely on recreational grounds.

Crossmaglen
Co Armagh.   c. 1942

A Tearbhraith,

I got here damned tired and feel as if Horse Mc Kenna had been kicking me all day. I have a few scattered ideas so I tabulate them as I cannot start writing to any length.

(a) Keenan is suspended for 3 months calendar ie 12 weeks this is up on 24th June. If there is an Ulster Council meeting on 27th Ham might be OK.

(b) Pay Andy Jock + give him coupons.

(c) If Anthony J. comes give him £17 in envelope in my room

(d) Send on my pay immediately it comes

(e) Drop me a note about that Monghan chap + maybe I could square things at Blayney on Sunday

My letters home were the best way to keep in touch in those days before email and mobile phones.

Cʀom-Ⱥbu

It was on my proposal in 1934 that the Magherafelt club was called in honour of O'Donnovan Rossa. This is the club crest, marking the Hawk of the Hill.

Bronnⱥd ⱥʀ P. Mⱥc Floin
Ⱥᵹ Comⱥiʀle Ulⱥd C.L.C.
Uⱥctⱥʀⱥn 1961 - 63

The plaque on my living-room cabinet which I received marking by term as President of the Ulster GAA.

SOUVENIR
OF THE OFFICIAL OPENING OF
ROGER CASEMENT PARK
Andersonstown   ::   Belfast
From 14th till 21st June, 1953

The opening of Casement Park was a major event in 1953 and I still retain the ticket from that occasion. This is the official souvenir programme from that day.

TEACHER'S CERTIFICATE EXAMINATION—PASS LIST, 1939.

ST. MARY'S COLLEGE—continued.

1321.	Davies, Reginald Paul	ED	hy	—	E	e	H	—	—	—	—	—	F	—	—	— HK
1322.	Deegan, John	ED	hy	pt	E	—	H	—	—	—	—	—	—	—	mu A HK
1323.	Diggle, Thomas	ED	hy	PT	E	—	H	—	—	—	—	—	—	—	mu a hk
1324.	Doran, Francis Maurice	ED	hy	pt	E	—	—	—	M	—	P	—	—	—	a HK
1325.	Dowling, Edmund	ED	hy	PT	E	—	H	—	m	—	—	—	—	—	a HK
1326.	Duffy, Bernard Dennis	ED	hy	pt	E	e	H	—	—	—	—	—	—	—	— hk
1327.	Duffy, Thomas	ED	hy	pt	E	e	—	G	—	—	—	—	—	mu	— hk
1328.	Dusting, James Edward Bernard	ED	hy	pt	E	e	—	G	—	—	—	—	—	mu	— hk
1329.	Eccles, John	ED	hy	pt	E	e	—	—	m	—	—	—	—	—	a HK
1330.	Egan, Gerald	ED	hy	PT	E	—	H	g	—	—	—	—	—	—	— hk
1331.	Farren, William John	ED	hy	PT	E	e	H	—	—	—	—	—	L	—	— hk
1333.	Ferguson, George	ED	hy	pt	E	—	H	—	—	—	—	—	—	mu a	hk
1334.	Flower, Francis Bernard	ED	hy	pt	E	—	H	G	m	—	—	—	—	—	HK
1335.	Ford, James	ED	hy	pt	E	e	H	—	—	—	—	—	—	mu	— hk
1336.	Fowles, Bernard John	ED	hy	pt	E	e	H	g	—	—	—	—	—	mu	— HK
1337.	Gallagher, Edmund	ED	hy	—	E	e	H	—	—	—	—	F	—	—	— hk
1338.	Guilfoyle, Herbert	ED	hy	—	E	—	H	g	—	—	—	—	—	—	a hk
1339.	Hackett, Henry Francis	ED	hy	pt	E	e	—	—	m	—	—	F	—	mu	— —
1340.	Harrison, Edmund	ED	hy	pt	E	e	—	g	m	—	—	—	—	—	— hk
1342.	Hodgson, James	ED	hy	PT	E	e	—	G	—	—	—	—	—	—	a HK
1343.	Hulme, Thomas Joseph	ED	hy	pt	E	—	—	g	m	—	—	—	—	—	a HK
1344.	Hunt, Kenneth Wreford	ED	hy	PT	E	—	—	g	m	—	—	—	—	—	a HK
1345.	Kelly, Ernest Joseph	ED	hy	pt	E	e	—	—	—	—	—	F	—	mu	— hk
1346.	Kilgallon, Patrick	ED	hy	—	E	e	H	—	—	—	—	—	—	—	a hk
1347.	Kirrane, Michael Joseph	ED	hy	pt	E	e	H	g	—	—	—	—	—	—	— hk
1348.	Larrissey, Joseph	ED	hy	pt	E	e	H	—	—	—	—	F	—	—	— hk
1349.	Lewis, James Stanley	ED	—	pt	E	e	H	—	—	—	—	—	—	mu	— hk
1350.	Loughran, Lawrence	ED	hy	pt	E	e	—	g	m	—	—	—	—	mu	— hk
1351.	McAllister, Hugh Alphonsus	ED	hy	pt	E	—	H	—	m	—	—	—	—	mu	— hk
1352.	McAndrews, John Robert Little	ED	hy	pt	E	e	H	—	m	—	—	—	—	—	— HK
1353.	McCarthy, Vincent Benedict	ED	hy	PT	E	—	h	G	—	—	—	—	—	mu	— HK
1354.	McCaughan, Hugh Albert	ED	hy	PT	E	e	—	M	—	—	—	—	—	mu	— hk
1355.	McCavana, Edward Francis	ED	hy	pt	E	e	—	g	—	—	—	—	—	mu	— HK
1356.	McCormack, Gerald James	ED	hy	pt	E	—	H	—	—	—	—	—	—	—	a hk
1357.	McFarland, Patrick Pearse	ED	hy	pt	E	e	—	G	—	C	—	—	—	mu	— —
1358.	McFlynn, Patrick Joseph	ED	hy	pt	E	e	—	H	—	m	—	—	—	—	— hk
1359.	McGlynn, James Patrick	ED	hy	PT	E	—	H	—	—	—	P	—	—	—	a hk
1360.	McGuiggan, John Anthony	ED	hy	pt	E	e	—	m	—	—	—	—	—	mu a	hk
1361.	McGuinness, James Joseph	ED	hy	PT	E	e	H	m	—	—	—	—	—	—	— hk
1362.	McHugh, Francis	ED	hy	PT	E	e	h	—	—	—	—	—	—	—	a hk
1363.	McKay, Alexander Patrick	ED	hy	pt	E	e	H	—	m	—	—	—	—	—	— hk
1364.	Mahoney, Diarmudd McCarthy	ED	hy	pt	E	—	H	g	—	—	—	—	—	—	a HK
1365.	Marsh, Francis William	ED	hy	pt	E	—	h	G	—	—	—	F	—	—	— hk
1366.	Mayland, Cyril Frederick	ED	hy	PT	E	—	h	G	—	—	—	—	—	—	a hk
1367.	Molloy, Thomas	ED	hy	pt	E	e	H	g	—	—	—	—	—	—	— hk
1368.	Monaghan, Francis Joseph	ED	hy	pt	E	—	—	g	m	—	—	—	—	mu	— HK
1369.	Morgan, John	ED	hy	PT	E	e	—	m	—	—	—	—	—	—	a HK
1370.	Mullany, John	ED	hy	pt	E	—	—	g	—	C	—	—	—	mu	— hk
1371.	Murphy, John	ED	hy	pt	E	e	H	—	m	—	—	—	—	—	— hk
1372.	Murray, Wilfred Gerrard	ED	hy	pt	E	—	H	—	—	—	—	—	L	—	a hk
1373.	O'Brien, Martin John	ED	hy	—	E	e	H	—	m	—	—	—	—	—	— hk
1374.	O'Brien, Thomas Edward	ED	hy	pt	E	e	h	—	—	—	—	—	—	mu a	hk
1375.	O'Byrne, John Leonard	ED	hy	pt	E	—	—	g	—	C	—	—	—	mu	— —
1377.	Power, Richard	ED	hy	pt	E	—	h	G	—	—	—	—	—	mu	— hk

A moment to savour was when I graduated as a teacher from St Mary's College. The names of those who joined Patrick Joseph MacFlynn are listed here.

DUPLICATE FOR TEACHER.

SIX PENCE

Registered in the Ministry of Education for Northern Ireland,

James L. E. Gormley

27th day of November, 1942

MEMORANDUM OF AN AGREEMENT, made the _____16 th_____ day of _____October November_____ One Thousand Nine Hundred and _____forty two_____ between _____Rt Rev Mons. Ward P.P._____, Local Manager of the _____St Joseph's Boys'_____ Public Elementary School (hereinafter called the Manager), of the one part, and _____Patrick Mac Flynn_____, Teacher of the said School (hereinafter called the Teacher), of the other part:

I. The Manager agrees to employ the Teacher as the _____assistant_____ Teacher of the _____Magherafelt St Joseph's Boys'_____ School, from the _____16 th_____ day of _____October_____, 194 2, henceforth until the expiration of three calendar months from the date at which notice in writing shall have been given by either side to the other to determine the said employment.

II. The Manager shall have absolute power to determine the said employment at any time without previous notice to the Teacher; but in every such case (not coming under Article III) he shall be bound to pay to the Teacher three months' salary, recoverable as a debt, or such smaller sum as, having regard to the circumstances of the case, the Ministry of Education for Northern Ireland shall determine to be equitable.

III. The Manager shall also have power to determine the said employment without previous notice, for misconduct or other sufficient cause; in which case the Teacher shall not be entitled to any compensation.

IV. In case the Teacher shall determine the said employment at any time without giving three calendar months' notice, as hereinbefore provided (except for good and sufficient cause), he (she) shall pay to the Manager three months' salary, recoverable as a debt, or such smaller sum as, having regard to the circumstances of the case, the said Ministry shall determine to be equitable, and the Manager hereby undertakes to apply any sum so forfeited and paid for such purposes and benefit of the said School as the said Ministry may direct or approve.

*Where inapplicable this paragraph may be struck out.

* Provided always that, notwithstanding anything to the contrary in this agreement contained, the Manager may in his own absolute discretion determine this agreement in manner provided in Clause I hereof upon or at any time after the marriage of the Teacher.

V. The duties of the Teacher shall be such as are in accordance with the Rules of the said Ministry.

VI. The salary and emoluments of the Teacher shall be such amounts as are payable under and in accordance with the Rules and Regulations of the said Ministry.

The contract of employment when I began my teaching career at St Joseph's National School in Magherafelt.

Relaxing with friends at home in Laurencetown in 1966.

There was always a chance to holiday with family as well, including Eddie. On this occasion we stayed at home and travelled to Donegal.

SPREADING THE GAA MESSAGE

The GAA's Ard Comhairle pictured at a meeting in 1942. This historic photograph shows Ulster GAA Presidents, Padraig McNamee and myself, as well as long-time secretary and close friend, Gerry Arthurs.

Back to the GAA and Derry's growth

My qualification as a teacher had the knock-on benefit of providing me with some more time to concentrate on the task of putting the Derry GAA on a more solid footing.

By then matters were settling down very quickly and nicely within the county. Lavey and Ballinderry were the two most established teams, so it was a case of trying to increase interest further as county secretary. As a result, I became a founder member of a number of clubs. I recall talking to some people in Bellaghy and the decision was taken to have a meeting to establish the club there. It was my job to meet them and 'preach the GAA gospel' as it were. They at least some support. My line was that we were trying to promote the Irish games in Derry and as Irishmen we each had a role to play. "There is no club here and we need one," was often my mission statement. A similar situation happened in Slaughtneil.

Affairs were also strengthened in Derry City, where three of us travelled there to hold a meeting with Eddie McAteer, Phonsie Deane and several others to set up the City Board. Typical of Derry, there were about fourteen teams who had expressed an interest in becoming involved and were all enthusiastic. Unfortunately that didn't last too long.

The county board meetings were generally held in schools or after a club championship match or whenever Derry played. But the fact that I was still playing and was also county secretary did lead to some occasional problems.

There was no such thing as emails and all the secretarial duties were completed longhand and then posted. The work involved back then obviously wasn't as onerous as would be the case now. All we had to do was organise the championships and other bits and pieces like inter-club transfers.

Correspondence from Croke Park and the coaching seminars and other issues which are so prevalent in the twenty-first century were virtually unheard of.

Another job completed at this time was the purchase of Celtic Park. The ground was far from being a suitable venue initially. There was a corrugated hut at one end and the gasworks and pigs at the other end.

Most clubs at that time were relying on the usual farmer's field, not only in Derry but also throughout Ulster. The purchase of Celtic Park, the County Grounds in Magherafelt and other venues went a long way towards putting clubs and counties in the north on a more solid footing and improving the GAA and the games.

Firstly, the ownership of a ground provided clubs with a sense of belonging, something that was their own and that they could do with what they liked. They were no longer depending on the goodwill of people and had the capacity to train when required because they now had a pitch at their disposal. It was wonderful the way clubs reacted to the challenge. My experience in Magherafelt and Tullylish proved just how vital a step forward pitch ownership was.

My job as county secretary also entailed making the various arrangements attached to Derry matches. We played in the Ulster Junior Championship and it says a lot when among the best footballers was Harry Owens. Formerly of Tyrone, he was well into his 40s during that period.

It was often a case of ensuring that all the fixtures were fulfilled. Some things were similar to today, including the transport and meals for the Derry seniors when they were playing. At that time the after-match refreshments consisted of the famous 'meat-tea.' This was salad with roast beef and white bread and margarine. That was the standard and it amuses me to think about the steaks, pasta and so on which is the staple diet of county players. In the 1940s, the meals were always generally taken in hotels. McGuckian's was one such venue and O'Neill's on Rainey Street in Magherafelt another.

Barney Murphy was the leading light and we had the three or four Tyrone men from Ballinderry! Mick McGuckin, Gustie McGuckin, and a few from Newbridge and Ballinderry were also there. They only played Junior Championship, so it wasn't the greatest standard. [1]

Sent off in the County Final

For me, the Rossas of Magherafelt always came first, and this was certainly the case in the early 1940s. But then there was the famous 1942 county final when I was county secretary and also had the dishonour of being sent off.

Glenullin provided the opposition and during this period the county finals were usually alternated between north Derry one year and South Derry the next. But a problem arose in 1942 when the final ended in a draw. The venue for the replay was the next big question and Glenullin argued that the replay should take place in North Derry.

The county board supported the Rossa viewpoint that it should be relocated to South Derry. Consequently, the issue was discussed by the Ulster Council and the end result was that the title was awarded to Magherafelt.

It would have been interesting to see how the replay might have gone, but one thing for certain was the drawn tie was very tough. Pat 'Mugsy' Keenan was one of our main players and hadn't been well in the run-up to the game. He was receiving a fairly tough time from one of the Glenullin players. Our captain, Patsy 'Sticky' Maguire told me in no uncertain terms that to 'do something about' the treatment being dished out to Pat.

So, the next time this player went up for the ball, I hit him full force and sent him out over the wire at the side of the pitch. They got him gathered up and then Paddy Larkin, the referee, said to me. "you better go off." That ended my involvement in the match, the referee, said to me. "you better go off." That ended my involvement in the match, but the most amusing aspect of the whole thing was afterwards when the county board meeting was held to discuss the final and the repercussions arising from it.

This generated some problems for myself due to having been sent off earlier in the day and under suspension. Every so often some of the other members would come outside to ask advice on some topic or other.

The Glenullin player definitely was definitely hit hard and was challenged coming down from a high catch. So, he was off-guard and just went sailing out. It's still fresh in my memory. Although we were awarded that title, there's no doubt that this Magherafelt team should have won far more championships.

At the time of the final my visits to Magherafelt were usually at weekends because of my teaching in Crossmaglen. There was no trip home on the weekends when the Rossa weren't playing. As a player, I was strong and a trier. Obviously the rough football around Culloville and Crossmaglen wasn't suited to Derry.

Apart from my own disciplinary issue, the various appeals were great craic altogether at the County Board meetings during those years. The officials, though, probably didn't think that at the time. There was no shortage of disciplinary issues investigating the numerous rows which seemed to be a feature of matches. The litigants were invariably outside cooking up their stories in unison and the mantra of 'heard nothing, saw nothing, nothing happened.'

My tenure as county secretary lasted from 1941 until 1945 and it was at this time too that I first became a member of the Ulster Council.

Horse hair seats and the redoubtable Gerry Arthurs

Our journeys began with the Rosary, complete with all the trimmings. Then, Gerry Arthurs would start recounting stories of the GAA in Ulster during the 1920s, the difficulties faced and his role in helping to smooth things.

That was my first experience of the man described as someone who did more than anyone to shape the Ulster GAA. It coincided with my becoming part of the Ulster Council for the first time, an association which has continued in some form or other right to the present.

This was prompted by my involvement as Derry secretary. Nobody from the county was able to attend as delegates to the Ulster Council. Paddy Larkin and myself took up this duty and the meetings were usually held in the old Imperial Hotel in Portadown. The first one was rather in inauspicious as we sat on a sofa with horse hair on it wondering if we would be admitted as delegates.

Gerry Arthurs, pictured extreme left, with the Ulster team in 1943.

The ruling was that there was no official representation from Derry, which meant that myself and Paddy Larkin were effectively nonentities. While we were permitted to sit at the meeting as observers, there was no such thing as taking part in the debates or voting.

Paddy McNamee was the president at that time and permitted our entry until there was official ratification of the Derry County Board. [2] Fortunately, that proved to be a short-lived difficulty, a meeting of the Derry County Board was held and our position was formalised. One of the others who joined with is was Eddie McAteer. There was only the South Derry Board at that time, so the GAA in the county was in a poor enough state.

At that time there were some great men on the Ulster Council, Alf Murray and, of course, Seamus McFerran from Antrim. Seán Ó Cinnéide from Dungloe was a great character and they were all tremendous GAA people.

Gerry Arthurs served as secretary for decades and his name is now perpetuated in the stand at Clones. [3] When I was based in Crossmaglen, we used to travel on a regular

2 – The GAA in Derry has its roots in the late 1880s before being reformed on a number of occasions in the early 20th century. Paddy MacFlynn was among those who put the association on a firm footing from the late 1930s onwards.

3 – Gerry Arthurs is seen as the architect of the modern GAA in Ulster. He served the Ulster Council in an official capacity until 1976. The main stand at St Tiernach's Park in Clones is named in his honour.

basis to matches, because there was very little transport available during those days of the Second World War. As a result, my routine would take me by train through the old Derry Central Line from Magherafelt to Portadown and on to Armagh. From then on, the journey would be completed by bicycle to Keady, with a meal at Trodden's Hotel in Armagh City, a popular GAA meeting place.

The challenges of holding meetings As Gaelige

A big feature of that period was the decision of the Ulster Council to change to holding its meetings entirely in Irish. This was something, though, which caused problems because it restricted the selection of counties who subsequently had to pick people who were fluent in Irish.

As a result, there was a belief that this seemed to favour teachers, something which wasn't accepted much. The motion to revert to Irish was proposed by Fr Éamonn Ó Doibhlinn, who later became the Parish Priest of Donaghmore.

The decision was taken and there were both positives and negatives. It caused difficulties and was perhaps a bit premature. However, the move also proved that Irish was a vehicle through which both counties and provinces could conduct their business and there was no doubt that this happened. Alf Murray, Seamus McFerran and Seán Ó Cinnéide were very dedicated to the language and encourage and promote its more widespread use.

But the extraordinary amazing thing about Gerry Arthurs was that he could never learn Irish properly. He understood what was going on and his brother Seán, who was professor of Irish at Queen's University, used to translate the minutes for him.

It wasn't a hindrance to him even though he never took part in discussions at the Ulster Council meetings. Instead, Gerry was someone who always had a lot of preparatory work done and he invariably relied on some other delegate to put his point of view across.

An example of Gerry's ability to organise things came some years later when a game between Donegal and Cavan finished in a draw. The two teams didn't come out for extra time and then, as now, this caused much confusion and annoyance. There was a full investigation and Gerry phoned to inform me that my presence was required at the subsequent meeting to discuss the issue.

As ex-officio chairman, I was moved to the chair and Gerry gave me very strict instructions that the game was to be replayed. We initially listened to the views of both teams as to why they didn't appear for extra time. Then, in typical GAA fashion, both counties were met privately outside the meeting. As chairman, it was my job to put it up to them that they would both be eliminated from the competition and the easiest solution was to replay the match. We got agreement, much to the delight of Gerry Arthurs.

Later, when I became President of the Ulster Council, Gerry would often receive a call from some club or county wanting a ruling or some problem resolved. He would invariably tell them that 'he'd have to contact the president.' There was no telephone in the school at that time. So, rather than waiting until the evening to contact the house in Laurencetown, Gerry waited an hour before phoning the person back to tell them that he'd been

Church Street in Magherafelt as it was before departing for Co Down. Note the delivery lorry outside MacFlynn's.

speaking to me and we both had made a decision. Then, when I'd come home from school, the call came through from Gerry telling me who had been on, what the problem was and how it had been sorted out. Of course, I didn't mind because he always did the right thing.

He was a great believer in the old adage that "the GAA is not run for money, but it takes money to run it." As a result, a lot of care was taken with admission prices. For instance, if the entrance fee to a game was two shillings he'd raise it to half a crown just to make it easier for change or for those at the gate. He was very good at big matches in Clones or elsewhere of having someone to keep an eye on things.

One such person on occasion was Billy Byrne, who became a great friend of mine later in life. Billy was usually stationed at the Fermanagh end of St Tiernach's Park and would stay around there making sure that everything was going according to plan. On one occasion, there was an incident when the man collecting the tickets went and handed them to his friend outside who sold them a second time. Billy became aware of this and promptly warned them that if this happened again, the Gardaí would be called.

Gerry Arthurs, of course, is seen as one of the people who really helped the growth of the GAA in Ulster from the 1930s onward. He was elected treasurer in 1934 after beating General Eoin O'Duffy. B. C. Fay of Cavan was the Ulster secretary, and he was succeeded by Gerry.

Finances were always a big problem in Ulster and Gerry sorted them out. During my time as president, there was one year when the income reached around £15,000. That was a huge amount of money, but could now be raised at a minor championship match alone. But the high levels of organisation from people like Gerry paid off. As a result, the Ulster Council was able to provide grants to clubs and counties to purchase and develop grounds. Overall, he was very efficient in money matters.

Another quality which Gerry Arthurs had was his great wit and way with people. On many occasions the two of us would travel together to meetings and the Railway Cup in

Croke Park. He was very careful about the number of people who stayed in the hotel at the expense of the Ulster Council. No hangers-on were allowed, and he'd remind them nicely that they weren't entitled to a free ride. A bit of a sideline for him during the 1940s was in the supply of jerseys and footballs from O'Neill's. He dealt with the founder of the company, Charles O'Neill.

Perhaps one of his and the Ulster Council's main achievements was ensuring that the competitions were properly organised. It was on Gerry's prompting and initiative that the Lagan Cup became recognised as a section of the National League for Ulster teams, with the exception of Cavan.

Delegates to the Ulster Council always had to be very vocal in fighting their corner for their county. I would occasionally have made my views felt about some issue or other affecting Derry and the sustained efforts of Sean O Cinnéide to highlight the plight of Donegal were well known.

On one occasion, there were sixteen appeals at a meeting. Another time I recall a meeting being held prior to a match at Croke Park. Hughie Beag was representing Donegal and there had been a big match due to take place in Croke Park which was scheduled to start at 3 pm. The throw-in was delayed until 4.30 pm and somebody asked Hughie what caused the delay. He responded, "the weather is good and the evening is long." All the Donegal men were native speakers, so the proceedings were very interesting.

We always checked that things were in order in terms of the type of paper used which had to be Irish watermark. The aim was to get a technicality to rule something out of order and save a lot of bother. There was an army of amateur lawyers in the country at that time writing appeals.

Fixtures were a constant issue. Sean O Cinnéide regularly raised concerns about the distances which Donegal teams had to travel due to the fact that they were fairly isolated. He knew the mileage from every club in Donegal to various venues in Ulster. When Gweedore purchased their new grounds he was even able to obtain a Gaeltacht grant.

Pádraig McNamee, who later went on to become President of the GAA, was also deeply involved in the Ulster Council on my arrival. It was strange because, while he wasn't a great orator, he was very sincere and able to run meetings efficiently, giving everyone their say and able to control things as well. The fact that he had good Irish also helped. The extension of his term from three years to five speaks volumes about his abilities. He was also extremely close to the Ard Stiúrthóir at the time, Pádraig Ó Caoimh.

Selling tickets at the big matches

The large attendances were a feature at the main Ulster Championship matches in the 1940s. Members of the Ulster Council were among those with the task of selling tickets. My base was at the school just at the top of the famous hill before entering St Tiernach's

Park.[4] This was particularly suitable because the low wall provided an ideal seat.

When stewards reported for duty they got a roll of tickets, and the required amount of change, the money in a brown leather bag with a satchel. The name of the ticket-seller was written on the first ticket. When they reported back, the ticket number was noted and an estimate made of how much money should have been collected. Everything was checked very carefully to ensure that the money corresponded with the number of tickets. As well as selling the tickets, I also helped to count the money at the finish.

The Rossas was more than simply a club and our membership cards helped create a sense of belonging.

After the match, all the stewards went into the school for a bottle of stout – or a mineral for the non-drinkers – and a couple of sandwiches. There was no such thing as a dinner.

Gerry Arthurs was also astute in ensuring that all the accounts were kept by one person. This helped to ensure that they didn't fall into the wrong hands. My job as Treasurer was a very simple one indeed and rarely involved much more than signing the cheques. Gerry often came with the cheque book to the meetings for me to sign each one.

At that time also, the number of county grounds developed was also increased. St Tiernach's Park became the main venue for games because it was one place that the trains passed through. It was a rail centre during the war years, and even had a direct line from Armagh. Castleblayney could also have been developed to the same extent. But Clones was eventually chosen because of the trains. Breffni Park was another venue, although it wasn't used too regularly.

Gerry Arthurs was also keen to obtain a ground in Omagh because of its geographical centre. The aim was to develop a second main provincial venue which would be easily accessible from all areas of Ulster. Parking wasn't as big an issue during this period. Most spectators came by train and many others hired buses. There simply wasn't the same number of cars. Pat McGrane after whom the McGrane Stand in Clones is named was always the right hand man for Gerry Arthurs and the both of them organised the stewards.

4 – St Tiernach's Park was purchased and developed in the early 1940s. It was chosen as the venue for Ulster Finals chiefly due to its central location on the railway and proximity to the dominant county at that time, Cavan.

More than just a club

A cherished memento from the early days of the GAA in Magherafelt is the Rossa membership cards. The citation on the back of the 1948 version reads "we ask of God such unshakeable purpose, such high and gallant courage and such unbreakable strength of soul as belonged to O'Donovan Rossa." There surely weren't too many clubs in Ireland that had membership cards during at that time. But we were one of them.

Jim Taylor was the 'Clubroom Chairman.' The club hired an outhouse in Rainey Street belonging to the Kielts and activities like table-tennis and darts provided great enjoyment. A club began and proved successful for a number of years. The only problem was that people had to ring a bell on the street to gain entry into what was really a private yard. This required somebody to go out and open the door for them. Like many similar initiatives, the enthusiastim eventually diminished. Willie John Halferty was the secretary and a great Rossa man, Tommy Walls was the treasurer and Sean Agnew the captain. [5] The card also lists five committee members, so our affairs were certainly well organised!

Our best ideas were developed when a group of us got together a night and began talking in Nan McKee's. Someone would suggest a bright idea and suddenly we'd decide to take action. Bertie Christie printed the membership cards and also the large posters which were prepared for the weekly céilí. It used to be 'Rince 8-10 pm' and Bertie always asked us, "what time is the rinco?" He was a great character.

Everybody in the club seemed to be capable of coming up with these ideas. One of the best was the weekly publication called 'The Hawk.' It was a big task ensuring that it was printed each and every week on time. Hugh Glancy completed regular articles and my future wife, Kathleen, who was in England at this time, contributed one about being in exile. Then, there was also the match reports and news about the forthcoming céilithe. The copies were initially sold for 3p each, but then handed out after Mass. As well as that, we went religiously weekly to Peter and Mrs O'Kane with a few paragraphs for inclusion into the Mid-Ulster Mail.

All of these things were seen as important signs of progress and reflected the growing self-confidence of GAA clubs. They also fitted into the general feeling during this period about the need for loyalty to the club. There was also the fact that a club was about more than the Gaelic games themselves, important as they obviously were.

In the 1940s clubs began to think in terms of the wider GAA, taking in the games, culture and language. These aspects of the Association were put on more solid footing. There were four clubs in the parish of Magherafelt: Rossa's, Castledawson, Loup and Ballymaguigan. South Derry for instance was very compact.

---

5 – Sean Agnew ran a busy shop in Magherafelt famous for its ice cream. Tommy Walls became a journalist with the Northern Constitution and WJ Halferty served as Secretary of the Rossas from 1944 until 1964.

Each of them held an Irish class, many organised history lessons and a céilí was usually held each and every Friday night. It was all Irish and céilí dancing, and the events were well organised and attended.

For example, in Magherafelt, the Irish and history classes generally took place in what's now St Mary's School. About a dozen people – mostly club members, but also others who were interested – attended. Miss Campbell, who was from Carrickmore, was the teacher in Castledawson. There was another teacher from Ballymaguigan who helped out.

Then, every Monday night, there was a class in the New Row School in Castledawson. The father of the present Derry chairman, Seamus Keenan and his uncle, Pearse, were central to establishing the new St Malachy's along with Theresa Martin and Jim Mackle. Before attending the class, I used to go up to the Nissen hut, in which a man called the Beaker Graham did a bit of cobbling. The two of us sat there for a while talking about the events of the day.

It was seen as important to learn Irish, but also to speak the language. During the summer holidays there was the annual trip to Rannafast to improve my ability in Irish. Fr Laurence Murray was very encouraging and learning the language in the heart of the Gaeltacht was very enjoyable.

The Magherafelt céilithe were held in the town hall, which is now the Bridewell. The building could be hired by anyone from Willie John McLaren in the Market Yard. The lighting cost 50p and we had to be careful not to run out of 50 pence pieces or light. The Rossas broke new ground by bringing from Belfast the Ard Scoil Céilí Band which was very well regarded.

Sunday nights and the weekly Ceili

A fond memory is of each Sunday night when some of us attended St Patrick's Hall in Dungannon. For us, and undoubtedly other clubs, the weekly céilí was the main fundraising activity. The first céilí organised in Magherafelt took place in a small hall at the bridge in Newbridge which was owned by Murphy's. Willie Taylor's Band cost 10'6, and the admission was 1'6. A small profit resulted from that night. Back then, a pound was a substantial amount. Indeed, I'd arrive back following the Christmas holidays with maybe £1 which would suffice for some time. Things were very cheap, as evidenced by the fact that a ten stone bag of coal cost two shillings.

My ability to speak Irish resulted in my appointment becoming fear an tí at these dances. All the dances were introduced as Gaeilge. Our dances and other events were all known as Rossa Productions. Members were organised to be in place to get up once the first dance was called. This ensured that the night always got off to a good start, rather than the band playing for five or ten minutes without anyone making the first move.

Derry's success in winning the 1947 National League title was certainly a major boost. The Magherafelt representation on the team made all of us extremely proud.

We were fortunate in having a lot of good dancers associated with the club. Frank Niblock's sisters were among them and, of course, the English dances were very much frowned upon.

At the wider level, clubs had a strong feeling about the ethos of the Association, and what it was about trying to achieve. The political scene, where the nationalist people were second-class citizens also increased the sense of pride and belonging within the GAA. It was ours, we were very proud of it and the Association was a reaction against the treatment which we were receiving.

In that respect, the GAA definitely gave a spur to the people. Alf Murray, Pádraig McNamee and others spoke about the GAA being more than just a sporting organisation and this feeling grew organically from within many clubs. It's important to remember that setting up a club during that period wasn't easy, and took an awful amount of self-sacrifice and money.

When a club was established, it gave the population of a particular area something to attach to. They then advance further, purchasing grounds and facilities for dressing-rooms and meetings. Even then, the great strength of the GAA was that it was so much part of the local community.

If you look at any club in Ireland, there are family names still involved whose parents or grandparents were helping to establish things sixty, seventy or more years ago. I can see that very clearly in Derry, where I meet people whose surnames resound through decades of involvement.

EDITORIAL.   Again we offer our congratulations to the Derry Senior
Football team on the McKenna Cup victory.   The three cups now on
view in a window in Magherafelt should certainly make any Derryman
feel proud. · We understand that these cups are to go on "tour"
through the County so that all have a chance of seeing the trophies.
May the collection be added to throughout the year.
    This month we include an article on the "hand-passing versus
catch and kick" controversy.   We would like further opinions on
this much discussed topic and on the other great question of the
All-Ireland final being played in New York.   We would even welcome
a contribution on the hoary and ever arising questions of the "Ban"
or "What does the G.A.A. do with its money?"   While on this subject
may we appeal to our contributors to send in their matter as early
in the month as possible as "we go to press" in the last week of
the month.

GLIMPSES OF ROSSA HISTORY

    After the 1956 Minor football game in Omagh the minutes for the
next few months record nothing out of the ordinary.   Goalposts were
bought and Joey Taylor is being continually removed from office only
to be re-instated at the next meeting.   Jerseys were bought at the
ridiculous price of 4/9 each and a ceilidhe was arranged with Tom
Murphy as M.C.   Then comes the annual meeting of 1937 and at this
meeting the following officers were elected :- Chairman James Bradley,
Vice-Chairman, Pat MacFlynn; Treasurer, Gerry Gallagher; Secretary,
Patrick Keenan with Gerry Gallagher as team captain.   Here again
the minutes lapse into the routine brightened here and there by
members resigning or being removed from office.   In the 1938 annual
meeting there is little change in the office bearers, C. MacFlynn
moves in as treasurer and J. Taylor is secretary.   Then various teams
are recorded for the following months and it is interesting to see
that the majority of these matches were won by the Rossas.   At this
period some Castledawson men were included and S. MacCann after
appearing as a sub. finds a place on the team.   The following year
with the foundation of St. Malachy's these players were no longer
available.   The 1939 annual convention is worth noting for this
year saw the Rossa club as county senior champions for the first
time.   Chairman, James Bradley; Treasurer, C. MacFlynn; Secretary,
C. MacFlynn; Captain, Francis ("Mike") McGlade; Vice-Captain,
Patrick ("Sticky") Maguire.

MOUSTACHES

    ·The moustache is definitely coming back.   Walk along the streets
of any town or city and you are sure to meet young men with a thin
dark line across the upper lip.
    Many reasons have been advanced for the returning popularity of
the moustache and perhaps the soundest of all is that a moustache is
manly looking.   In fact a delve into history reveals that a family
celebration always took place when the son of the house was able to
trim the hair on his upper lip, and was regarded as more important
than the attainment of his twenty first birthday.
    A moustache gives strength, character, individuality, and
distinction to the face and bearing.
    In their hearts women like moustaches secretly they respect and
admire moustached men.   A few remarks by a woman about the charm of
Robert Taylor's moustache or Errol Flynn's works wonders.   The male
"forgets" to wield the razor across his upper lip and in a few days
time fancies himself the screen idol's rival.   In fact, I read
recently that with the coming back of the moustache, man's old
authority over women would return.   The cultivation of one entails
a lot of trouble and trimming but, of course isn't it worth it.

/In

An extract from the Hawk from 1947. The Hawk was the popular weekly organ of Magherafelt
O'Donovan Rossa during these years.

This was an exciting team to be involved in the GAA because of this growth in so many areas. The number of clubs was increasing, those which had already existed were being put on a firmer footing by starting to purchase their grounds. This was the biggest push forward of all.

My role in helping Derry win their first NFL title

Maybe my main claim to fame should be that I was in charge of the Derry team which won the National League title for the first time in 1947. However, the truth of the matter is just a bit less glamorous and my role wasn't that of a Mickey Harte, Brian McIver or Brian Cody.

There wasn't a great interest in the county teams before the mid-1940s. Indeed, playing for the county wasn't really regarded as the major honour which it has become during the intervening period. There was no high-powered manager either, and instead the team was voted upon by the board and I remember doing that on many occasions.

In Derry, the big step forward was winning the Junior title in 1946 which gained us promotion into senior ranks for the first time. The Junior grade might seem meaningless to the modern reader, but then it was the second best team and filled with players who were either just past their best at senior level, or young lads coming up through the ranks.

We were an improving team with the help of the three biggest clubs of Lavey, Newbridge and Ballinderry. Our success in winning the Lagan Cup put us into the semi-final of the National League, where we defeated Longford in Derry to reach the final against Clare at Croke Park.

The big snow of 1947 delayed the match for weeks. My good friend, Pat Keenan, was the captain and, if my memory serves me correctly, the game was played on Easter Monday. [6]

Appropriately, the match was delayed even further because the curtain-raiser was a Colleges game which ended in a draw. This caused me some consternation as I had a date with my future wife, Kathleen, and she had to wait until our game against Longford was finished.

I had to arrange the hotel, transport and make sure the jerseys were there ready for the match. It was generally the county chairman who made the decisions on the sideline, but that happened very seldom and teams generally kept the same fifteen players on for the full hour.

The advent of training made a big difference to that team. I remember it being seen as a tremendous thing when Derry began training one night in the week to get themselves fit. They had charts for keeping fit and stuck to them within their own clubs and grounds, running and practising kicking and the other skills.

---

6 – Derry's success in the 1947 National League was the first national triumph for the county. The competition had been delayed due to the heavy snow of that year.

For the 1947 final, we had terrible trouble getting an hotel. Pádraig Ó Caoimh ended up getting us some small hotel because everywhere else was booked up due to the Easter Holidays. After that, we arrived back in Magherafelt to great celebrations.

One of the key players on that team was Patsy 'Sticky' Maguire, of the Murray, Armstrong and Maguire half-forward line. Patsy was a famous footballer, having represented Ulster in the very important Railway Cup success of 1942 which I feel proved a big inspiration to each of the counties and undoubtedly played a part in paving the way for Derry's rise to prominence five years later.

The Railway Cup success was like winning an All-Ireland for Ulster, especially since they'd been narrowly beaten by small margins on a number of occasions previously. It was a real breakthrough because the players from the smaller counties like Derry were getting on the senior stage. It did more to liven things up.

The performance of Iggy Jones in the 1946 Hogan Cup final was another sign that our footballers could compete with and beat the best. We all attended that final because Larry Higgins from the Rossas was playing and Iggy produced a brilliant display. He was unbeatable, jinking all over the place. That final was one of the best matches I ever witnessed.

The story behind the 1947 All-Ireland in New York

It was the cars parked outside Croke House which confirmed to me that I was on the right track. You see I barely knew where Croke Park was when I was first appointed to the Central Council in the early 1940s.

I knew you went up Drumcondra and turned left at the bank on the corner. I turned and saw the cars outside the house and suspected – correctly as it turned out – that this was Croke House. My knowledge of Dublin was scant, and add into that the fact that travelling to Dublin from Magherafelt was very awkward because I first had to go to Belfast and get the train from there and had to stay in Dublin because the journey was so arduous. But that was all made worthwhile in 1947 when I had that first-hand experience of what must rank as one of the most significant decisions made by the GAA up until then – to play the All-Ireland Final in New York for the first and only time.

Canon Hamilton stood up in the small and packed room where the GAA Congress was held. He was from Clare and both him and the other delegate began reading these tear-jerking letters from exiles in America about how much they looked forward to seeing GAA matches That was start of bringing the 1947 All-Ireland to the Polo Grounds in New York, although it was later alleged that they'd written the letters themselves.

Congress that year had approved staging the final in New York with the provision of 'if possible'. Later, the Central Council meeting to discuss the issue was adjourned after the decision was taken to send Tom Kilcoyne, the Connacht secretary and Pádraig Ó Caoimh to New York to investigate the feasibility of such a move. When they returned, the

Central Council then had a secret meeting at which the two men reported that staging the match in New York would be very doubtful due to the terrible problems involved. [7]

A vote was subsequently taken against going to New York. However, Dan O'Rourke was in the chair as President and his son was playing for Roscommon who had yet to meet Cavan in the All-Ireland semi-final. He made the comment that 'no son of his would get on an aeroplane,' and back then flying was still a major issue. This annoyed the Ulster contingent who felt that Roscommon were presuming that they'd reach the final.

Then, the vote was taken again with the press present and after a fairly colourless debate it was decided to go by a very small majority. I remember Dan O'Rourke was very annoyed about this and Pádraig Ó Caoimh was also very concerned because he foresaw great difficulties. A re-count took place with the same result, and there was no doubt that a number of the Ulster counties had turned their vote. Nothing could be done only accept the result, and of course there was obviously no way in which the previous vote could be disclosed.

The Executive committee of the GAA had been very much against travelling. But then when it came to deciding who would make the trip, all of them were in the official travelling party. Martin O'Neill, the Leinster Secretary, was referee, Gerry Arthurs, another provincial Secretary, was umpire.

The biggest concern centred on getting a field which would be big enough to play on. Baseball pitches had this height on them, there were also concerns about the sale of tickets and a fear that the Association would sustain a loss if it was a wet day because the Americans are famous for not coming out in the rain. There was also the logistical questions of getting the two teams to travel.

A lot of problems were arising, one of them being getting time off work to spend two or three weeks away. Getting to America wasn't easy either, and there were the costs because the players had to get expenses and an allowance for food.

I didn't have very much to say during that debate because I'd never been to America at that stage and would have understood what was involved. But I think I did support the decision as a good PR exercise to boost the GAA in New York which was fairly strong. I didn't have a chance of going to the game, although it would have been interesting to have attended.

As a result, myself and everybody else in Ireland had to listen to the game on the radio at home and the famous plea by Michael O'Hehir looking for five minutes more so that the people back home could hear the closing stages. Later on I saw the film of the match and clearly recall Gerry Arthurs smiling as he waved the white flag for a late Cavan point.

---

7 – Although the minutes of the private meeting are not recorded, an 'informal discussion' is mentioned by then President, Dan O'Rourke. Paddy MacFlynn's account is also verified by Michael O Ruairc, another central council member at the time.

Cavan, of course, were still the main team in Ulster standard-bearers and we all supported them. John Joe O'Reilly, Big Tom O'Reilly, Phil 'the Gunner' Brady whom I remember well, Simon Deignan, who had a bad name in Derry after 1958 and the 'Babe Ruth of Gaelic football', I knew Mick Higgins well, he was like Down's Greg Blaney in the way he could control the game from centre-forward.

But there's no doubt that playing that All-Ireland Final in New York was a gamble which paid off and much of the credit for this must go to Pádraig Ó Caoimh. He had a way of rousing and motivating people and carried the weight of the whole organisation. He was known as the architect of the modern GAA and I knew him very well after arriving as a young man on the Central Council.

I got on the Central Council because the executive council at that time was made up of the chairman, who was the President, Pádraig Ó Caoimh as secretary, two trustees, the four provincial chairman and three from each province making a total of fifteen. In the nine counties of Ulster each county got its turn and it was Derry's choice. So, for some reason or other I was on the Central Council for two years representing Ulster. The executive made all the decisions, with Pádraig and Briege running the whole show very efficiently from Croke House, one of the distinctive red-bricked houses on Jones' Road. A big room to the front was the main office.

In later years Pádraig requested an invitation to the opening of the new grounds in Ballykinlar because a friend of his had died while being interned there in the early 1920s. He asked me could he be asked to come and officially open the ground and we had a very enjoyable day.

BROADENING HORIZONS
WITH LOVE OF MY LIFE

VALUE STORES.

IN OLD LINEN MARKET ARCHWAY.

VALUE STORES - A CHILD'S TREASURE PARADISE.

The Value Stores in Magherafelt. There was no doubt that I was sad to leave the town of my birth.

Kathleen and myself were married in 1948 and enjoyed many happy years of life together. Here we are in 1984.

My involvement with the GAA in Derry was by now very extensive. Indeed, it would probably have been reasonable to anticipate that this would continue to be the case. Yet, in 1948 I made what eventually became the life-changing decision to take a post as principal in Ballynahinch, Co Down.

Now before this I had very little connection with the Mourne county. So, the decision to move to Ballynahinch was very strange considering how much I was attached to the whole Derry GAA scene and, of course, my life around Magherafelt. What happened was that a vacancy appeared for the principalship of the primary school in Ballynahinch. My uncle was married to a woman from there and her sister was visiting when she mentioned to me about this job and whether or not I would be interested in applying. She encouraged me, with the result that I duly sent in the application even though the prospect of actually moving wasn't something that I contemplated too much.

It was with a certain amount of apprehension, then, that one of my first visits to Ballynahinch was for the interview conducted by Canon Michael McCrory PP, VF. He decided to appoint me to the post, so here I found myself Principal of Ballynahinch school. At this time I was keeping company with my future wife, Kathleen, who was completing her master's degree at Queen's University.

There's no doubt that this was an extremely big break from the norm for me. However, the extent of this wasn't immediately apparent at first because each weekend came with the required trip home to Magherafelt, completed by bus into Belfast and then onwards. In addition, I continued to play with Rossa's.

It really was an inexplicable decision because there was no such thing as me falling out with anyone or having a row. I was content with the way things were progressing through my work in Magherafelt and no reason why that should change. I was very much involved in all things Derry, and this move to Ballynahinch was a tremendous step to take which thinking back I didn't give an awful lot of thought. One memory which stands out, however, is the advice of my father who was very definitely of the opinion that I should move on. I was very close to him and he advised me to give this opportunity a go.

Ballynahinch at that time comprised of separate sections for both boys and girls. The boys part consisted of one room with the assistant at one end and me at the other. This really was a case of learning the hard way because when the first inspector came he told me the only remark he would pass was that I was still sane. It took a lot of organising and work to ensure that we were able to have a productive teaching environment in those difficult circumstances of two different classes proceeding at the one time. Needless, to say that the two schools were later replaced, by which time I had left in any case.

At the same time, Ballynahinch was somewhere that I liked very much. Kathleen had cousins there named McKay so we would visit them at least twice a week and play poker. I also played badminton in the hall and then, of course, became involved with the local

GAA at the time. I stayed with John Mooney, who had a farm on the edge of the town and was a brother of the lady who was married to my uncle. His house was only about a mile from the school on the Crossgar Road, so the whole arrangement was very suitable.

Maybe all of this fitted in with my general attitude to life. I was always someone who tried to take everything as it came, in my stride. Consequently, the move from Magherafelt wasn't something which I worried about and that was probably for the best. I had a very happy upbringing there, a lot of friends at primary school with whom I was still in very regular contact.

I spent five years in Ballynahinch between 1948 and 1953, before moving to Gilford. The 11-plus was only beginning at that time, and ensuring that the children were properly prepared was always a big concern. Needless to say, I used to be glad to see the summer holidays. Perhaps what helped me was my ability as a good delegator and I was fortunate to have had great help from

The move to Laurencetown created new challenges. This is one of the insurance policies for Laverty's Bar and surroundings.

the other staff. I couldn't have carried on without them.

My first car was an Austin with a canvas roof called 'Betsy'. The vehicle arrived around that time as well and had previously belonged to the curate of Ballynahinch, Fr Mick McConville, who sold it to me at the knockdown price of £100. I found the money hard enough to gather up, but eventually I managed it alright.

Leaving my beloved Rossas

Now taking up the teaching post in Ballynahinch was one thing. Leaving my beloved Magherafelt O'Donovan Rossa's was a completely different matter. But it was probably inevitable that this move would also become necessary in due course.

Regular weekend trips home ensured that my involvement continued for a while and I've mentioned how I continued to play for the Rossas in 1948. However, my marriage the following year and the demands of full-time work in Ballynahinch ensured that the decision had to be taken.

It was, therefore, with deep regret that I announced my intention to move at the 1948 Magherafelt annual general meeting. [1] This was a big moment, because of my great love for the club, the fact that a few of us had been involved right from the start and suddenly my allegiances would be elsewhere.

A lot of those who were involved in the club were definitely shocked when I told them I'd be leaving and going to live in Co Down. They couldn't understand the motivation for my decision and if I'm being honest, I couldn't really understand it myself either. However, the club was strong enough to keep going, they won the county title again in 1949 and I thought it was in a very strong position with lots of young people who were sons of the founders and were beginning to work very hard for Rossa's. At this time, too, the very proactive juvenile policy was beginning to reap dividends and that has continued to the present time. In addition, there was also a fairly successful camogie team. However, there was no tradition of hurling and on the few occasions that we had tried to start a team, the lads got no satisfaction because the field wasn't suitable. It's not so pleasant when you're poking about trying to retrieve the sliotar from a hole in the ground.

Initially, the break hadn't really dawned on me because I was returning home each weekend. Of course, my interest in the GAA had grown to such an extent by this stage that I was very anxious to maintain my involvement and it was only natural that this would be through the local Ballynahinch club. At that time, they were based in Ballynahinch, but drew most of their support from Drumaness and, of course, the club is now known as Drumaness. Nevertheless, it was then that I felt the wrench because I had been at the centre of all things GAA in Derry and no longer had any part to play.

It was a very conscious decision of mine to become involved with Ballynahinch. The GAA was there and I wanted to play a part. There was no way that I was going to return to Derry each weekend and try telling them what should be done. A clean break was required from both Rossa's and Derry because I'm a great believer in letting the people on the ground in a particular area do the work.

My name had gone before me and a few of the club officials met me and asked me to attend a meeting. I immediately joined the committee and became chairman in due course.

There was just one junior team in Ballynahinch at the time and they did all that was required of them in the minimal way that was so prevalent during this period and which wouldn't be acceptable now. A man called Herbie Noad was the club secretary and if the team were short it was between Herbie and myself to toss to see which of us would go into battle. By then I was past my best because I never had any great skill as a footballer and in those days when the game was heavy and physical I was strong and fairly fit. This stood to me, particularly in the later stages of my career.

---

1 – Paddy informed the Rossa club that he was leaving Magherafelt at the annual convention on Christmas Day, 1948. He regretted that he could not let his name go forward for the post of chairman and that this was in all probability the last time he would act as an official of the club. Pat Keenan assumed the role of chairman subsequently.

Our one success during this period was an appearance in the Junior Football Championship final when, above all clubs, we were defeated by Laurencetown. When I came to Laurencetown subsequently, I soon discovered that the team which had defeated Ballynahinch had three or four county players from Lurgan playing for them. Included were a number of well-known personalities who must have made some difference because it was a very close and low-scoring match. We should have won!

Another interesting change came with the fact that in 1948 I had represented Derry on the Ulster Council of the GAA. The following year my allegiances had switched to Down and one of the chief reasons was the need for an Irish speaker and, as I was already on-board because of my fluency, it was quite simple to remain only this time as a Down delegate.

Suddenly I had gone from a large duck in a small pond to a small duck in a much larger lake. Nevertheless, I suppose my association with the Ulster Council and Central Council made it slightly easier to become involved within the Down scene pretty quickly.

By 1954 I had become assistant treasurer on the Down County Board. Then, George Tinnelly, who was the chairman, came to me and said that the treasurer was resigning and that he wanted me to take the job. So, I became treasurer in Down and, like most jobs which have come my way in the GAA, I was kind of 'pitch-forked' in without any election. [2] Nevertheless, this was a new role which was to give plenty of tasks during subsequent years.

East Down at that time was also very badly organized. The annual convention was a bit of a disaster. So, I went in and took over as chairman to start to reorganise the board. There were always mix-ups about fixtures, so a first task was to address those problems. I always attempted to run a very 'straight to the point' meeting where there was no time wasted.

Without boasting, I think I left in a better state than what I found it in. I was involved for about five years in total. My past experience in Derry definitely helped, and there were many of the same chores and challenges.

There was big excitement in 1950 when the news spread that the one and only Éamon de Valera would be the latest high profile figure to address the very popular Feis An Dúin. He was following in the footsteps of Pádraig Pearse who gave the oration in 1915 and I was fortunate enough to be a member of the organising committee when the 'Long Fellow' was invited to attend.

Everyone in Down has always been extremely proud of St Patrick's Park in Newcastle and the venue has always been a very popular location for the Feis. Gerry O'Donughue

---

2 – Paddy became Down Treasurer in the spring of 1954, replacing Liam Stewart who was unable to continue in the post for personal reasons. The new incumbent resigned the post of Ulster Treasurer to take the job in Down.

was the chairman at that time and I remember us making arrangements for de Valera's coming.

Most of the GAA presidents, including myself, and others were asked at some point or other to give the oration and unsurprisingly, there were massive crowds to hear de Valera. The organisers worked through Frank Aiken, who had south Down connections through his wife and was very close to him.

My role in the organisation came through by chairmanship during that period of the East Down Board. However, even though I am currently a patron of the Feis and was an examiner for a number of years, I was never very active apart from the involvement at that time.

Unfortunately, I didn't get to meet Dev on that occasion, but the opportunity did come years later through my involvement in the GAA. By that time he was quite old and didn't have an awful lot of chat as a result.

My years spent as Down Treasurer

One month in 1948 I was Derry's delegate to the Ulster Council. The following month I was still on the Council only this time representing my new adopted county of Down. It was an easy transition and one which led to me becoming Down Treasurer in 1954, a post which I subsequently held until 1973.

This was, of course, just before Down's great breakthrough of the 1960s and I worked hard at the role with the help of a small finance committee. We met at my home in Laurencetown to pass all the accounts and then it usually took me about two days to write out the cheque, fill out the slip and then address and post it off.

In those days the amount of money was very small compared to now. If I remember correctly, the income and outlay during my first year as Treasurer amounted to around £600. The vast sums of money involved now were unheard of. Travelling expenses of players were running to about 5p or 10p per mile and meals at hotels were quite cheap. All this changed when Down began to improve, and were provided with steak dinners in good hotels after games.

Gate receipts from club championship matches were the chief income. During my time as treasurer we introduced the rule that all money went to the county board rather than the old system of splitting it three ways with the two clubs. There was also income from the Ulster Council for county team expenses, a flat rate for home games and then according to the distance travelled for away matches.

Thankfully, the finances during those years were in fairly good shape and the county board was rarely in much debt. We provided a grant of £30 to clubs for the purchase of their grounds, as well as supplying the county team free for the opening to try and encourage them. There was a great emphasis at that time on helping clubs buy their own grounds, and it was certainly one of the biggest revolutions in my view because now local clubs owned a property which could be called the GAA's.

This solved the major problem of finding a regular pitch to play on and dealing with the local farmer. Many clubs played a variety of different venues, often of a poor standard and the availability was regular due to the whim of the landowner.

The need to vest these grounds legally was also important role for me during this period. Later, Dan McCartan did a very useful survey in which he required clubs to produce their deeds, rather than just saying that they were in the bank or with the solicitor.

Trustees were appointed and now in Down if a trustee dies the club is notified immediately to replace them. This was a terrible weakness because a lot of the time clubs weren't aware of where their deeds were and never replaced trustees. This is covered in the deed of trust and when I pass on the solicitors will have a field day because I'm a trustee of so many clubs.

At the beginning there was some resistance from clubs to this outside organisation because they viewed the grounds as their own and perhaps resented outside interference. But the importance of making sure that everything was legally watertight had to be stressed. Now the trustees are technically the owners of the ground, holding it for and on behalf of the club and the GAA. All of this took quite a bit of work to put in order, especially because the deeds of many clubs weren't in order. Indeed, on a number of occasions clubs lost their grounds due to a faulty legal situation.

Alf Murray began this initiative during his presidency in the mid-1960s. It was an idea generated by his own experience with Clann Éireann in Lurgan who, as I stated, had opening their grounds about 20 years previously.

By purchasing and developing their own grounds, club were also able to offer something to the local community. The venue could be used for events, sports days and other activities.

Meeting and marrying Kathleen

THE love of my life was Kathleen Laverty and we first met at Queen's University in Belfast through a group of common friends. It wasn't long before we began going out and I remember, of course, keeping her waiting while I attended to the task of watching Derry in that 1947 National League Final.

At that time I was doing a Diploma in Education and with other friends we met and got to know her. Thankfully, Kathleen was prepared to wait and in or around 1948 I decided to pop the big question and ask her to marry me.

A lovely photograph from our wedding day in 1948. Charlie was the best man and Kathleen's sister the bridesmaid at the ceremony which took place in Ballymena.

I said, "It's near time we got married,' and she replied 'Alright.' It was all very straightforward, which maybe suited the two of us. Kathleen was always great craic and the one great thing we had in common was our fondness for reading. This brought us together a lot over the years. We married in July 1949 in Ballymena and the whole marriage ceremony was conducted in Irish. [3]

Now the only difficulty which arose was that the priest, Canon McAlister, got stuck in the Irish on the way through. So, he handed the lines to me, telling me to 'finish it yourself.' I had to marry myself at the finish.

I have great memories of a tremendous honeymoon. Initially, we travelled to Paris and stayed with friends there and then I got into a pair of shorts and we carried two knapsacks, travelling by bus to the Louvre Valley. That was great because we visited all the chateaux right down to the Louvre Valley, we stayed locally and conversed with the locals because Kathleen was fluent in French. It was a wonderful experience and my first visit to France.

It was then that I lost my pioneer pin when I started to drink white wine.

3 – The wedding took place in All Saints Church Ballymena. Miss Gertrude Laverty, sister of Kathleen, was bridesmaid and Charles MacFlynn, brother of Paddy, was best man. The ushers were Dr Eddie MacFlynn and Sean Laverty.

We spent about three weeks in total on honeymoon. At that time in Paris, they were still building the bridges following the devastation of World War Two. As a result, they used to have a very bad word on the British Airforce, describing them as very inaccurate in the way that they blew up most of the bridges.

On our return, our first house was situated out in the direction of Spa. It was very well laid out and in beautiful surroundings and was somewhere that I was definitely sad to leave when we then moved into Laurencetown.

Home from the early 1950s onwards was Laverty's Bar, Laurencetown Co Down.

Each weekend the two of us would come over to Laurencetown to visit Kathleen's aunt and uncle who were at that time living next door to the pub. Each week I would come over and give them a hand with bottling the beer. I had the little Austin car and drove over on the Friday night, staying the two nights and then returning home on the Sunday. Sometime later, Kathleen's uncle David Laverty died, with the result that her aunt became more dependent on us. [4]

We were in the house a lot as a result and, then when she died, we became heirs to the pub. It was a natural progression and the pub was a good going concern, one of the main reasons being the fact that pigeon-racing was so popular. Each weekend and especially when there was a show, the fanciers would be here checking their receipts. My experience having being reared in a pub eased the transition, even though it was very tiring in later years when I was teaching during the week and then working on a Friday and Saturday. It was after midnight before things would ease.

By the early sixties, myself and Kathleen had appointed a barman to look after things during the day and ease the pressure on ourselves because I was very tired at times trying to keep all the pokers in the fire what with the teaching, being involved with Down and also the Ulster Council. Kathleen was, of course, a great help and each Sunday evening I got a few hours to sit down and clear up all the little administrative tasks demanding attention.

It was in this house, where we spent most of our married life, that Kathleen was actually born, three years after me in 1921. Her father was postmaster in Banbridge, before being changed to Ballymena. As a result, Kathleen stayed here with her aunt and uncle,

4 The bar is still going strong and is currently being run by Denny and Margaret McInnes.

attending Banbridge Academy. She then went from here to Queen's and spent most of her time here, while the rest of her family were in Ballymena. Her father went on to become postmaster in Derry City, travelling there each day from his home. He then retired and came to live with us and was very good at helping with the paperwork and accounts in relation to the pub.

Anyhow, on one of these visits, after Mass that the Parish Priest, Fr John Joe Lennon, who was a wonderful character, called me over to tell me

Contemplating the growth of Down and Ulster GAA on holiday in Norway.

that there was a vacancy in Gilford and asking me to apply. "Will I get the job if I apply?," was my response, to which he quickly retorted, "What the hell am I asking you to apply for it!" That is how I came to get the job in Gilford and in addition there was the fact that Kathleen's aunt and uncle were very keen for me to move.

So, it came that I took up residence in Gilford in 1953. Gilford was always a very pleasant place to live and both myself and Kathleen took our employment in education very seriously indeed.

Kathleen eventually finished up as Vice-Principal of Lismore Comprehensive School. She was very interested in education and worked hard at it to do the best that she could.

Settling into the routine of life

A PARTICULARLY enjoyable part of life was the opportunity to travel to so many different countries. Whether on a personal basis, or as part of my official GAA duties, the chance to see many of the sights aboard has left me with cherished memories. Sometimes I take a flick through the photographs taken by myself and Kathleen during those happy visits.

Of course, the three big commitments of our lives demanded most attention. My work with the GAA, our teaching and the pub in Laurencetown meant that spare time was at a premium. However, the long summer holidays did provide us with the opportunity to travel and each year brought a new destination.

Every year after our honeymoon, we used to hire a house in the French countryside and spend almost a month staying in various parts of France in places like Brittany, the Dordogne Valley, Loire Valley and a little place called Ag on the Mediterranean.

Kathleen was a very keen French scholar. French was her language and this was the motivation for many of these trips. Our honeymoon in France was my first trip abroad and I still occasionally get in contact with Christiane, one of the girls with whom we stayed. She taught in the university.

One of our visits to France co-incided with the 14 July celebrations. I remember the big lady with a sash 'Liberté Egalité Fraternité'. The people from the local town came out to give them support. So, the Republic was declared and that night there were fireworks. It was an appropriate time to be there. The commune works by the state paying the teachers and after that they are on their own. They had all sorts of local services for collecting rubbish and other things.

In later years, then, Kathleen learned Spanish and this opened up a whole new range of opportunities. We then switched our attentions to Spain and I got to like Spain very well, especially the food. We had friends in Madrid and a great benefit was Kathleen's sense of direction. She was able to navigate the centre of the city just the same as going around Banbridge.

I remember the grandfather of the people we stayed with in Madrid lived in the north of the country in a little town outside Burgos. We went up by train to his house and outside he made a nice flat outside what used to be an outhouse. At night we were sitting under a big horse-chestnut tree playing cards with the neighbours. I couldn't understand the card game being played, but I soon caught on and used to cheat a little bit, much to their consternation. Felix was a great old character.

The Spanish culture was something which appealed to me very much. In subsequent years I attended a number of weddings over there, one in Madrid and another in the Basque country. One of them, Ines, previously spent time with us here in Laurencetown and then invited myself and Kathleen to the wedding in 2002. It was a Basque wedding and took place in this little country church and when it was finished they were firing shots in the air with great celebrations. At the reception afterwards, we started at about 4 pm with a whole range of different courses. We were still eating at about 11 pm.

One of the ways that we got to know these various people was through a friend of Kathleen's who worked in the civil service. It was through her that Spanish students who came over here on exchanges ended up staying with us here in Laurencetown.

They were very passionate about their culture and a memory which stands out for me is of a young man showing us around in Valencia. He brought us to the cathedral, showed us the door and told us to go in. But he didn't enter himself because Franco had murdered a couple of his uncles and he was very sore about this. In the evening his mother prepared for us a lovely Spanish dinner for us and, because her husband wasn't a big eater, she would urge me on to partake of this beautiful food. I didn't speak Spanish, but was still able to pick up a basic understanding of what was being said. During the day we took tour trips to Bilbao and neighbouring cities.

Like Ireland, the Spanish have a great love for what they call 'my village.' Their hearts are still in their homeplace, even though they might be living in Madrid and have little or nothing to do with their native place. It was an opportunity to remain in touch with their identity and that's something which is also very familiar among the Irish.

Every few weeks there was a festival and I recall one called the 'Festival of the Blue Blouses.' It began in the morning at 9 am, yet nobody was ever drunk and drank small cups of coffee. People with bagpipes and drums marched around the streets, without much ever happening. These festivals allowed the people to relax and let off steam as it were.

I enjoyed very much going over to Spain and other countries, and the chance to experience a different way of life and cultures. Then, there was the time I attended a bullfight in Madrid, complete with the matador finishing off the bull with his sword. It was something which appalled me and the only relief I got was when the bull came out and refused to fight. There is great skill among the matadors, although to be honest, the treatment of the bull and the unfair nature of the fight didn't appeal to me.

At the same time, the bullfights are great occasions. The spectators get very involved and, if the bull doesn't do its stuff, they throw the cushions for the concrete steps into the arena. The farmer who owns the bull sits in the royal box and if the bull doesn't fight well, they shout all sorts of obscenities at him.

I also visited Santiago de Compostela, home of the Camino, and saw those completing the famous walk with their seashells and certificates for completion. One year, near the Portuguese border, we saw lorries from Gilford driving over Taco.

In 1961 we spent about three weeks in Norway, and also travelled to Switzerland. It was a great experience and I suppose we got accustomed to driving on the European motorways. This gave us great freedom to see all the local sights.

Norway was a very interesting country. When we visited there were restrictions on money which meant that everything had to be paid for up front. We flew to Bergen and then got a taxi to the hotel, before going by bus along the coast. It was a very clean and well-organised country.

In Switzerland we visited Interlaken, where in the nineteenth century the royalty and all sorts of people visited. The big attraction there was the highest mountain which we visited.

Overall, these visits helped to broaden my horizons and the trips abroad were something which I took a great interest in. They were also something which we enjoyed thoroughly because the good weather was guaranteed and I also had a very inquisitive mind and I'd be asking all sorts of questions while Kathleen would be busy translating.

Usually, we drove over and I recall driving from Rosslare to Lavere and then over the mouth of the Seine and straight down the dual-carriageway right to Age in the south of

France. We travelled through the night, with three drivers. Two would sit in the front and then after a certain number of miles you would get out half a cup of coffee and take a stroll in the mild night. Then, the driver would get into the back seat for a sleep and the routine carried on.

Myself and Kathleen and Kathleen's two sisters were regular travelling companions and a Fr Murray who was Parish Priest of Lurgan and was at that time in Craigavon,. He said Mass each day, including one day in an enclosed convent just outside Paris. When there was a problem with the language, Kathleen would be called upon.

There were six major roads all going straight to Paris. Then, we entered the Pherpique which required great care to get into the right lane and get off at the right junction. A mistake could result in hours of needless driving to get back on track. Paris is in a lovely valley called the Plain of Beauc. I remember driving across it, a road in the middle of the wheat, and the whole scene was just gold as far as the eye could see. We were in no hurry and able to enjoy the scenery.

I never had any real difficulty driving in France, although I did once get a terrible fright. We were on a roundabout and this big lorry came gradually edging me towards the junction. Suddenly he changed tack and moved off, and I noticed that he must have been trying to avoid the traffic police sitting nearby. Fortunately, I never had any crashes. The local cars, though, were difficult to drive and one of the key problems was that the other drivers didn't show the same level of patience as would be the case if you had been in a car with IRL on the back.

On another occasion myself and Kathleen flew initially to Paris and stayed with friends there prior to flying onto Madrid to spend some time with our friends there. But while we were away the travel agent with which we had flown went bust. But the GAA came to my rescue in the form of a prominent Dublin official who also held an important position in Aer Lingus and thankfully the tickets were cleared. It's amazing how even the most worrying situations usually resolve themselves.

Flying at that time was, of course, a lot more comfortable then is the case now. There were far fewer people, although I found Charles de Gaulle airport in Paris hard going. One problem which comes to mind is the manner in which passengers travelling between the terminals had to be bused. In contrast, the Madrid airport was better because of the train which took you around and then another major advantage was the fact that Kathleen was fluent in French and Spanish. We were never stuck as a result, no matter what happened!

A few years ago we went on an Irish News-organised twelve-day trip to Sardinia in Italy. The first person I met on the plane was Tom Scullion from Bellaghy and we had great craic the whole time. He has, of course, a record of having the most Derry titles.

**PRESIDING
AT PROVINCIAL LEVEL**

The famous Derry team of 1958 which reached the All-Ireland Final. There was great excitement at their progress, but unfortunately things didn't work out against Dublin.

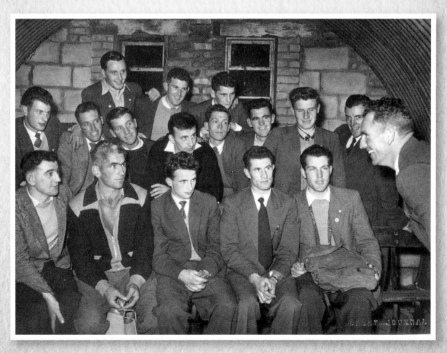

A picture of focus on the faces of the Derry players prior to that All-Ireland campaign. People like Jim McKeever were great thinkers about how gaelic football should be played.

The Ulster Council Tax issue

For many years the whole issue of whether the Ulster Council should be paying tax on income generated in the six counties was a big bone of contention. It led to me for political reasons having to step down as treasurer, something which I was very annoyed about.

Finance was something which occasionally brought us into conflict with the authorities in the north and this was one such important example of that. What happened was that Revenue officials were chasing the Ulster Council through Gerry Arthurs to pay tax on things like gate-receipts. [1]

However, he avoided them by forwarding the argument that we were merely a sub-committee of the main GAA which had its headquarters in Dublin. As a result, he told them that all correspondence on the issue should be sent there. Consequently, all the letters were answered by the auditors in Croke Park and all the bank accounts and funds were in the south.

He never replied to anything and stuck rigidly to the policy of sending absolutely all correspondence to Croke Park. It was a fairly brave move to make in the political climate of the period.

I was treasurer at the time and carried out the political resignation to further bolster our position. Harry Carey from Donegal and crucially across the border took over. Despite my disappointment, I did see the reasoning behind the move and to be fair the Revenue were never able to force the Ulster Council into paying tax, a situation which continued right into the 1980s.

Around the same time, the GAA in Ulster was compelled to pay valued added tax (VAT) on gate-receipts. This change amazingly took place following a match which was played in Omagh. The money was put into the bar-account and the Revenue subsequently saw this large sum of money, amounting to a couple of hundred thousand, going in and coming out and wondered what was going on.

How Ulster teams came to the fore

Ulster teams at club and county level have enjoyed great success since the mid-1950s or so. The contrast between the years prior to that and nowadays is amazing when you think how so many teams struggled even at junior level.

But the success of Derry in reaching the 1958 All-Ireland Final, Down in the sixties and then the progress in the 1990s to the present day has been really noteworthy and welcome. I can remember the sense of jubilation after each of those All-Ireland Finals,

---

1 – The Ulster Council were under pressure from the authorities in the north to pay tax on gate receipts. This continued to be an issue for many years subsequently.

not forgetting the other big games which have been won at minor, under-21, club and all the other levels.

The province is definitely competing the best on a permanent basis now and I feel that the drive towards encouraging clubs and counties to purchase their own grounds was a catalyst. Two significant factors were the size and standard of the pitches.

Half a century ago, many teams weren't even playing on pitches which were the regulation size, something which put them at an immediate disadvantage. It was obvious, then, that it was bound to help, along with the provision of better facilities which represented a tremendous step forward in helping players reach their potential.

I have mentioned about how the 1942 Railway Cup win and the Iggy Jones performance in the Hogan Cup final in 1946 were important in highlighting Ulster's rise to prominence. Cavan were always the very dominant team in Ulster and almost unbeatable.

Mick Higgins was the great general in chief up front, there was Big Tom O'Reilly and Tony Tighe. I knew them all way through my involvement with Ulster teams in the Railway Cup.

The Railway Cup helped the rise of teams like Armagh, Tyrone and then Down. They realised that they were able to compete against players from the other counties. Tyrone and Armagh won three All-Ireland Minor titles in 1947-49 and the breakthrough began to come gradually.

Everything changed utterly in the 1950s and things have never been the same since.

Up until then Ulster teams were content with welcoming any crumbs at all which fell on the table. That's one of the reasons why an Ulster team in an All-Ireland final gets the support of the whole province. Around this time the success at Minor and Railway Cup, which we nearly dominated, gave our counties great heart. This combined with the decline of Cavan left the whole provincial championship far more open than had previously been the case. [2]

Derry's progress to the 1958 All-Ireland Final is a case in point and gave me great satisfaction as they progressed all the way to Croke Park. They really should have done better and it's unfortunate that they only got the one opportunity to prove their worth at national level. There were some great players on that 1958 team, like the Gribbins and Jim McKeever. A widespread view still is that Roddy Gribbin, who was the unofficial manager, could have made the difference in the final against Dublin if he had gone on at some stage. He had been training and was very fit. Maybe the county lacked self-confidence because there were a number of stages in the match when they could have pushed on to win and didn't.

---

2 - Tyrone's success in winning the 1956 Ulster title heralded the end of Cavan as a major force in Ulster football. While the Breffni men came back to win a number of titles in the 1960s, they have managed to win just one Angloe Celt since 1969.

Jim McKeever was, of course, the star. I remember a man in Dublin who told me about going to the matches and, rather than watching the whole game, he would follow just one player throughout. Derry were playing Kerry one time and he followed Jim and Mick O'Connell. We went out to see the film and it was tremendous because both of them were such clean players who didn't indulge in pushing, shoving or other tactics. Nowadays, there's the terrible problem of players catching at midfield and being immediately bottled up.

Down's big breakthrough

Those of a certain age in Ulster will readily recall the big breakthrough enjoyed by Down in 1960s and the golden decade which followed. While I had no direct involvement in the team, my role as county treasurer throughout that time gave me some insight.

Maurice Hayes became secretary in 1955 and even then there was a belief that Down had the players required to do well in Ulster at least. There's no doubt that the 1960-61 team was something special, and they were very nice people as well.

In 1962 I travelled with them to America and knew a lot of them as friends. They were always very personable, and never in my time as treasurer did I have a word or any

Down's breakthrough and the performance of players such as Sean O'Neill (pictured) is recalled with great pride.

problem with them about expenses or anything like that. [3] A special committee on the county board looked after the arrangements for matchdays such as booking hotels and meals. This meant that my only real role was to look after the expenses, and make sure they got anything required. Mind you, the handouts were nothing as compared to now.

As footballers, too, they were very talented and came together almost by chance. Looking back at the films of those games from the vantage point of today, the style of play and the skill of the players was excellent. The McCartans, Sean O'Neill, Tony Hadden, Paddy Doherty, Leo Murphy and all of the rest were very accomplished footballers.

---

3 – Down travelled to the US in the spring of 1962 and visited a number of cities where they were feted by Downmen's Associations and played challenge matches. Within two weeks of returning they defeated Fermanagh in the Ulster Championship but the trip was seen by some as a factor in them relinquishing their provincial and All-Ireland titles.

Those players were naturally talented who were, importantly, ambitious. Barney Carr and Maurice Hayes came in with this plan to win an Ulster and All-Ireland within five years. The technical side of things was completely looked after by the management team and a key thing was that they became like a family. It was a case of one for all and all for one. The number of times that substitutes were brought on during that spell was limited because the players were extremely fit and had dedicated themselves to winning the Sam Maguire Cup. I always admired them for their ability to hammer home their advantage if they got on top in a match. There was no going back.

THE EMPIRE STADIUM, WEMBLEY

Admit

Mr. P. Mc Flynn.

to

The Royal Box

Date *May 16th 1964*

ENTER AT STADIUM RESTAURANT ENTRANCE
This Card admits to Car Park

My ticket for the Royal Box at Wembley in 1964. A nice momento of a special period.

The atmosphere in Down in 1960 was just electric. Everybody – Catholic, Protestant and Dissenter – took an interest because they were neighbours, very likeable and everyone knew them. That year the county went wild in its excitement and one aspect often quoted is the cross-community aspect of that support.

Working in the bar here at Laurencetown also gave me an opportunity to see Down's progress from two angles. Many people who wouldn't necessarily have had a big interest in Gaelic games listened in and watched the matches if Down were playing because of the affinity to these players who were the children of neighbours.

Everybody was talking about them and when they won it was a tremendous achievement. The way they played in that final against Kerry was brimming with resolution and determination. The teamwork and the style developed by them opened up a new era for football generally. Barney Carr never got the credit which he merited for his role in shaping that Down team. He had a good footballing brain and I'd have no doubt about his work.

One of the features of that Down team was the support which they received from the other counties in Ulster, something which has continued right through the years. But they also generated a great impression throughout Ulster and I remember someone in Dublin who was able to recite the names of the Down players from goalkeeper through to the full-forward line.

The fact that they had taken the Sam Maguire to the north for the first time was also significant and that set the standard for the likes of Derry, Armagh and Tyrone to follow. To think that they could go into Croke Park and beat Kerry was brilliant. In every way, that Down team stood out, including their strip. For instance, they began wearing black togs to apparently make them easier to recognise on the television.

1961 was another tremendous year of excitement and the reward for winning the All-Ireland that year was the great month-long trip to America. I represented Pádraig Ó Caoimh. We began in New York, but didn't play there because of an ongoing row between John Kerry O'Donnell and Croke Park.

That was the only occasion on which I actually travelled with the team. After beginning in New York, we went on to Philadelphia, where there was a strong contingent of people from Derry and Tyrone. Fr Peter Campbell, the former Tyrone player, was there with the Columbian Fathers and he was very excited when we played a game in aid of them.

It was on then to Cleveland and then to Los Angeles. In total the trip lasted almost a month. One of my jobs was to carry a sum of money for any of the players or party who perhaps encountered financial problems. The way it worked was that the players got expenses to buy their own meals for which there was an allowance. The money for that came from gate receipts and sponsors, including a number of big fundraising dinners which we attended.

In Chicago, George Tinnelly was speaking to thank the Down people there who had organised various functions there. As well as my role as Treasurer, I also got the chance to spend time with Hugh Byrne, the then president, seeing some of the sights.

For a lot of the party, this was a first time abroad. The players were under no pressure of work or training. They played local teams in challenge matches and the whole trip was extremely enjoyable.

Of course, there was always the concern that the trip, which took place in May, had left them tired for the 1962 championship and I think there could be something in that. They weren't long home until they were facing Fermanagh in the championship and eventually lost their title to Cavan. Some supporters blamed the trip to America as the reason for that defeat, but you have to remember that the players thoroughly deserved that tour.

My workload as treasurer increased quite a bit during this period due to Down's success and the financial arrangements to recompense the players for any expenses which they might incur. The county gained a reputation for raising the standard in terms of the treatment of players. There were no more 'meat teas'. This was a big change which helped the morale of the players. They began to

The US and its skyscrapers were a new experience. This is the Manhattan Hotel.

feel that they were being respected and thought about, rather than being stuffed into some small eating-house. Now they went to a decent hotel for something decent to eat and this added to the generally good feeling surrounding the whole set-up.

This was in contrast to the situation which had prevailed previously and one of the things that I insisted on was equal treatment for the county hurlers. It was the start of the more professional approach in terms of travelling arrangements, meals and so on and began the whole movement culminating in the situation which we have today.

The county board and indeed the whole county appreciated the team and the fact that they weren't complaining about their treatment. Indeed, we as officials went out of our way to treat them properly and I would be all for that.

Many of the friendships developed then have remained. I am still in contact on a regular basis with Leo Murphy.

Looking back now, those players were also great thinkers about the game, as evidenced by the likes of Joe Lennon and Sean O'Neill especially. That team will always be remembered by anyone who saw them for their attractive and clean style of play. Sean O'Neill had a great footballing brain, Joe Lennon gave everything great thought and played with immense efficiency.

Becoming President of the Ulster Council

A PLAQUE on the cabinet in the corner of my room commemorates my three years as President of the Ulster Council. It was an important role which I held between 1961 and 1964 during an exciting period for the GAA in the province.

By the early sixties I had been involved at provincial level for quite a number of years, so the top post was definitely a natural progression. But my work during that term certainly didn't have the high profile enjoyed by people like Aogán Ó Fearghail or Martin McAviney who are now called upon on a daily basis to carry out TV or radio interviews.

Just like today, I had served a number of positions since that first meeting in Portadown in the late 1930s. They included being treasurer until stepping down to allow someone from the 26 counties to take over due to the tax issue in the north.

After that I stood for president and was elected at the convention in Donegal. Frank O'Neill from Coalisland had beaten me for the position in 1958, so there was a desire on my part to make amends when standing again. Ultimately, I can remember winning the poll reasonably comfortably. My fluency in Irish was certainly an advantage.

The post was available and it was my desire to make a contribution. The three years were definitely very enjoyable, and the work a lot more straightforward than in the modern

---

4 – Paddy remarks about having to deal with the neighbouring Collegeland and Moy clubs on the Tyrone/Armagh border. He recalls the story that they used common players who lined out bi-weekly with the two clubs in the Tyrone and Armagh Leagues.

era. One of the responsibilities was to make all the fixtures and, just like at Central Council level, the hearing of appeals occasionally provided immense enjoyment. [4]

Every club in Ulster during this period appeared to have volunteer lawyers ready to act on some the most minor of points. An unregistered player, teams not turning up or appeals against rulings by the County Boards were just some of those issues. The old traditional method of hearing both sides was followed by a vote of the members present. Some of the Ulster Council meetings went on throughout the day, even with Gerry Arthurs running the whole show.

One of the big developments of the late 1950s and early 1960s was the rise in attendances and there was one year when the level of income reached the pinnacle figure of £15,000. Of course, at that time expenses were kept to a minimum, and hotels and transport was cheap.

The main areas of expenditure during that time were a small stipend for Gerry Arthurs, printing and the general office stationery. The expenses of one of the two county delegates were covered and a big thing was grants for the development of club and county grounds.

Because of this, the task of maximising the main source of income of the Ulster Championship was vital. We had the fortunate situation of having an extra match and Gerry Arthurs usually tried to ensure that there were two good semi-finals. I wouldn't say he rigged the fixtures, but he organised them to suit the financial concerns of the Ulster Council.

Eddie Devlin of Tyrone receives the old Anglo Celt Cup in 1957. It was my duty to present the Cup as President of Comhairle Uladh in the early 1960s.

Today the names are taken from a hat or bowl on television. But at that time in the early 1960s, the draw was arranged and agreed by the counties involved. Gerry Arthurs compiled statistics of how often teams had met and each county took its turn in the preliminary round.

On one occasion both semi-finals were decided by last-minute points and Gerry expressed due disappointment. "I don't know what sort of referees we have now," he remarked before adding, "they have no commonsense at all." Two draws would have been more appropriate.

The odd number of teams made things more awkward which is why the Lagan Cup which included everyone except Cavan was so convenient. This was subsequently changed by Central Council. But the Lagan and McKenna Cups were treated very seriously, compared to now when teams are less concerned about subsidiary competitions.

My aims for those three years as Ulster president wouldn't have been described as a vision. Nevertheless, the two topics in which I was particularly interested were promoting the Irish language and grounds.

Clubs often contacted the Ulster Council for advice on purchasing new grounds. On a regular basis, Gerry Arthurs and I met with club committees to discuss their plans. We did a lot of work looking at the fields which they wanted to develop and examining whether or not they were suitable.

This was something which interested me because of my own experience of how clubs benefited from owning their venues. It was always a great morale-boost, providing them with immense pride. One of the problems was that clubs always felt compelled to plan a stadium on a par with Casement Park or Clones. As a result, the big danger was the potential for debt.

At that time the grants from the Ulster Council usually amounted to £50 or £100. An awful lot of work was carried out voluntarily. Applications were made for this money and the case for the club was always made by the county delegate. The grants were only given when the work had been completed, and generally an Ulster Council official visited the club.

It was often a case of 'keeping up with the neighbours.' Two or three people invariably had harebrained schemes. Some of the plans were amazing and I felt a responsibility to ensure that the plans remained realistic. Now the requirement on clubs to seek approval from the Ulster Council to borrow money is very beneficial. Great advances were made in terms of club development during those ten years starting about 1961.

Of course, it wasn't all rosy in the garden and a big problem in each of the counties was fixtures. The number of games cancelled because teams didn't turn up simply wasn't acceptable. There's no doubt that the fixtures situation in every county could only be described as chaos.

Maybe clubs were badly organised and players didn't give the same loyalty to their teams. I remember that on occasions it was a nightmare due to the absence of reports from referees.

Gradually, the mindsets of clubs began to change. We spent time trying to stress the need for a regular programme of fixtures throughout the year and that it would have to be adhered to. That has been achieved and it's satisfying to hear clubs discussing a match in January that might not be scheduled to take place until July or August.

Dealing with the RUC for Ulster Finals at Casement

There was absolutely no contact with the authorities in Northern Ireland during the 1940s and 1950s. This was to continue for many years afterwards. Despite this, they did keep a close eye on us and I remember the RUC coming to my home searching for documents. It was around the time when Sean Dolan was interned. He was communicating with me and the police wanted to see what he was saying. Sean was a great man, but internment didn't help his health and he died soon afterwards.

Later, in the 1960s, the relationship between the GAA, the Stormont Government and the Northern Ireland authorities was non-existent. There was a feeling of them against us in the dealings with them. We felt that they didn't pay much attention to us, and that we were second-class citizens.

But that period also saw a number of Ulster Finals and other big matches taking place at Casement Park. Consequently, there was a certain amount of necessary contact with the RUC. Casement Park was a popular venue for our provincial showpiece during those years. To be fair, they were very up-to-date with the demands posed by traffic managements. Their maps explained where cars would be coming from and they knew precisely what to do.

There were also meetings held with the police and the discussions were very business-like. We began by explaining that a big match was being staged there, who the competing teams were and the likely routes that the supporters would be taking. They approached it in a similarly professional manner. It didn't seem to matter to them who we were. Their job was to regulate the traffic and they did that.

As far as the RUC were concerned, this was another occasion. It was in their interests not to disrupt things or cause bother because that would only lead to matters being thrown-back at them later on.

Both the 1961 and 1962 finals were played in Casement Park. One of the reasons why the venues were rotated was because everyone thought Clones was too close to Cavan. A vote was taken and Antrim were always justifiably complaining that Casement was being under-utilised.

The increasing attendances at Ulster matches is vividly shown in this picture from the 1957 Ulster Final between Tyrone and Derry.

After that, Clones became the automatic choice as the only venue capable to hold the growing attendances coming to see the great Down team. Ulster final day in Clones compares well with all the big GAA occasions. Over the years I have always enjoyed the hustle and bustle and still relish my annual visits to St Tiernach's Park. There was the tradition of going there and the venue gained the same kind of reputation as enjoyed by Thurles for a Munster hurling final.

Parking was easier and the facilites generally better in Casement, but the tremendous atmosphere at Clones was the key. It became a social occasion and even the adventures of going to and from the match were a story in themselves.

The new Casement Park will definitely become a regular venue for Ulster finals in the future. It seems inevitable to me that Clones will become increasingly sidelined because there is no room for two large venues. This is a perennial debate and around the early 1960s Gerry Arthurs had this vision of a big ground in Omagh as the prime Ulster venue because of its centrality. The prospect of a 40,000-seater stadium in Casement is very exciting.

My role on that Ulster final day changed little over the years, even when I became President of the Ulster Council. There was no point in me standing about doing nothing, so like everyone else I continued to sell tickets on the low wall outside the school. But the fact that I was holding the presidency did give me a greater insight into the organisation involved behind the scenes.

Gerry Arthurs was the main man. Both of us travelled to Clones twice beforehand to check that all the arrangements were in order. The hill at that time in the early 1960s was a great asset, even though it belonged to the local parish and was purchased by the GAA years later.

There wasn't half the number of stewards as is the case now. But the traffic is much heavier and the number of cars is in sharp contrast to the days when the train took supporters to this central spot on the railway lines of Ulster. The traffic was becoming a problem at all venues during this period, especially with the then-emerging doubts about the future of the trains.

We were fortunate because the same template was used each year. A meeting was held with the Gardaí to discuss the traffic plans. On one occasion, a problem arose with the building from which the tickets were sold because it was roofed only by zinc and wasn't very safe. I had asked the Garda superintendent whether people could be prevented from climbing up on it because there was the real danger of someone falling through. Halfway through the match, then, I went around to check that everything was alright and there were two Gardaí sitting up on it. I was understandably very annoyed and expressed myself to the superintendent who, to be fair, got them removed.

The Irish course at Rosgoill Gaeltacht

One of the most innovative initiatives during my time in the Ulster Council was getting into its stride when I assumed the presidency in 1961. This was the Irish course organised annually at the Rosgoill Gaeltacht in Donegal.

It was officially opened in 1960 by Kevin Boland, Minister of Defence, and had been set up by Alf Murray, Gerry Fegan and myself. The big attraction of the course was the fact that it was exclusively orientated to the GAA and club officials. As a result the various elements were specifically geared towards equipping people with what they needed to effectively run the Association. The writing of minutes, appeals and objections were among the topics covered.

Much of the initial success of the course could be attributed to Harry Carey from Lifford who proved to be a massive help. He worked in the Donegal County Council office and was able to ensure that a lot of the typing required for the course was completed.

The course lasted for around two weeks and a lot of young people came. Among the highlights was the annual visit from the then Tomás Ó Fiaich, who was attending

Maynooth at the time. He came and gave those attending a number of informative talks on Irish history and culture. [5]

The idea for the course came from Seamus Ó Riain who went on to become president. He had organised a similar course in Munster, although not on the same scale as what we planned. When the decision was taken, we got the schedule of what was happening from him and improved and extended by

My good friend Alf Murray and his wife were lifelong friends. Alf's advice was a great source of inspiration for me for many years. Here we are at a function with Kathleen.

basing the classes on the GAA specifically. Seamus was a man with great ideas, and later on became one of the founders of the Féile na nGael.

Each year we travelled to Downings, and as well as the organisers, there were guest tutors and speakers. In addition to the future Cardinal Ó Fiaich, there was also Seán Ó Cinnéide from Dungloe and Eamon O'Cannon who were both teachers in Donegal. Unfortunately, the course stopped during the Troubles due to the travel difficulties. However, the course has been revived again and has been renamed Cursa de Faoite.

My close friend Alf Murray

TRUE friends are so important in life. One of those who most definitely fits that category for me was Alf Murray. We spoke almost daily for the best part of sixty years and in later decades I visited him almost every weekend. The two of us always spoke in Irish and, even when his body failed him, Alf's mind was still razor-sharp.

Even now, I get regular visits and phone calls from his family. This contact really pleases me because my contact with Alf and his family goes right back to our first meeting in the early 1940s when I began teaching temporarily in Crossmaglen.

One of Alf's uncles was a man called James Campbell, who had played on the Dundalk team which won the 1887 All-Ireland football final. Alf himself was born in Dromore, Co Down, and reared in the small area of the county which touches Lough Neagh. He was a famous figure in Ulster GAA circles at the time and served as President of the Ulster Council from 1946-1949. But from those years onwards, he was a massive help to me, and especially when I stood and was eventually elected as President. Alf had been

---

5 – The Rosgoill Galtacht course run by the Ulster Council continues to be a popular event for gaels from throughout the province. Paddy was due to address a 25th anniversary debate at the event in 2013.

defeated for the presidency previously by Seamus MacFerran and was rewarded a second time around.

Our association began when Alf was fundraising for the purchase of Davitt Park in Lurgan. Its development was a testament to his drive and foresight and the example set by the Clann Éireann club was one followed by clubs throughout Ulster and further afield in the 1960s. Considering Alf's influence, it was no wonder that club development was among my main priorities when I became Ulster President in 1961 and subsequently.

A raffle was organised to raise some money for the pitch and the club sent tickets to various places, including our school. I sold what came and asked for more and I remember becoming very friendly with him. There was a dress-céilí held also to help the fundraising and on occasion I would have stayed with him, his sister and parents on occasional weekends. Some time later the pitch was opened and Roscommon were supposed to come. But they let them down, so I got the urgent call asking for Derry to do the honours. We got a team gathered up a duly fulfilled the fixture.

But as well as this, Alf was an orator in the mould of someone like John F. Kennedy. It was very inspirational to hear him give an address. This was perhaps understandable because he certainly went to great lengths preparing. I remember him having two or three points which had to be put across. Of course, he often rehearsed so effectively that no notes were required.

A letter inviting me to apply for the post of Director General in 1964. Sean O'Siochan was the obvious choice having worked under Padraig O Chaomh previously.

The GAA and the Irish language were everything to him. His presidency from 1964 to 1966 was marked by some great innovations. Chief among them was the Coiste Iomána and his desire recalled Michael Cusack's motto of 'bring back the hurling'. Joe McDonagh of Galway always refers to the crucial impact that the supply of free hurls to schools during this period was to the subsequent success of the Tribesmen. Even yet, my friend Pat Guthrie will still talk about how effective this hurling drive was in promoting hurling in many of the weaker counties. This can be attributed to Alf's determination and organisational ability. He was constantly pushing out the boundaries and the kept to success was that Alf picked very good hurling people who were excellent organisers and men of action.

It was during Alf's time as President, too, that the first coaching seminars and courses for club and county officials were held. These have since became the norm and their importance cannot be over-emphasised in shaping the GAA which we know today. I had a close first-hand view of Alf's term as president after being elected as Central Council delegate from Down in 1964 when I defeated Maurice Hayes.

My desire was to be on the Central Council when Alf was president due to our close friendship. I also wanted to help him in whatever way possible. It also has to be remembered how well he dealt with the death of Pádraig Ó Caoimh. He had to organise Padraig's replacement and ensure that the huge vacuum was filled because of Padraig's huge contribution since 1929. Alf was strong-minded and effectively ensured good continuance in the immediate aftermath of this massive change.

Of course, Alf continued throughout to take a keen interest in Clann Éireann. Many of the activities which they carried out during this period are still viewed as the template for how a club should link with its local community. Suil Fada was a walk organised as a fundraiser through the schools. I remember Alf having all the income and scholarships organised so perfectly.

Clann Éireann were the first club to have their own clubrooms and they worked in conjunction with the Department of Education in the north, a rare occurrence for the period. I remember there were whispers about them taking money from the Stormont Government. Nevertheless, they worked with the authorities to start a youth club. A big hall was constructed and on one occasion I recall going down to see the progress and was greeted by the sight of Alf mixing cement. A handball alley was built and much of the expense was covered by grants which was a very new innovative departure.

Ambrose Lavery worked closely with Alf and the meetings with the Ministry officials were enlightening for the simple fact that both of them knew exactly how many young people would benefit and what activities they would be engaged in. The people taking the various activities such as boxing and cycling were paid through grants and everyone was looking at the development with amazement.

Not only that, Alf and Ambrose subsequently advised clubs on starting similar projects. Even today, their work is still reaping benefits in this deprived area.

Some people might have viewed Alf as very unbending and tough. My experience was so different. On a personal basis, he was great craic and could always accept a joke against himself. We had the same interests in the GAA and the language and each year the two of us also attended the Gaeltacht at Rann na Feirste together.

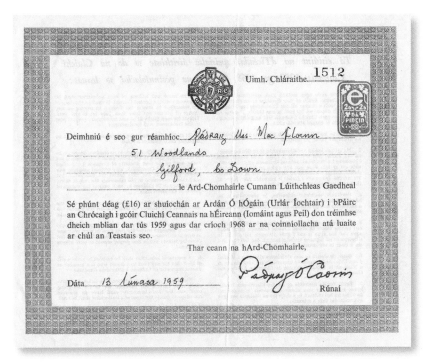

The rising confidence of the GAA was clear. Here's my certificate for a five-year ticket scheme which began in 1959.

He was always capable of rising to an occasion, something recognised in later years when he was the recipient of Gradam an Phiarsaighfor his contribution to Irish culture. The event was organised and held in the headquarters of Comhaltas Ceoltóirí Eireann and both myself and Kathleen were very proud to attend. His acceptance speech was magnificent.

Alf, of course, was also an accomplished player. He never put on any weight, and kept himself very fit. I refereed against him on one occasion and blew him up for taking too many steps. It was in a game between Monaghan and Armagh and he wasn't too pleased. In later years he always reminded me about my bold decision to penalise him. Ultimately, it was me who forced his retirement when I told him to "go before they're asking why you're still about."

In 1979, I think he was even more delighted at my election than anyone else. During the next three years Alf was somebody who I always consulted whenever any problems or challenges arose. This was particularly the case during the hunger strikes crises and I always got very sensible advice. There were many qualities which he had and which I wanted to adopt. There was his clear thinking, the positivity, the ideas and his great knowledge of the GAA from grassroots upwards.

For me, there were about four presidents who really led the way. Pádraig McNamee was outstanding, Pat Fanning from Waterford and Con Murphy of Cork. Alf was in that bracket. Many presidents were elected, served their term and worked hard without any great push for progress. Alf had great verve and vision and was an excellent president and friend.

The advent of TV coverage

Modern technology means that the old black and white pictures of All-Ireland finals from the 1940s onwards are now more widely available for people to watch at their leisure in the comfort of their homes. What a change from the debates and controversy which surrounded whether the GAA should allow the All-Ireland semi-finals and finals to be broadcast live by RTÉ.

It was me who initially proposed that RTÉ be given the rights to the All-Ireland Finals for the nominal fee of £10 as a promotional exercise. However, this was the least of our worries from an Ulster vantage-point and, as president, I felt it was important for me to articulate the views of our members.

My knowledge of the TV world became fairly extensive, but I would never claim to be an expert. In the early 1960s I made a great oration on behalf of Ulster about how badly we were being treated in being denied excess to national TV. Shortly after that, Fr Ignatius Andrew who was the religious correspondence at the BBC gave a lecture at

The Derry players relaxing before the 1958 All-Ireland Final. The advent of TV coverage meant the association had to be increasingly aware of its rights and responsibilities in the media.

Gormanston. Pádraig Ó Caoimh rang asking me to attend. Fr Ignatius presented a very interesting summary of how television worked. He explained how it was possible to impress TV, and the fact that every letter was examined very carefully and if they got a whole lot of letters from the one place it didn't have the same impact.

As a result, we in the GAA were able to get organised to get the clubs to put the pressure on for the matches. The GAA headquarters were based at Croke House, where the front room was the meeting place for the Executive and the big debate in 1962 was the whole issue of live TV. [6]

There was a great fear among the delegates at the Congress in this period that the televising of games would result in a dramatic drop in attendances. The opposite has in fact been the case. Nevertheless, the trepidation was clear and prolonged because even up until quite recently the number of matches has been restricted.

My thinking behind proposing the token fee of £10 for the rights was based on the belief that television could be a useful tool for promotion. A vote was taken and passed at Central Council. Now the situation is dictated by the GAA management who make a plan in conjunction with the competitions control committee.

The situation was so different in Ulster where we had absolutely no coverage on either TV or radio. This was exacerbated by the fact very few people were able to receive RTÉ. This was brought up at the Ulster Council where the strong view was that the national television service should cover the whole nation. We were, however, operating at a different scale. Some international TV agreements precluded RTÉ from erecting booster stations. Thankfully, this was resolved fairly quickly.

BBC and UTV were a different proposition altogether. There were constant negotiations with them trying to secure an improvement in coverage without getting anywhere. I met the person in charge of sport and they always made the point about our games being the minority sport, something which we obviously rejected. Nevertheless, their attitude was extremely anti-GAA at the beginning. To begin with, they wouldn't even meet us.

Some progress did materialise and the live broadcasting of the 1966 Ulster Final was significant. This was also important in allowing people, not familiar with the GAA and whether they agreed with the Association or not, to watch the game if they wanted in the privacy of their own homes.

The unfortunate thing is that, even yet fifty years on, the coverage of Gaelic games on BBC and UTV remains limited. A survey carried out in Down a few years ago emphasised the disparity in both newspapers and on radio and TV and still holds true today.

---

6 - The first matches broadcast live on RTE were in 1962. In 1966 the BBC broadcast the Ulster Final between Donegal and Down. Commentary on that occasion was by Jim McKeever of Derry.

SPORTS COVERAGE SURVEY OF THE BELFAST TELEGRAPH
(Issues 14-10-1982 — 30-10-1982 inclusive)   COVERAGE IN COLUMN INCHES

SPORTS	Th. 14/10	F. 15/10	Sa. 16/10	M. 18/10	Tue. 19/10	W. 20/10	Th. 21/10	F. 22/10	Sa. 23/10	M. 25/10	Tue. 26/10	W. 27/10	Th. 28/10	F. 29/10	Sa. 30/10	TOTAL	%
SOCCER	197.3	94.7	17	111.3	119.8	201.8	113.9	86.1	18	97.3	126	104.1	44.2	71	10.1	1472.6	29.4
HOCKEY	105.7	2.1	7.8	17.9	—	24.6	81.4	26.4	6.1	5.9	17.9	20.9	80.1	—	12.8	409.6	8.2
RUGBY	—	57.3	—	2.6	26.5	38.4	3.6	63.9	—	29.0	26.6	40.1	35.6	45.7	15.6	384.3	7.7
MOTORSPORT	22	34.2	8.7	37.2	16.6	45.4	15.5	20.9	—	24.7	52.7	20.1	36.9	29.7	—	364.6	7.3
GOLF	26.2	21.8	47.9	18.9	21.5	10.6	31.1	15.8	—	8.5	13.0	31.3	34.8	5.8	18.2	305.4	6.1
SNOOKER	—	3.3	79.1	12	4.0	5.0	12.9	3.8	57.4	5.0	6.5	5.6	30.4	—	70.5	296.5	5.9
EQUESTRIAN	3	5.1	—	—	170.2	—	40.4	—	—	2.9	2.2	—	8	21.8	6.2	293.8	5.9
CRICKET	—	4.4	31.8	19.8	10.4	—	—	21.8	57.9	35.8	9.8	45.1	18.9	14.1	10.8	280.6	5.6
DOG RACING	—	—	—	—	22.8	18	20.7	31.8	16.2	16.0	15.2	4.5	14.0	27.1	15.8	202.1	4.0
G.A.A.	—	21.6	—	26.8	—	15.6	—	17.7	—	25.1	—	10.8	—	20.9	—	138.5	2.7
BOXING	14.1	—	16	—	—	4.9	1.3	—	—	7.5	—	—	53.3	—	3.5	132.1	2.6
SQUASH	28.4	—	—	5.8	—	—	27.6	—	14.8	6.2	—	4.5	6.3	5.3	11.8	110.7	2.2
BOWLS	—	15.8	2	2.8	23.5	3.7	6.9	3.6	2.8	—	3.5	24.9	2	1.9	2.4	95.8	1.9
ANGLING	11.6	17.9	13.3	—	—	—	—	22.1	—	—	—	—	—	20.5	—	85.4	1.7
TABLE TENNIS	—	11.4	—	7.4	—	—	—	18	—	12.9	—	—	4.9	24.4	—	79.0	1.5
TENNIS	—	1.2	10.4	1.1	—	—	19.1	—	—	9.4	9.7	—	4.3	—	—	55.2	1.1
BASKETBALL	—	16.8	—	1.1	—	—	9.4	8.3	—	6.9	—	—	—	—	—	52.4	1.0
ATHLETICS	—	16.8	7.7	2.4	—	—	—	—	—	1.6	—	—	—	13.1	—	41.6	less 1%
SWIMMING	—	—	5.5	—	—	—	—	—	—	25.2	—	—	—	—	7.5	38.2	''
KARATE	—	—	—	—	—	—	31.4	—	—	5.1	—	—	—	—	—	36.5	''
WATER POLO	5	3.0	—	10.3	—	—	—	—	—	6.1	—	—	—	—	—	24.4	''
ROWING	—	—	—	—	—	—	—	24.3	—	—	—	—	—	—	—	24.3	''
CYCLING	12.2	—	—	—	—	—	1.4	—	—	—	—	—	2.2	—	7.7	23.5	''
SAILING	—	4.4	—	1.8	—	—	2.3	—	8.5	4.0	—	—	—	—	—	21	''
BADMINTON	—	—	—	—	—	9.2	—	—	—	—	—	—	5.3	—	—	14.5	''
NETBALL	—	—	—	—	—	—	—	—	—	10.1	—	—	—	—	—	10.7	''
VOLLEYBALL	—	—	—	—	—	—	—	—	—	—	—	—	5.3	—	—	5.3	''
SKI-ING	—	—	—	—	—	—	—	—	—	—	—	—	—	4.9	—	4.9	''
HANDBALL	—	—	—	—	—	—	—	—	—	2.7	—	—	—	—	—	2.7	''
DARTS	—	—	—	—	—	—	—	—	—	—	—	—	—	—	—	2.2	''
	—	—	—	—	—	—	—	—	—	—	—	—	—	—	—	1.3	''
																5009.5	100%

A REPORT
ON THE COVERAGE OF
GAELIC GAMES
IN THE NORTHERN MEDIA

by
Down G.A.A.
Communications Committee

It was important that views in the north were able to receive TV coverage of the major matches as statistics showed that the TV, radio and newspapers were less interested in providing extensive coverage.

HELPING TO SHAPE
THE MODERN GAA

THE modern GAA has its origins in the 1960s which was a very interesting decade to be involved. Down's success, the advent of television, the increasing role of the Association within the community, the revival of hurling and the evolution of the games were all important factors.

By then I was also ready to take on a greater role at national level, having served my time on the Ulster Council for many years. Perhaps this desire was generated by the high profile enjoyed by Down on the All-Ireland scene. As a result, there were numerous occasions when my role as a Central Council delegate required strong representation from me both there and at Congress.

One of the more significant issues arose in 1968 just after the third All-Ireland win. A proposal was forwarded that the team should travel to Australia the following spring, 1969. At the time the international dimension to Gaelic games was being increasingly probed, facilitated by the increasing ease of international travel.

However, this Australian trip never really got off the ground because of the costs involved. It was hard to obtain sponsorship there, compared to the United States visit six years earlier. We had been on an enjoyable trip to San Francisco in 1962 when we played at least six games and then returned to New York in March 1969.

Those trips were certainly interesting, not least because the travelling was a great adventure. Everything was extremely well organised by a man called Michael J. Kavanagh. A notable feature was the way in which the Americans cut down on speeches by just getting those at the top table to stand up and bow, rather than having the requirement for each person to speak.

Down's 1968 team was not as good as that of 1960 and 1961. Nevertheless, the players still had great heart and really should have won again in 1969. My role, though, never went beyond the tasks involved with being county board treasurer. A great tradition was that only the immediate team and management travelled to the big matches. I strongly agreed with this and instead went to the games my own way.

Developing an international dimension

The large-scale emigration from Ireland developed an international element to our games similar to what prevails today. While the focus is now on every continent, at that time in the late 1960s, the presence of Gaelic games was limited to England, America and to a lesser extent Australia.

In the winter of 1968, Hugh Byrne from Wicklow and myself, were appointed by the Central Council to compile a report on the state of international competition.

The situation in America demanded attention. The difficulty was that the New York and North American divisions didn't agree, and then there were also constant problems in their relationhip with the Central Council.

The Down style and the county's success made them an attraction far beyond Ireland's shores.

Many of the issues stemmed from players travelling from Ireland who played under the auspices of both boards. Our remit was to resolve the perennial and complicated problem of players going out from here, even for just a weekend. It was something which has continued to cause concern.

In addition to this, there was the issue of students travelling to work for the summer. Clearance from Croke Park was required and the aim was always to try to restrict the number of visiting players for each team. A free-for-all would have been unfair to the local players. [1] It would have undermined the interest and enthusiasm of those non-Irish who wanted to participate. Facilities were also poor. Gaelic Park in New York belonged to the railway company and was leased out to John Kerry O'Donnell.

We eventually recommended regulations about visiting players and the number of emigrants permitted. Those were and still are the key issues and that 1968 report did help to sort out a situation where nobody knew what players were legal or illegal.

Thankfully, there has been an acceptance more recently about the need to extend the games to the non-Irish. A few years ago a club from London reached the final of the Féile na nOg in Celtic Park in Derry and were being coached by a lad from Galbally who had recruited help from Mickey Harte. [2]

---

1 – The problems with visiting players have persisted down through the decades and the drip of inter-county players to the US when their championship is completed remains an issue demanding attention from the GAA.

2 – Feile Na nOg s the football equivalent of the highly successful, Feile Na nGael in hurling. The event has been hosted by Derry on two occasions, most recently in 2013.

This is better than just restricting the games to Irish emigrants because it was too easy for clubs to field the emigrants rather than cultivating their own homegrown talent. I was amazed and satisfied to see some black players taking part.

Maybe we started the ball rolling in 1968, and the momentum is being maintained by the Overseas committee in Croke Park. Progress is also evident in England where Gaelic football and hurling are being coached in a number of secondary schools. Much of the credit for this can be attributed to the young breed of emigrant who is prepared to reach out.

It's hard to know whether or not teams from England, America or elsewhere can ever compete effectively with their Irish counterparts. In the 1960s the winners of the National League and other competitions travelled over to New York after winning what was called the 'Home Final.' This was a kind of international dimension, but was abandoned for various reasons, including the gap in standard.

Mickey Harte often proposes a 'world club championship.' There is no doubt that the presence of Gaelic games in Europe, America, the Middle East and Far East, as well as England, America and Australia, would make this a viable proposal. However, the question as always would centre on the standard. However, it must be hoped that these countries will be in a position to produce minor teams in a few years.

Unfortunately, unlike rugby and soccer, the same development of gaelic games overseas has never really occurred. The whole British legislative system was involved in the spread of rugby, soccer and cricket, whereas all the Irish had were a couple of Christian Brothers teaching in a school and they had their own work to carry out.

This was in contrast to the civilian employees working in military establishments who were glad to become involved. For them, the ability to play the games of your masters was a status symbol. The same thing happened in Ireland where the Garrison towns like Omagh and Longford were always strongholds of soccer or rugby. The legacy of that is still evident in these towns.

The infamous John 'Kerry' O'Donnell

Few figures in the wider GAA world of the 1960s and early 1970s matched the redoubtable John 'Kerry' O'Donnell. He ran the Association in New York for many years. But while he was a major figure, I have mixed views on the true worth of the contribution made by him.

There was a period years ago when the opportunity arose for the purchase of land in New York which could have been used for Gaelic games. But John Kerry had this desire that Gaelic Park should remain as the centre for the GAA in New York.

He and Harry Bietzel from Australia were great pals. A story is told about John Kerry once taking a team to Australia for three weeks. Then, when he returned, John Kerry went through to the county board minutes removing anything which he didn't agree with.

I knew John Kerry well for a time in the late 1960s. This was around the same period when he described the members of Central Council as 'nobodies' who were merely 'keeping the seats warm.' He then wrote to each and every one of them telling them that he was not referring to them personally.

John Kerry could be arrogant and difficult to deal with and there was little point reasoning with him. If he took a decision then that was set in stone and it was impossible to change his mind. It was his way or no way.

Down travelled to America in 1968 and part of the proceedings was a speech by Joe Lennon at the end of the match. However, John

John Kerry O'Donnell's distinctive handwriting. He was a real character in GAA circles.

Kerry pulled the plug on the microphone and this really annoyed Joe and the Down contingent. It was also tradition in the 1970s for the GAA president to attend an annual dinner in New York which was usually attended by around 1100 people. On another occasion I was seated between two people whom John Kerry didn't like. He said to me, "You're seated between two thieves today." Later, John Kerry made a speech during which he launched a shocking attack on the Allied Irish Banks representative, despite the fact that AIB were sponsoring the event.

As a Kerryman originally, he was understandably preoccupied with their fortunes. They were always treated royally when they travelled to New York.

There was no shortage of opportunities for John Kerry to exert influence. Trips to America by the top inter-county teams were a very regular occurrence at that time as the National League 'Home' champions' played New York in the final proper. Indeed, I recall Down doing badly in a match in 1968 and Paddy O'Donoghue took them in at half-time and delivered a real fire and brimstone speech. Suffice to say Down won the next game easily after that talking-to. [3]

---

3 – Down completed the National League and All-Ireland double in 1968. This was to be their last Sam Maguire triumph until 1991.

Attendances of about 11,000 were usual at these matches, and the whole occasion was obviously a source of pride for the Irish community in New York. However, the surface on Gaelic Park was terrible and not suited to the showcasing the skills of the top players form Ireland. Some work was eventually carried out and I was invited over to see what had been done. John Kerry was lined up to take me on a tour, but the day of the trip coincided with a heavy snowfall, so we couldn't see anything of this newly resurfaced pitch. John Kerry was enraged at the misfortune.

The New York GAA at that time was chaired by a man called Jackie Salmon. He had strong square shoulders and made his own decisions, much to the annoyance of John Kerry.

As well as being such a prominent figure in the New York GAA, John Kerry also came regularly to Ireland very often. Each year he attended the All-Stars, including on one occasion when he came wearing the full regalia of the Knights of St Gregory. Someone said to him, "You didn't bring your sword." Quick as a flash, John Kerry responded by saying "No, I was afraid I might use it." He was a great wit as well.

Overall, he probably did more harm than good to the GAA in New York.

Why I voted against removing 'the Ban'

Over the years I have been fortunate to witness at first hand many of the seminal events which affected the development of the GAA. Among them was that famous occasion in 1971 when the ban on the playing of rival or 'foreign' games was removed.

Congress that year took place in Belfast. So the decision was taken in the unlikely surroundings of the Whitla Hall in Queen's University. But the decision to rescind the rule wasn't as dramatic as is often portrayed.

It was in fact very much a fait accompli because the clubs had all been given a chance to air their views through the respective county boards. Pat Fanning was president at the time, very pro-ban and the last man in the world who would have wanted the rule removed.

However, he had to accept the inevitable that the members of the Association had spoken through the clubs and county boards. These GAA people gave a very clear view and obviously the counties' delegates arriving for Congress had already been mandated to vote in a particular manner. Consequently, it was merely a case of going through the motions. A highlight was the very gracious speech given by Pat in accepting what to him was a decision which he wouldn't have accepted normally.

My personal view on the ban was divided, despite having played rugby at Strawberry Hill in the 1930s. Three decades later I was very much in favour of retaining the ban. This belief was based on the view that its removal would affect the numbers participating in Gaelic games. My compromise was that the ban on attendance should be the only part of the rule to be removed. [4]

This thinking was based on self-preservation and my view that young players in an area should have allegiance only to Gaelic games and not other sports. There was also the question about what would happen when there was a clash of fixtures between sports. Such a scenario could lead to all sorts of problems and ill-feeling.

Everything was going well, the ban had stood to the GAA's benefit and there was no need in my opinion to fix something that wasn't broken.

Mistakes were made in relation to the implementation of the ban and the restriction on attendance was stupid and unnecessary. This was evidenced by the experience of Douglas Hyde when he was President of Ireland and expelled for attending a soccer international. Eddie Devlin of Tyrone was observed walking through crowds on their way to a rugby international while returning from a colleges GAA game. The vigilance committees introduced to identify and report breaches of the ban were obnoxious, going around spying to see if people were attending foreign games.

Looking back now with the benefit of hindsight, the decision taken in 1971 was the correct one. The ban couldn't have lasted much longer. It had run its course and that was quite obvious from the vast majority of members who supported its removal.

It was a very historic moment when the rule was formally removed, although I felt we were still entering unchartered waters. The big questions centred on how the decision would affect the GAA, whether or not it would weaken us, if it would cause problems in terms of divided allegiances. Thankfully, it worked out and was the obvious thing to do considering the way modern society developed.

Of course, the ban would be even more difficult to enforce. In the early 2000s, I showed I had learned my lesson by voting in favour of removing Rule 21 barring the police from taking part in Gaelic games.

Incidentally, the removal of the ban wasn't the only big issue up for debate at that 1971 Congress. Another one was the proposal by Down to introduce an open draw for the All-Ireland Football Championship. Our motivation was based on the fact that we had been caught for a couple of years by having to play in the Ulster preliminary round. As a result, there was a lot of displeasure within the county.

But there wasn't a great groundswell of opinion in favour of such a move. The open draw has occasionally raised its head during the intervening period, including the suggestion that there should be four groups of eight in the championship.

---

4 – The Ban on foreign games was eventually removed from the GAA rule book in 1971 at the Congress held in Belfast. A number of previous attempts to have the rule struck off had been made in the previous decades.

Of course, this is never going to happen because the provincial finals are first great occasions and secondly of vital financial benefit. If the Ulster Council had no Ulster Football final, then the level of employment and grants to clubs and counties would have to be severely restricted. Munster would be particularly badly affected because both its hurling and football finals are major occasions.

A new system would, of course, be much easier to implement with the ease of travel throughout Ireland compared with a few years ago.

Going for the GAA Presidency

The words of one delegate to me after my election as President in 1978 are especially appropriate. "We're so tired of looking at you going for the presidency every three years that we decided to finally elect you to get you out of the road." His comment sums up my quest for the post throughout the decade.

The presidency was a position which I made a conscious decision to seek in 1970 and subsequently. It was going to be a great honour and privilege and my inclination was inspired by a good grounding in a number of different positions.

By then my record of service was year. As well as having been Ulster President from 1961 until 1964, there was also the experience as a Central Council delegate from 1964. So, this was the perfect time stage and time to make a move.

In saying that, though, it was still probably a mistake to stand so quickly. My first challenge came in 1970 against Pat Fanning. He was the overwhelming favourite and it would have been better to have pulled out because there was no chance of me or anyone else defeating him.

It was a similar situation in 1973 against Donal Keenan of Roscommon. That was a lost cause as well because Connacht had very few presidents. As a result, if a worthy candidate did stand, he was nearly certain to get in. Donal Keenan filled all those credentials and duly won as anticipated.

Limerick captain, Eamonn Grimes, lifts the Liam McCarthy Cup in 1973, with Donal Keenan pictured alongside.

My third attempt arrived in 1976 when Con Murphy of Cork was the main candidate. He was strong and popular and duly won.

However, it wasn't all disappointment on my part. On each of those three occasions, my vote increased to the point where I had polled fairly well against Con Murphy and given him a good challenge.

Looking back now, I wasn't really disappointed following those three defeats. The simple fact was that the opposing candidates were extremely strong. Pat Fanning turned out to be an outstanding President and very articulate. His qualities were apparent in the manner which he handled the removal of the ban so exceptionally well in 1971.

There is always great excitement when Congress meets to elect a new president. The names and credentials of the various candidates are discussed and a favourite usually emerges. Potential candidates are nominated by an individual county who were then asked whether or not they accept.

Success finally arrived for me in 1978 when the Congress took place in Mayo and I beat Jim Roche from Wexford. The experience gained from those earlier failed attempts definitely stood to me that year when I was finally elected.

Both Derry and Down put my name forward on each occasion that I stood for the presidency. Delegates are mandated by their respective counties on what way they should be voting, although some are given a free choice. I could always rely on the support of the Ulster counties, but the key in 1978 was the support from Connacht and a group of counties in north Leinster.

In both 1970 and 1973, people advised me to withdraw on the day of the election, but I ignored them. One of the reasons for this was that the experience of having stood before.

This was emphasised in 1973 when my vote actually increased from three years earlier. In 1976, there were a number of counts before Con Murphy and myself were separated. If I had been able to gain the support of just a few more counties, then my bid could have been successful then.

At that time it was merely a case of letting my own record speak for itself, unlike today when a certain amount of canvassing takes place. My chief adviser in all of these things was, of course, Alf Murray and he encouraged me to stand. The decision to start putting my name forward in 1970 was definitely a big one which required a lot of thinking and contemplation on what the job entailed, how it would affect my life and what sacrifices were required.

One of the first things I did upon my eventual election as president was to resign from my teaching post at the end of that school year. That probably could not have happened eight years earlier in 1970. The workload even then was very extensive. For me to be away the whole weekend on GAA duties all over the country and then return for school on Monday morning was going to be extremely tough.

At that time, I was also principal, so the situation was going to be very nearly impossible. While I was still reasonably young, there was still a lot of pressure. There was also the issue of taking time off work.

This had been something which became apparent in 1968 in relation to the proposal that Down travel to Australia. It was also an issue when I travelled with the Down team to San Francisco in 1962.

I had to pull all sorts of strings to be able to travel. Eventually, I was able to get leave of absence without pay. A substitute teacher was appointed to cover my absence and there was the added challenge of dealing with officials from the Department of Education who often did not appreciate this GAA involvement.

There was no such thing as early retirement when I was elected as GAA president in 1978. At the age of 60 I had only a few years to complete my teaching career. However, the Department were extremely reluctant to grant the request for early retirement and this led to long and protracted negotiations. They were covering themselves against the question of why I had been granted early retirement when so many others might have had their requests rejected.

Even at Ulster level in the 1960s, the task of combining the attendance at functions and meetings with the teaching was difficult at times. It was always a problem, because there were five teachers in Gilford during this period. The school was quite big and I was still teaching. Now the GAA is more generally accepted and quite respectable and teachers are able to obtain concessions. But back then the attitude to the Association by the Stormont officials was more hostile.

MOVING ON TO
A NATIONAL STAGE

A role on the new Games Administration committee lead to responsibility for arranging fixtures in both hurling and football, and the appointment of referees, including John Moloney who is seen here with the Cork and Kilkenny captions prior to the 1978 All-Ireland Final.

Getting a place on the GAA's new Management committee

Big changes were taking place within the GAA at the start of the 1970s. This was partly arising from the report of the special Commission on the GAA in 1971. As someone who had stood for the presidency twice by 1973, I was very definitely putting my credentials on the line.

That year saw my appointment to the GAA's new management committee which has become such an integral part of the daily organisation of the Association since then. The other members included Con Murphy, Jack Fitzgerald, Johnny Mulvey and T. P. O'Reilly from Cavan and Sean O Siochan.

It was decided that one person from each province and the GAA President would be elected to serve. T. P. O'Reilly was Ulster's representative and then I stood and was elected to the extra position. My membership of the management committee added further to my workload. It also raised my profile during the subsequent years as I was called upon to discuss a range of very important and ongoing issues within the Association.

The meetings took place on a weekly basis and sometimes more often. Each month the management committee reported back to the Central Council when any decisions made by us were rubber-stamped. On a regular basis, tricky problems which arose at Central Council were referred back to the Management Committee for resolution.

The management committee appears to have taken over, leaving the Central Council to merely approve decisions. However, things weren't as simple as this 40 years ago, and the

Central Council could be extremely critical. During my presidency, myself and Liam Mulvihill usually met to discuss the Central Council agenda, the issues which might arise and how they could be dealt with.

It was a case of being extremely careful to foresee what was coming up. The President had to be ready for a member of the Central Council raising something contentious. Part of the job was also to get the correct result each time and avoid a wayward decision.

The management committee is arguably the most important group within the GAA now. It currently comprises the President, the four provincial presidents, the two trustees and one other representative from each province.

My appointment to that group was undoubtedly an honour and required me to be very active and aware of the issues affecting the Association. Our meetings usually began at 7.30 pm on a Friday and continued until 10.30 pm that night. Things would then resume at 10 am on a Saturday morning and not finish until around 3 pm.

The facilities at Croke Park were quite primitive before the construction of the Ceannáras building. While the meetings of the Central Council took place in Clonliffe College, the Management committee met in Croke Park. A big aim was to ensure that each member had a say and there were all sorts of issues which needed to be dealt with, from questions of national significance to problems from within counties.

Discussing suspensions with Tony Hanahoe at the GAC

Tony Hanahoe and I retreated to a quiet corner in Croke Park one famous evening in the mid-1970s. He was the star Dublin player of the time, someone with forthright opinions and a talented lawyer. I was Chairman of the new Games Administration Committee.

There was no shortage of issues to deal with at the time. Major incidents at big matches were the most high profile, although there were plenty of equally contentious issues from club games which demanded attention.

But Tony's case was different and one of the most interesting which I've ever dealt with. He had written an article passing comments on the then well-known referee from Kildare, Seamus Aldridge. [1]

So, we summoned Tony and after discussing within the committee, myself and Tony retreated outside for an 'eyeball to eyeball' encounter. "Tony," I explained, "You have to be suspended and I have no option in the matter, but if you make any effort in apologising we might be able to reach an agreement." However, being a lawyer he wasn't prepared to move at all and was duly suspended

1 – Tony Hanahoe was a star player from Dublin during their All-Ireland successes in 1974, 1976 and 1977. He remains one of only a small number of players to captain their counties to two Sam Maguire Cup titles.

Dealing with Dublin's Tony Hanahoe was certainly an experience to remember.

Like many roles within the Association, the job of chairman of the GAC gradually increased in terms of profile, pressure and responsibility. Con Murphy appointed me to the post and the duties included appointing referees, making fixtures and deciding on venues. This was a post which took up a lot of time and Con always backed up our decisions.

Fixtures were a difficult issue, and this was compounded by drawn games and officials canvassing in relation to referees and venues. Jimmy Smyth of Clare was secretary and very knowledgeable about hurling. The canvassing was especially prevalent at the time of the All-Ireland finals and Jimmy and I usually discussed who was the best candidate.

The GAC members were then asked to discuss the various possibilities. One would remark that a particular referee didn't have a good game a few weeks previously. That candidate was then eliminated and by this process we always arrived at the preferred person.

For instance, the provincial referees pushed the referee from within their own province. This would usually have followed some representation being made to them by the native county of the candidate.

There was one All-Ireland semi-final which was expected to be extremely tough. Unfortunately, John Moloney had retired, but I spoke to him and he came out of retirement to take charge of this big match. One man whom I helped promote was George Ryan from Lattin in Tipperary. [2] He was recommended to me as someone

---

2 – George Ryan refereed the 1978 and 1985 All-Ireland hurling finals and has remained a close friend of Paddy MacFlynn.

capable, an opinion proven by his expert handling of an All-Ireland final.

Another time, a hurler was up before us for striking with the hurl. Two of those who had witnessed the incident were Pat Fanning and Paddy Buggy. They, being two hurling people, told me that it was an awkward pull rather than deliberate striking. So, the player was exonerated.

My aim was always to be on the side of the players, unless the incident was clearly malicious. I always took any mitigating circumstances into consideration and our meetings were often very lengthy due to the workload.

Overall, it was an enjoyable time to be involved in organising the games and one of my additional tasks was to at least attempt to develop a more effective structure to the organisation of fixtures.

My good friend, George Ryan, who refereed the All-Ireland Hurling Final.

Fixtures were usually something of a mess, and often reached the stage where it was virtually impossible to complete all the competitions as required. The aim was to produce a plan which would be adhered to for the remainder of the year. Of course, draws and other issues often played havoc with these best-laid plans.

It was important to introduce some order to this so that people would know exactly when and where matches would be played. We were running two major games at senior, intermediate, minor, under-21 and Junior level. The number of county teams was immense and things have now become even more complicated due to the club championships.

There was also resistance to the playing of matches on a Friday night or Saturday, the chief fear being that supporters might turn up. The association was a bit conservative in that respect. But time has yielded a sea-change in the mindset and now games are played on week-nights under floodlights. Saturday is also just as common for games as a Sunday and is accepted by players and supporters.

This was definitely something of a headache trying to get everything sorted. I think, though, that I did make a worthwhile contribution. In 1978 – my last year – we were able to announce dates which were adhered to for the most part.

This better organisation has benefited the under-21 grade which is no longer confined to Sundays. The dual player has also been helped because clashes between the two main codes are not as regular as in the past.

The change in more recent years has happened out of necessity because, unlike the 1970s, there are All-Ireland qualifier series and other competitions to be accommodated with the result that Saturday games are vital to ensure that the fixtures schedules are completed.

Things have definitely improved immensely since then, even though the problems during the spring need to be address when there is a proliferation of colleges, under-21, Minor league and National League games.

Deciding whether to stand again

Three failed attempts to win the GAA Presidency lead to a certain amount of soul-searching in the early spring of 1978. Would I stand again for the post after losing out in the three previous elections during that decade?

It would probably have been easier to give in. Fortunately, a lot of friends encouraged me to try again one final time. So, while I wasn't very keen, a number of people talked me round.

Chief among them was Alf Murray, and another person who was very encouraging was Donal Keenan, who had served as President from 1973 to 1976. He had beaten me in 1973 so his advice was much appreciated.

Future Ulster Council President, Peter Harte, is among those congratulating me after being elected President at Congress in Ballina in 1978.

So, there were a certain amount of nerves as the vote loomed in March 1978. At the same time, I was fairly confident of victory because on the previous occasions the people also in the running were all big names and defeat was perhaps inevitable.

On this occasion, though, Jimmy Roche didn't represent the same obstacle. He had been a provincial chairman and had followed the same kind of career path as myself. In addition, the Ulster counties were, as usual, fully supportive. When Connacht joined them, my destiny was confirmed.

Of course, there was no such thing as canvassing or an opportunity for the nominees to set out their vision. Instead, each relied on their individual records of past service to the GAA.

As well as Jimmy Roche from Wexford, the other candidates that year were Jimmy Gray of Dublin, Dr Mick Loftus of Mayo and George McGuigan, a native of Moy. The three of them were eliminated at the first count at which stage I was ahead on 87 votes to 80 for Jimmy Roche. On the second count, I polled 106 to Jimmy's 82, while Mick Loftus and Jimmy Gray were eliminated as their combined totals didn't match Jimmy's 82.

Now the race for the Presidency came down to a straight two-way tussle with Jimmy Roche. Thankfully, that that third and decisive ballot was won by the convincing margin of 156 to 99.

Unlike previous years, the vote in my favour was strongest and the support from the Connacht delegates was vital, including the large Galway contingent. The support of the other Connacht counties and those in north Leinster was also very important. Jimmy Roche from Wexford was my closest challenger, but the Leinster candidates generally do not carry the support of their whole province.

After ten years of effort, and forty-five years after my first involvement in the GAA back in Magherafelt, the journey towards the presidency of this great Association was complete.

Cheers in the pub for their new President

A number of emotions were going through my mind as the enormity of that announcement sank in. Relief was perhaps the primary one initially and then pride that at attaining to the highest office in the Association.

There was certainly no hiding my pride when that announcement was made at the Town Hall in Ballina on the weekend of Sunday 26 March 1978. After three failed attempts, success had arrived on the fourth.

It was also a great honour for both myself, my family and the county. I definitely felt that I had reached my destination by achieving this position.

The local club for racing pigeon enthusiasts was based out of Laverty's Bar. It was drawn from both sides of the community and many of those pictured were among those in the bar who offered me congratulations when I returned home after that 1978 Congress.

My travelling companions to that Annual Congress were the Down delegation, including Paddy O'Donoghue. Alf Murray was also there and probably most excited of all because he had coached and advised me so well down through the years and was consistently pushing me to stand. Most of the Ulster people were very pleased because of my record of service with the Ulster Council for 25 years.

"You're not going to read all that," Alf Murray said to be as I got ready to deliver an acceptance speech. Pre-prepared speeches have never been a strong point, so it was a case instead of reverting to the tried and trusted method of delivering a shorter acceptance speech drawn from a few brief notes.

Strangely, none of my relatives were in attendance. That has all changed since and now the President's wife is also introduced to the crowd, something which is certainly more emotional. However, I phoned home immediately and told Kathleen. She was understandably delighted as well and congratulated me.

That day also Down were playing in Mayo and a large cheer went up from the supporters when the result of the election was announced. My minder was Bill Casey who introduced me to many of the delegates and looked after me.

Alf Murray had been the most recent president from Ulster, so it was definitely time for another. There was always a feeling that the post should move around the various provinces regularly.

However, there were no great celebrations on my return home, although some of the local clubs here in Down did organise functions. Tullylish were understandably very pleased that they could count the President as a club member.

One of the most memorable moments was back at the bar on that Sunday night. The punters had been watching the television news and gave me great cheer. This was much appreciated because a lot of them were not GAA people and didn't have much interest in it ordinarily. Indeed, many of them were non-Catholic neighbours, but they still appreciated the fact that this was a significant honour.

It was a big moment as only twenty-seven men had held this position previously. [3] At a practical level, the only outward memento was the presidential medal, shaped like an All-Ireland medal, which I received the following year. This practice was initially proposed by Derry and was something that Tommy Mellon was very keen on. The option of a chain of office rejected, so the medal was introduced instead.

The first President-elect

The decision of Congress in 1975 to appoint a president-elect was a momentous one for me. Fortunately, the GAA gave me a year to become accustomed to the post of President. Previously, of course, a president was elected and immediately took up the position. But that was changed, so my presidency was historic in that respect.

Ever since, every new president serves a year of preparation before assuming the role. This role of president-elect has become increasingly important since 1978 and is undoubtedly a far more preferable situation than the one which preceded it. [4]

In 1970, 1973 and again in 1976, myself and the other nominees for the presidency were briefed on the Friday night of Congress about the issues and motions on the agenda. This was vital because any of the people standing could – if elected – have been thrust into the limelight dealing with any number of pending motions and debates.

It was an auspicious occasion indeed in the spring of that year when I was finally elected President. My term of office was due to begin officially at the 1979 Congress, leaving me with a year to become accustomed to the role and what it might entail.

There's no doubt that the role proved to be a great advantage for a number of reasons. Firstly, the President-elect was appointed to the GAA Management committee. This gave them an insight into the issues affecting the association for that twelve-month spell.

Con Murphy was the President and after my election the two of us met to set down

---

3 – Paddy was immediately preceded by Con Murphy in the post of President. There have now been 38 GAA Presidents since the first, Maurice Davin.

4 – Pat Guthrie, who was deeply involved with Paddy in the National Feile Executive, initially proposed the position of President-elect at Congress in the mid-1970s.

lines of demarcation. "Con, you're the President and I will not in any way cut across you unless requested," I said to him. Thankfully, our relationship worked very well, I stayed in the background and only attended functions when requested. He was extremely easy to work with and very committed.

Sometimes people needed to be reminded that Con was still the President. My comments did not matter. After that spring of 1978, there were constant questions about possible priorities and policies. However, it would have been inappropriate to try and upstage the incumbent President.

At one stage I described my role as not being relevant. However, this did not mean irrelevant. As Chairman of the Activities Committee there still had an important role to be fulfilled. The twelve months from spring 1978 afforded me the opportunity to formulate more fully ideas for how the GAA could continue to move forward.

The role of president-elect has become an important one, although this wasn't guaranteed when it was established. Consequently, I had to tread wearily to ensure that the new position wasn't messed up accidentally or otherwise. The 12 months from 1978 until 1979 would be used as a template to govern the future President-elects. If guidelines were to be established then my actions during that period were vital.

During that year my visits to clubs and various functions began. When Con Murphy was unavailable, the chance to fill the breach provided valuable experience of the GAA at grassroots level. Needless to say, this a distinct advantage during the three years from 1979.

Assuming the role of President did not come without sacrifices, including leaving the Down County Board. This was particularly poignant considering my service there since 1954 in various different offices.

T. P. Murphy was elected as the Central Council delegate and the changeover took place officially at a county board meeting in Newcastle. There had been a lot of contact with many different officials during the previous twenty-five years or so. It was important to thank them all for their co-operation and help since 1951.

There was no time to sustain any great involvement in the Tullylish club either. They made a special presentation in the early part of my presidency, and a bouquet of flowers for Kathleen. Then, in June 1978 my retirement from teaching at Gilford after twenty-seven years was also marked by a party.

This enabled a full and uninterrupted devotion to the role of president, although the roles of teacher and president were combined for the first few months. It was nice that the teachers and staff at the school held a party towards the end of the 1979 summer term.

My great friend Billy Byrne

It became clear immediately that becoming President would also involve a massive amount of travel. This is where my great friend Billy Byrne from just up the road in Laurencetown came into his own.

He was much, much more than a solid and reliable driver during the next three years. The two of us had been friends for years and travelled together to matches all over Ulster and further afield. There was nobody else who could have provided the assistance which he did during that period.

Billy was great and my constant companion for those three years. He was also a fanatical GAA supporter and a good judge of character. He often told me that someone 'wasn't up to much' and was generally correct. One night the Parish Priest in Tullylish remarked to Billy that he wasn't very charitable, but nearly always right!

We travelled to functions and events all over Ireland. On our return journey, he would mark my speeches out of ten. "Six out of ten," he'd said, before adding to my surprise, "You made no sense and I thought you were never going to stop talking." He was extremely forthright in his views. His advice was appreciated, especially if something had been done wrong.

Billy organised everything before each journey, including the time of departure, how long it would take and the best roads to travel. The fact that he was there was a massive relief. This was particularly useful

Billy Byrne, without whom, the role of President would have been so much more difficult. He was a steadying influence, a good friend and great company on many long journeys.

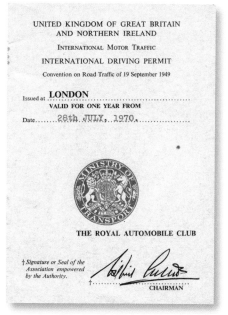

My international driving licence. It was something which occasionally proved very valuable on GAA trips.

on the many occasions when the two of us were leaving some far-flung part of the country late at night. I merely had to sit back and relax as he drove home along roads which were a lot less comfortable than is the case now. It was a considerable journey leaving somewhere like New Ross in Wexford at 1.30 am. He also kept my car in order, checking the tyres and oil gauge and ensuring that it was properly serviced.

At the functions, he usually disappeared for a couple of hours while I did my duties at the top table. But coming home in the car, there was chapter and verse on all the local GAA politics.

Over the years, Billy served in a number of positions with the Tullylish club and also as treasurer of the Down County Board. Before that, he had played football and was also an accomplished referee. Not surprisingly, the people in clubs got to know him very well and I think he enjoyed the chance to meet them.

On one occasion, myself, the former president, Donal Keenan, and Dr Mick Loftus were appointed to adjudicate on a row between a number of clubs in Westmeath. But Billy knew the case far better than me. He had been outside talking to the officials before they were called into the meeting, they opened up to him with their grievances and he was able to brief me on the way home about the two sides of the story.

An example of his commitment came at the time when Con Murphy's mother died. The two of us were in Mayo at a club function and Billy thought nothing of leaving there and driving to Cork for the funeral.

Another role which he relished was the task of collecting my allocation of All-Ireland Final tickets at Croke Park and delivering them to all sorts of locations, including the Northern Ireland Office at Stormont.

Thankfully, my friendship with the Byrne family continues through Billy's daughter, Caroline. She takes me to Mass each Saturday night and looks after my financial arrangements through her work with the Bank of Ireland.

My aims for the Presidency

After one year as President-elect, it was at Congress 1979 when my term as President officially began. My acceptance speech was short and hopefully to the point. The completion of the new Ceannáras development at Croke Park and the preparations for the GAA's Centenary Year were among the main priorities.

One of the other challenges was to increase communication between Croke Park and the clubs. At that time – and indeed in the modern era as well – there were a feeling of 'them and us' and my belief was that the two should be in regular contact. Some of the clubs might not even have known who the President was. In an effort to address this, a number of club manuals and other publications were produced for distribution to clubs.

Con Murphy presents my All-Ireland medal as I assume the role of President at the 1979 Congress. The year spent as President-elect to Con was extremely important.

It was very important that there was access to GAA material, such as the All-Stars posters.

There was a steady stream of invitations to attend club events and it was important to accept as many as possible. This was a way of showing the ordinary grassroots member that they weren't alone. They always appreciated a visit from the President. The message was that we were all part of one Association one with the same objective and there were no different grades or second-class citizens.

This was also achieved by ensuring that there was club representation at the main GAA functions. Coaching courses were also organised more regularly and a big highlight was the opportunity for schoolchildren and clubs to organise tours of Croke Park.

A third target for me was to develop a greater efficiency within clubs. A problem back then, which still exists to a lesser extent, is an attempt for officials to try and make the Guinness Book of Records for their length of service in a particular position. Some people were chairman or secretary of a club for twenty or thirty years and had run out of enthusiasm. As a club official myself, my aim was always to only stay in a position for two or three years and then develop someone to take over.

This has led in more recent years to the introduction of the five-year rule at county level. However, whether or not this regulation has been effective is debatable due to the amount of recycling of officials that goes on. A similar rule at club level would not have been possible, but a more regular change would still be desirable. Positions like club chairman and secretary have become a lot more onerous due to the increase in fixtures, fundraising and development.

Proposals for change along these lines created the sense that a new brush was sweeping clean within the Association. Liam Mulvihill had just been elected as Ard Stiúrthóir, Pat Quigley was the PRO, and the three of us were friends and very much on the same wavelength. [5]

I described the experience of becoming President as a frightening one because the workload was so daunting. The number of meetings to be presided at was immense, and there were huge demands in terms of attending functions.

It was also an enjoyable time meeting so many genuine GAA people and I always tried to meet the ordinary member at functions. Visits to schools and clubs was one way of achieving this.

---

5 – At aged just 34, Liam Mulvill originally from Longford was appointed Director General and held the post until his retirement. He was replaced by the current holder of the position, Paraic Duffy from Co Monaghan.

A Life in Colour

Aodhan O'Loughlin and (grandson of former Derry and Rossa legend Gerry), and on the right is James McCloy (grandson of former County Chairman Seamus). Also pictured are GAA President, Christy Cooney, Ulster President, Aoghan Farrell, and the Derry chairman, John Keenan.

ABOVE – The All-Ireland Hurling Finals during my Presidency were especially memorable. Offaly are seen here celebrating as I deliver a few well thought out words of thanks and congratulations.

TOP RIGHT – This photograph taken with Cardinal O'Fiaich has pride of place at my home.

BOTTOM RIGHT – Billy Byrne, Canon Trainor and myself pictured. Both men were great friends of mine over a long period of years and Billy's help and advice was always invaluable.

TOP LEFT – Meeting the Queen was definitely an experience. She had been invited to Croke Park as part of her trip to Ireland. I felt it important to honour the wishes of Mary McAleese by attending.

BOTTOM LEFT – The new President of Ireland, Michael D Higgins, greeted me earlier this year as current GAA President, Liam O'Neill looks on.

ABOVE – Martin McGuinness, the Deputy First Minister in deep conversation with me, Ulster Council President Aoghan Farrell and the Derry chairman, John Keenan.

The letter of congratulations from Mary McAleese on the occasion of my 90th birthday is much cherished.

UACHTARÁN NA hÉIREANN
PRESIDENT OF IRELAND

10 June, 2008

Mr. Pat McFlynn
c/o Mr. Pat Guthrie
32 Willington Green
Templeogue
Dublin 6

Dear Mr. McFlynn

I have learned with great pleasure that you will celebrate on Wednesday 18 June, 2008 the ninetieth anniversary of your birth.

Your immeasurable contribution to the GAA, an organisation in which you played many significant roles, has been sustained over a prolonged period and has been marked by many highlights and successes. Your career as a teacher has been characterised by dedication, commitment and concern for the health of the minds and hearts of young people. You have served the community of Ireland well and we thank you for it.

I send you my warmest congratulations and most sincere good wishes on this joyful occasion.

Yours sincerely

Mary McAleese
President of Ireland

ABOVE – Eoghain Rua hurling club Coleraine, Co Derry.

TOP RIGHT – Skills representatives from the 32 counties pictured with Paddy MacFlynn and John O'Reilly at Coca Cola Feile na nGael 2002.

BOTTOM RIGHT – The Magherafelt U-14 team which played some wonderful football in winning the All-Ireland Feile in 2007.

ABOVE – John O'Reilly presents the Feile na nGael flag to Denis Hanley, chairman of the Lar Tire Feile Executive while Paddy MacFlynn looks on.

TOP LEFT – Bellaghy camogie club on parade at the 2002 Feile in Belfast. It is great to see the growth of the GAA in South Derry. A far cry from when I began in the 1930s.

BOTTOM LEFT – Derek Ryan of Clare who was third in the SkillsStars competition receiving his trophy from former GAA President, Paddy MacFlynn with the Ulster Feile Chairman, John O'Reilly in 2002.

ABOVE – The opening of the commemorative wall in Tullylish was a proud moment for me.

TOP RIGHT – Frank Murphy of Cork greets me at Congress. This annual event is still something which I try to attend and was held in Derry in 2013.

BOTTOM RIGHT – Stalwarts from Tullylish pictured at the 125 celebrations in 2009.

My visits to Magherafelt have always been memorable. This picture was taken at the opening of their new pitch and facilities.

Hopefully those present enjoyed listening to my memories about the early days of the Rossa club.

In my 90s, I have tried to live life to the full.

CELEBRATING 90 YEARS
AG CÉILIÚRADH 90 BLIAIN

LEFT – A painting completed by Kathleen MacFlynn's nephew in law- Alan Mc Gowan from Edinburgh

BELOW – My nephew has always been a big help and taken me around my places, especially in South Derry. We are pictured here at the home of Seamus Lagan.

RIGHT – The wedding of Liam's daughter, Sinead, was a great family get-together.

LEFT – Myself, Eddie and Charlie reminiscing our childhood in Magherafelt!

BELOW – Four generations of MacFlynns. Here I am with my nephew Liam, his son Niall and Niall's son, Patrick.

Receiving an award from Liam Mulvihill, or is it the other way around. Liam was a great support during my Presidency and has remained a true friend ever since.

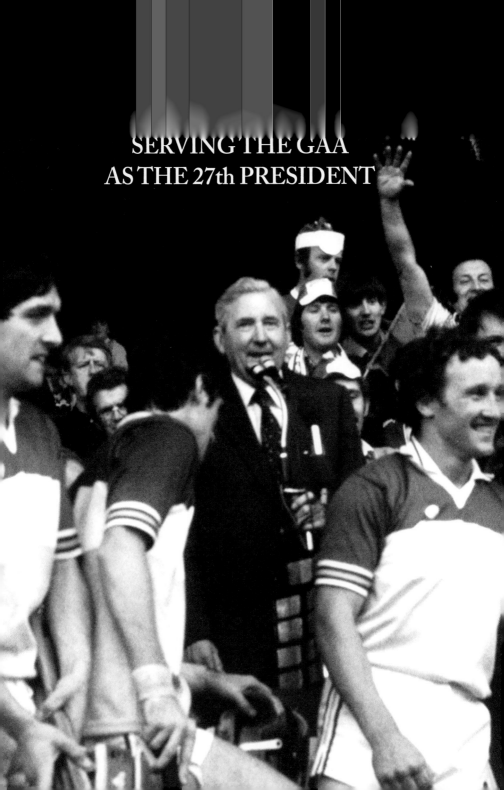

SERVING THE GAA
AS THE 27th PRESIDENT

With the 1979 Kilkenny captain, Liam Fennelly, Director General, Liam Mulvihill, and the Liam McCarthy Cup.

It was always a great honour to attend the opening of clubs grounds, such as this one in Co Kildare.

Busy times on the All-Ireland Finals weekend

There is always a great sense of anticipation in the building to an All-Ireland Final weekend. Being President brought a special responsibility to ensure that all the carefully laid arrangements proceeded without a hitch.

My weekend began on the Saturday morning. Unfortunately, it was practice during those years to hold a Central Council meeting on the day before the All-Ireland Final. This was completely unsuitable when there were so many other arrangements which required attention. That was completely ridiculous and made the whole weekend much tougher than should otherwise have been the case.

There was immense planning involved in putting all the arrangements in place, despite the fact everyone knew what was needed after years of organising the big day. It became something of a routine and was something which all of us involved certainly looked forward to.

My first All-Ireland speech as President was given following Kilkenny's hurling final win in 1979.

After all, this was my day in the sun as President. All-Ireland Final Day began by arriving at Croke Park at around 9 a.m. A short briefing meeting was held to ensure that everyone knew what, where and when particular things were happening.

An important job for myself as President was to meet the various guests of honour and

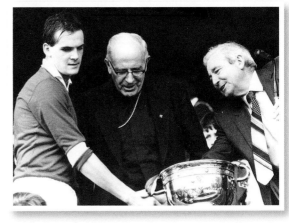

Unfortunately, Derry failed to win a minor or senior title during my three years. But they came close in 1981, only to lose to Cork, whose captain is receiving the Thomas Markham Cup here.

show them to their seats in the Ard Chomhairle. We would then sit with the Taoiseach or a foreign dignitary to watch the match.

Getting up to speak in front of 60,000 or 70,000 people was a strain, so there were definitely nerves on my part. Of course, it was important to realise that the speech was merely clichés about the standard of the game. Then, there was the fact that nobody wanted to hear me, they weren't interested and what had to be said almost wasn't worth saying.

The tradition prior to 1979 was that the President attended the banquet for the winning All-Ireland team. When Liam Mulvihill arrived, I suggested that the two of us toss for this honour. My first experience was at the function for the Galway team which lost the All-Ireland Hurling Final that year. That event was very sad and sombre occasion because they had let Kilkenny back into contention twice during the match before eventually losing.

It is extremely difficult to speak at an event like this. Fortunately, in 1979 Bishop Casey took over saying, 'we're not downhearted at all' and proceeded to launch into a rendition of 'The West's Awake'.

However, on the upside,, my toss-up with Liam Mulvihill resulted in my attending the winning banquets for Galway and Offaly.

The official reception for the teams took place on Monday morning, before myself and Liam Mulvihill visited Hugh Byrne who lived in the Wicklow Mountains. This was a great way to release the tension of the previous twenty-four hours. A walk along the quiet country roads was a welcome relief from the noise and excitement of the All-Ireland Final.

Happily upstaged by Galway and Joe Connolly

Ah, what memories! The final whistle had just been sounded and Galway had won their first All-Ireland Hurling Final in fifty-seven years. The outpouring of emotion and joy was something which nobody who was in attendance will ever forget.

It was a landmark triumph for the Tribesmen which created such a sense of euphoria in the whole county. Their success at Croke Park on that famous has to be the highlight of my term as President.

Fr Iggy Clarke was unable to play in the final against Limerick due to injury. He had nowhere to sit in the Ard Chomhairle afterwards and ended up taking my seat.

As President, it was important to remain completely impartial. Inwardly, though, there was an anxiety to see a particular county doing well. That was certainly the case in 1979 between Galway and Kilkenny because the former would definitely benefit the most from taking the title. Again, in 1981, my personal bias was towards Offaly who were contesting the Liam MacCarthy Cup for the first time.

What a moment! Galway captain, Joe Connolly lifts the Liam McCarthy Cup in 1980. It was great to witness the outpouring of emotion on that marvellous occasion.

The significance that the boost of winning an All-Ireland can bring should not be underestimated. In Ulster this has become very apparent from the success of Down in 1960, and then Donegal, Derry, Tyrone and Armagh in later years.

But back to 1980 and Joe Connolly's famous speech all as Gaeilge. Anytime we have met since, I always remind him that he was the man who showed me up in Croke Park after the All-Ireland that year. That whole occasion was also extremely emotional, not least because of the length of time which they had waited. [1]

Offaly's success the following year was also especially memorable. There are only 65,000 people in the county, yet they were able to produce All-Ireland hurling winners in 1981 for the first time and then the football in 1982. Bro Denis Minehane in Birr inevitably springs to mind as a leading light in the promotion of hurling and sowing the seeds of eventual success. Joachim Kelly became a close friend of mine in the years after 1981. He was from Lusmagh and I subsequently attended the county final which they reached and won.

It was fortunate that two of the All-Ireland Hurling Finals during my presidency proved to be so brilliant. Offaly and Galway capturing the Liam MacCarthy yielded a huge increase in the interest in hurling.

1 - The speech given by Joe Connolly following Galway's All-Ireland Hurling success in 1980 is generally regarded as the greatest ever. Galway won the Liam McCarthy Cup again in 1987 and 1988.

There was some criticism following the 1981 presentation when Garrett Fitzgerald assisted me in the presentation to the Kerry captain, Jimmy Deenihan, now a Fine Gael TD.

Some of the correspondence which was received following that 1981 All-Ireland Football final.

Meeting the politicians

A LETTER from the Fianna Fáil cumann in Cork was very forthright in its views when I opened it at home in Laurencetown a few days after the 1981 All-Ireland Hurling Final. It stated that Garret Fitzgerald had taken unacceptable liberties by lifting the Sam Maguire Cup on the previous Sunday and helping me present it to the winning captain.

Of course, the Fianna Fáil people were very angry at what they saw as political interference in the GAA, and that it was something which as president I simply should not have allowed.

The worst of all was that Garret Fitzgerald had not the slightest idea or interest in who was playing or what was going on. He did not even look at that match and as a result I found it extremely difficult to make conversation with him.

Then after the final, he was up with me holding the cup. A Fianna Fail Cumann in Cork wrote to me saying that they had seen this happening and raised great objections. They said it was a terrible breach of protocol.

Now I didn't do anything with the letter when it arrived that morning in Laurencetown. However, Gene Fitzgerald got in contact subsequently expressing concern at the fact that there had been no response to his letter. Apparently, the cumann in Cork were becoming restless that the incident had not been properly explained. As a result, it was diplomatically explained to them that the new Taoiseach was on his first official visit to Croke Park and was unaware of the protocols associated with the presentation of the Liam MacCarthy or Sam Maguire Cups.

Of course, in all of this I tried to learn from Pádraig Ó Caoimh. When he met all these politicians he treated everyone of them the same, showing no bias or favouritism to any of them. He was in turn accepted by them all as a fair and straight man with no leaning towards any of them.

Charlie Haughey and Garret Fitzgerald were to the two main political figures in Ireland during those years. There was a common connection with Haughey as both of us had strong connections to South Derry. His family had originally come from Swatragh, so there were regular opportunities to discuss common acquaintances from there.

It was also slightly easier to deal with him because, of course, he had a greater affinity with the games. His brother 'Jock' Haughey played for Dublin when they defeated Derry in the 1958 All-Ireland Final. I found Charlie easy to get on with and, as well as our conversations about the particular match, he would have used the opportunity to discuss the situation in the north and what my opinions on this were.

This knowledge of and affinity for Gaelic games on the part of Charlie Haughey was in stark contrast to Garret Fitzgerald who did not know or care what was happening on the field. Although he was a very talented intellectual in many others respects, having a conversation with him at these major matches proved to be extremely difficult. There was not even a mention of Northern politics, which might have been anticipated considering my connections.

Talking about the particular match which was taking place such as an All-Ireland Final was generally a good starting point for conversations. President Hillery also had a great interest in gaelic games.

Kerry's dominance was bad for the game

The excitement of the All-Ireland Hurling Finals in 1980 and 1981 compared to the three successes enjoyed by Kerry in the football which became tiresome. They swept all before them in the three finals of my presidency.

It wasn't good for Gaelic football that they were so dominant. After all, every sport requires the lifeblood of emerging new teams making a breakthrough. This was highlighted in 1991, 1992 and 1993 when Down, Donegal and Derry all captured the Sam Maguire. Those were tremendous years which provide a real tonic in the province.

My hope had always been that at least one Ulster county would have reached the All-Ireland Football Final between 1979-81. Unfortunately, none of them even came close. Roscommon reached the All-Ireland Final in 1980 in a game that turned out to be both nasty and bitter.

Offaly did better the following year and, of course, Paddy Buggy had the honour of presenting the Sam Maguire Cup to their captain after the famous 1982 final. Seamus Darby's goal has gone down in history.

My footballing experience did not fulfil my hopes or expectations. Peter Quinn did, of course, enjoy much better fortunes. He had the wonderful experience of presenting the Sam Maguire Cup to three counties from Ulster during his three years as President. Needless to say, I would have loved to have had a similar honour. Down would obviously have been my preference, but any of the nine would have been marvellous. The only Ulster All-Ireland winner was the Down Under-21s in 1979.

Apart from the All-Ireland Finals, the President generally attempts to attend the

There are occasions when the President has to stand firm for the GAA's ideals.

major All-Ireland and National League Finals in the various grades. However, for me the invitation to attend the opening of club grounds received priority. As a result, there were a few of the top underage and league finals which I did not attend.

The Kerry jersey controversy and why I would have resigned

There was no doubting Kerry's dominance of the All-Ireland Football Championship by the early 1980s. They were the all-conquering glamour team and attracted intense interest both inside and outside the GAA.

The GAA had a rule stating that only officially sanctioned and Irish manufactured sportswear could be used by counties. It was generally adhered too, but the controversy which surrounded the Kerry team prior to one All-Ireland Final led to a crisis of unprecedented proportions.

But then Kerry had a deal with Adidas and supposedly played the semi-final in Adidas jerseys which was a direct breach of the rule. It was important, therefore, to be tough on this.

In 1981, seemed to be intent on wearing an Adidas strip in the All-Ireland Final. It was clear that a stand had to be taken one way or the other. It was around this time that I phoned the Kerry Chairman, Frank King. The ultimatum to him from me as President was clear. Unless Kerry gave a cast-iron guarantee that they would wear an approved strip in the All-Ireland Final, then another of the semi-finalists would be nominated to contest the game instead. [2]

In the event, they did indeed wear the Irish-manufactured jerseys. However, they had been insistent on wearing the strip made by the foreign company, which would have been in breach of the GAA rules. I stood back and made it clear that they would be removed from the competition in accordance with the GAA rules. "The rules are there and I am here to ensure that they are adhered to," was my message to Frank King. There was nothing which the President of the GAA or anyone else could have done. He was extremely annoyed about all this and was very critical of me afterwards because of what he described as a 'dictatorial attitude'.

My strong view was that if Kerry got away with playing in non-Irish manufactured jerseys, then this was a basic rule which was broken. After all, there was a perfectly good manufacturers in Ireland without going outside.

All of this happened about a fortnight before the final. So, there wasn't much time to reach a solution which was satisfactory. As a result, the demand from me was for an immediate response to the request for the guarantee to abide by the rules.

---

2 – Kerry were involved in a number of disagreements with the GAA authorities over sponsorship in the early 1980s. However, the issue has become much clearer since 1991 when sponsors names on jerseys were first permitted.

Back to Derry for the official opening of new facilities for Ballinderry Shamrocks.

While they were adamant, they appeared to take seriously my threat to nominate one of the semi-finalists. A strong line was required to ensure that individual counties such as Kerry did not blatantly breach the rules.

There is no doubt that eliminating Kerry from the competition would have been a massively controversial step, especially considering their dominance during this period. Thankfully, my resolve on this didn't have to be tested, but there's absolutely no doubt that I would have had to do something to stand up for the rules of the Association.

Some of the people in the GAA's Management committee at the time felt that this approach was too stringent and they didn't support it. Indeed, it was quite possible that a vote might have gone against Kerry being eliminated in the way being proposed by me.

This outcome would not have been too popular and it's very doubtful whether there would have been complete support. Such an important move would have been discussed both at the Management Committee and Central Council level and there was the chance that Kerry would have swung a subsequent vote in their favour.

To have replaced Kerry in the All-Ireland Final with another county would have been an unprecedented move. Whether or not the President had the personal authority to authorise this was not ultimately tested.

However, the consequences were clear and it would have been interesting to see what might have happened. If both the Central Council and Management Committee had gone against my decision, then as President I would have had to consider my position and resigned.

It was Liam Mulvihill who represented the GAA at the official celebration function subsequently. Needless to say, my Presidency wasn't the most popular in Kerry. They were a law onto themselves and I found that the position did not carry the same importance there as in other counties. The chairman of the county board had far more influence.

Tickets were a big problem and the young schoolchildren responded to my praise about the work which they were doing by saying, "if we are such a great county, then why are there not more tickets."

Overall, though, that Kerry team of the late 1970s and early 1980s really was tremendous and comparable only to the Down side of 1960 and 1961. There was no return for the opposition when either of those teams raced ahead. It's difficult to say, though, which of them was the best.

The hand-pass rule was changed again in 1981. However, just like the modern era, that level of hand-passing was to the detriment of Gaelic football generally. The Kerry team had perfected its use. A lot of passes then and now were throws rather than hand-passes.

My trips to Derry were also enjoyable. Watty Grahams and a reunion for the 1947 National League team offered two such opportunities.

Returning as President to my native Derry

ONE newspaper headline in May 1979 described how I was a local boy returning to South Derry in something of a hero's role. On that occasion, the opening of Ballinderry's new pitch was to be my first opening ceremony and where better than so close to home.

The concerns of Pearses in Derry City were addressed in a letter, while the correspondence from Magherafelt District Council never should have been sent.

Replied 25/9/1981

3, Shantallow Road
Waterside
Derry
10-9-81

Dear Mr President

On behalf of the Pearses G.A.A club, Waterside, Derry. I as president of the club have been instructed by our members to lodge a very strong complaint and Protest at the central council inviting the Mayor of Derry City to Croke Park for the Minor semi final Champion-ship and we hope that he will not be invited to the All Ireland Final.

Our Reasons for this protest are that this man is anti G.A.A. and he connived with Unionist and D.U.P. to close the Lisnagelvin playing fields on the pretense that they were Unplayable. So as we could not play on them leaving Pearses Club without a pitch near at hand we have to travel four miles to our home matches now even though this ground is in our area within

---

260/79

17th July, 1979

Mr. P. McFlynn,
236 Banbridge Road,
Gilford.

Dear Mr. McFlynn,

I have been directed by the Magherafelt District Council to inform you that they are unable to offer their congratulations to you on the occasion of you being elected President of the G.A.A.

Yours faithfully,

Clerk to Council

It was to be the first of numerous trips back to South Derry which provided an opportunity to catch up with old friends from past decades. Just before taking up the post, I attended in February 1979, the annual Magherafelt annual dinner in Ballymena when the Rossa plaque was presented as a memento of the visit. As well as my regular visits home, there was also a talk-show during in 1981 which was held in St John's Hall. The presence of Jim McKeever and Tommy Mellon at this event ensured many forthright views on the new rules being introduced at that time.

It was good to return home for these kind of functions. Many of the old hands from the 1930s such as Pat Keenan were still alive and my visits gave us a chance to catch up on old times and the fortunes of the current Rossa team.

In June 1979 there was a big turnout for the opening of Pádraig Pearse Park in Kilrea. A challenge match between Derry and Antrim rounded off a day to remember for all at the club.

Over the coming years the trips back to Derry were become very regular and most were in South Derry. As one of the people who helped set up the Slaughtneil club they always sent me an invitation for any function being organised.

However, there was one event missed which I regret not getting the opportunity to attend. This was a reunion night at the Arches in Magherafelt for the 1947 Derry team which won the National League. Unfortunately, I had a prior engagement on that occasion.

As President-elect in 1978, one of my preparatory functions was the opening of Glenullin's new pitch named after Seán Ó Maoláin. That was an opportunity to see many old faces from the early days of the GAA in the county who had helped the Association from its infancy. Many of them had played against me in the 1942 county final.

A visit to St Martin's GAA club in Desertmartin was a first by the President to the area. This gave me another chance to stress the vital role which the association at local level can play in the development of community enterprise and spirit. The event was held in the partially completed new community centre which was being constructed at a cost to £100,000.

The official opening of the new playing pitch at Loup took place right in the middle of the republican hunger strikes 3 May, 1981. It was marked by a challenge game between Tyrone and Derry, the blessing was carried out by Cardinal Tomás ÓFiaich and I officially opened the facility.

One particular event which also struck a chord concerned a former Rossa's player, Eamon Gilmore. He was a former player with the club before being confined to a wheelchair after a work accident. I had the pleasure of presenting him with a pass to the special enclosure at all Ulster GAA games.

No reception from Magherafelt District Council

A letter from Magherafelt District Council told me that they would not be holding a civic reception on honour of my election as GAA President.

Amazingly, an official from the Council had decided to write confirming that as a native of the town and newly-elected President of the GAA, there would be no civic reception.

The background to the story highlighted the sharp sectarian divisions which existed in the area at the time. Tempers flared often at Magherafelt council meetings and this was just the latest in a long line of similar incidents.

Michael O'Neill of the SDLP proposed that letters of congratulations be sent to me, as well as the St Pius X team which won the All-Ireland Under-19 Gaelic football title and also the Rainey Endowed 1st XV in rugby who had recently enjoyed a successful tour of France.

However, the then Chairman, Rev William McCrea, had other ideas about the letter to the new GAA President. He forwarded a counter-proposal that the Council send a letter instead expressing how it had been grieved that a man from the district should have 'lowered its name' by heading what he described as 'one of the most biased and discriminatory organisations in the country'.

Similar sentiments were echoed by Robert Overend of the UUP who did not want Magherafelt Council to be associated with the GAA. The McCrea proposal was carried and the letter duly dispatched to my home in Laurencetown. The Nationalist members of the Council naturally supported the proposal to send the letter, complete with congratulations.

The then clerk of the Council was an old school pal of mine from the Rainey and lived in Rainey Street. He was stupid enough to actually write the letter. There was absolutely no need for it to be sent at all.

The only positive to the incident was the reaction of local councils down south who presented me with plaques on a regular basis. Tullamore Urban District Council made a presentation to me and there was always great amusement when the story of how Willie McCrea and my hometown council had turned me down for a similar accolade. [3]

It is easy to laugh about the whole incident now. But it certainly wasn't very pleasant at the time because of the rejection. There could be no great surprise considering Willie McCrea's attitudes to the GAA over the years. He is someone whom I have never met.

---

3 – Although Magherafelt District Council declined to provide Paddy with a civic reception in 1979, he did receive civic honours from a host of other local government organizations in Ireland and throughout the world.

Enjoying a joke at the 1979 Ulster Final with Cardinal O Fiaich.

Maybe he kept the plaque safe. In 1993 I was eventually afforded a Civic Reception along with the Derry team which won the All-Ireland title. How times had changed since 1979.

My living room is adorned with a whole host of plaques from a wide variety of organisations and groups. There's the one from Tullamore Urban Council, another from Queen's University GAA Club on the golden jubilee of its establishment and one was presented by Omagh District Council.

There is also a plaque from Big L Radio, a pirate station in Limerick who interviewed me for about two hours. They had three people questioning me about every aspect of the GAA and made the presentation afterwards. The station was illegal and the President of the GAA should never have been on in the first place.

Another event was the annual dinner of the Camross GAA club in Co Laois, home of the famous Cuddy hurling brothers. On that occasion they presented me with a book entitled The Flora and Fauna of the Slieve Blooms. A little while later in the course of my address, I spoke of my interest in this, prompting three people afterwards to offer me lodgings for any future visit. The caretaker of their grounds at that time was from Tyrone of all places, and conducted a guided tour.

These are all great mementoes of a very special time. However, Margaret McInnes, who runs the bar for me now along with her husband Denny, often bemoans about having to wash and polish all the cut glass and china received over the years.

My friendship with Cardinal O Fiaich

It was of immense benefit that Cardinal Ó Fiaich was able to exert such influence during the worst years of the Troubles in the north. His term as Catholic Primate of All-Ireland began at almost the same time as my presidency. As a result, we were in very regular contact.

Coming from Crossmaglen, he was a great fan of Armagh. How unfortunate it was that he died before the county's great breakthrough in winning the 2002 All-Ireland. That would really have completed his life story and the great interest in Gaelic games and culture generally.

Our roles, although very different, were similar. There was a desire on my part to ensure that the GAA did not become involved in the political wrangling. This was matched by Cardinal Ó Fiaich efforts to ensure that the Church did not become involved either. However, both organisations did have sympathy with those who were on Hunger Strike and the fact that these were young Irishmen who should not have been dying.

Due to this common aim, the two of us often met to discuss the H-Block crisis. These informal talks were an attempt to try and make sense of what was happening and see how the Church and the GAA could help while not becoming involved in a political sense.

Around that time, too, Cardinal Ó Fiaich became a Patron of the GAA. However, he declined to wear the medal, despite my urgings.

Shortly before Cardinal O'Fiaich died while on pilgrimage to Lourdes in 1990, he said a Mass in Irish in Lurgan. Alf Murray and I also attended and the Cardinal was very interested in asking questions about Alf's footballing exploits, much to Alf's bemusement. Eventually, Alf said to me, "he's getting them for my funeral so that all these facts that can be related during the sermon." Alas, Cardinal O'Fiaich died soon after that. [4]

His knowledge of all things Irish was immense. At the opening of St Oliver Plunkett Park in Crossmaglen he gave chapter and verse on the local connections with St Oliver and his significance to the Archdiocese of Armagh. He also attended the annual Irish course in Donegal and came in, sat on a table and began to give a lecture without notes.

Myself and Patrick Hillery were described as two generals in this picture from the 1980 Feile Na nGael.

4 – Cardinal O Fiaich died while on pilgrimage to Lourdes in May 1990, soon after the photograph with Paddy was taken.

The presentation of the All-Ireland Feile trophy climaxed a wonderful festival of hurling which I thoroughly enjoyed as President.

Walking in step with the Mayor of Galway and President Hillery following the 1980 parade.

Officials at the launch of the All-Ireland Feile. The whole Feile experience provided me with many happy memories and friendships.

Fond memories of Feile Na nGael

A few years ago the middle-aged man stopped me going into Croke Park on All-Ireland Final Day. "Do you remember," he asked, "the day you came into our losing dressing-room after the All-Ireland Féile? I'm the man you spoke to and we appreciated it." He was from that great hurling stronghold of Toomevara in Tipperary and my memories of that incident are still very vivid.

They had just lost the final and were understandably devastated. There was no point in me going into the dressing-room of the winning team where the celebrations had already begun. Instead, my first port of call was the losing team and that middle-aged man with the red hair certainly remembered the moment.

Toomevara played Glen Rovers in the final and were beaten by two goals in the closing stages. This big lad was sitting crying and in an attempt to console them I invoked 'Mat 'the Thrasher' Donovan and the 'honour of the little village.'

Féile na nGael is probably my most cherished memory of my time as President. Of all the GAA experiences, it's the one which provided me with the happiest memories. Established in 1971 under the presidency of Séamus Ó Riain, the emphasis was on participating rather than winning. A skills event was held, the teams were hosted by clubs and the representation from each of the thirty-two counties made the whole festival very special.

As President, one of the most important aims was to visit as many of the clubs and schools as possible. Arrangements for this were made in advance. I hoped this provided something of a morale boost to the coaches and the young hurlers themselves. Afterwards, I always made a point of writing to the schoolteacher thanking them for their co-operation.

During Féile na nGael four groups would spread out to complete these visits within the host county. There was a great feeling, not least because the school holidays had just started for the young players involved.

My first involvement came as President-elect in 1978. That year the Féile took place in Kilkenny. I thoroughly enjoyed everything associated with the Feile. A group of us travelled to as many of the matches as possible. The teams came from all areas, including some from counties which were struggling in hurling. The division one competitions had the top teams. The final was always a tremendous match.

Coca Cola were very generous sponsors. John O'Connor was their head at that time and had a great interest in the youth and hurling. Jim Whelan was another man who took an active part in the organisation. The company spared nothing in ensuring that the whole event went smoothly.

Pat Guthrie was the Secretary. He was the greatest man I've seen for having things organised down to the last detail and visits me regularly still. The strange thing is that I knew nothing about Féile na nGael prior to that. However, all that changed in 1978, Pat invited me to Kilkenny for a weekend filled with hurling.

Local clubs acted as hosts and great hospitality to these young players from all over the country. The organisation of accommodation was an experience in itself, as the players were allocated their houses for the weekend. The teams weren't allowed to stay in hotels because that would have been a snub to their host club.

My role was as Chairman of the organising committee. The main group of four included Jim Whelan from Coca Cola, Donal Hickey and of course, Pat Guthrie who was the main organiser. The organisations began with a visit to the host county in October for preliminary discussions. Everything was explained to them about what was required and they then in turn appointed a local Féile committee.

A person was put in charge of various sections, including pitches and referees, the parade and visits to schools. Each of them was told by Pat Guthrie about what was expected from them. People were recruited who weren't deeply involved in other aspects of the GAA.

The meetings got full attendance, something that amazed county board officers. The discussions started at 7 p.m. and finished promptly at 10 p.m. Pat Guthrie warned me to keep things moving on and the agenda inevitably included a report from the county

President Hillery was a dedicated supporter of the GAA. Here we are at a celebration marking his involvement with the association.

Admiring the Christy Ring trophy which is awarded at the All-Ireland Feile.

Féile committee. Sometimes, it even involved replacing someone who wasn't pulling their weight.

Most of the costs were covered by Coca Cola, with additional income from the production of a Féile programme. There were suggestions that there should be an entrance fee to the finals, but my view was that this wouldn't have been appropriate.

The actual weekend began on a Thursday with trips to schools on Friday. A Mass was also held and the big highlight was the national parade of the teams. I'll never fully understand how they got the thirty-two teams, plus the camogie teams and handball organised. Each club wrote a short history and, as the club passed, Micheál Ó Muircheartaigh gave some brief snippets of information. There were prizes for the best banner and best dressed teams, and some went to great lengths to ensure that they were properly dressed.

Pat Guthrie even had the route of the parade measured and knew exactly how long was needed for the procession to be completed. I found it very emotional speaking to everyone when they assembled at the field. Here was the future of the GAA, thousands of young players, standing there. My words were short. This was a proud moment not only for the organisers and myself as president, but also for the clubs. Big crowds always turned out to watch the parade and to a city like Galway in 1981 bedecked in such colour was truly remarkable. This was the GAA at its best.

There were always some great teams in the division one final. Ger Loughane trained a team from Clare which won the title three years running. I asked him a few years later how many of them progressed to senior level and, strangely enough, none of them did.

The games were central to Féile na nGael. There were four teams in each division, each guaranteed three matches which took place throughout the day. The winners then got through to the semi-finals. The compilation of the results was crucial and an office in some local hotel was recruited for the purpose. Then, the results were phoned in from the various venues and displayed on four big notice-boards.

It could be very busy because many people came in to see how the various divisions and their own teams were progressing. With good organisation, it was possible to attend three matches in a fairly short space of time by going for the start of one, half-time in another and the finish of a third.

This gave me the opportunity to meet the players and just encourage them to enjoy the games, keep practising and respect the people they were staying with. A feature of the Féile over the years has been the exchange visits taking place between clubs.

As well as the main divisional titles, the skills competition was also a big highlight. Players were tested on a wide range of hurling skills and the award for the winner was the Christy Ring Trophy. A player from one of the weaker clubs or counties won out. The then

President of Ireland, Dr Patrick Hillery was a hurling enthusiast and attended regularly. This tradition was carried on more recently by Mary Robinson and Mary McAleese.

Kathleen also enjoyed the weekend immensely. She was friendly with Donal Hickey and his wife Kay, who was from Camross originally. The two of them visited various sites in the host county while their husbands proceeded with their busy schedules.

These young players gave their all and put their heart and soul into the matches. A man from Cavan arrived at the Féile one year training and managing the team and driving the bus. That's the kind of commitment which makes the Feile unique. [5]

Unfortunately, I became disgruntled with Féile more recently. The national organiser, Pat Guthrie, was removed and out of loyalty to him I decided to step down. The Féile Committee was largely independent of Central Council, although a full report was present each year. However, this independence ensured a degree of unpopularity.

The way things ended for Pat was disappointing and I haven't attended the Féile too often subsequently. It's hard to envisage things being as well organised since he was such a great motivator.

A high profile post

The role of GAA President is an important one in the social life of Ireland. That importance has increased over the years and is even more relevant at the moment than thirty years ago.

Interviews were never my strong point because there was the fear of saying something wrong or being misquoted. This was often the case after a controversial match when the stock answer was usually that the due process for dealing with incidents would be completed.

It wasn't appropriate for the President to comment on the merits of a decision during a match. Something could be said that might be wrongly interpreted. This was particularly the case during the H-Blocks controversy when every statement had to be carefully worded.

My term officially ended at the Congress in 1982. This was a time for reflection because suddenly I was away from the centre of things, even though a year was spent as an ex-officio member of Central Council.

Fortunately, the incoming President, Paddy Buggy, was a great friend. He appointed me to a group called Coiste na gClub. This group helped clubs who were completing developments, helping them to ensure that all their legal requirements were fulfilled and helping them to access any grants which might be available.

---

5 – Paddy served as National President of Feile Na nGael from 1986 until 2003.

The acquirement of the deeds of trust and other legal documentation was the most significant task in relation to this role. After all, clubs could not access grant-aid until all of this was in order. A registrar of clubs and their trustees was proposed and established. It was important to ensure that trustees were replaced whenever they died.

In total, I spent three years in this post and it was opportune considering my retirement from teaching. Needless to say, there was still plenty of jobs to be done and meetings of the Management Committee and Central Council to attend. In addition, I returned as chairman of the Tullylish club.

Reflecting on the Presidency

On reflection, there were several aspects of the presidency which proved very satisfying. This was the heartbeat of the association and it was encouraging to witness the work which was going on.

Many clubs contacted Croke Park requested the attendance of the president at the opening of new facilities or some other event. A diary was kept and a 'first-come, first serve' approach adopted. There was no point in some big club receiving preference over a small club who had booked earlier. That would have sent out the wrong message, so the promise to attend had to be kept.

Of course, the attendance of the President was the primary concern with the office rather than the person. It was a great honour for the President to attend a club and, while my presidency might not have been a great one, the chance to meet people was of the utmost importance.

A visit to Inishowen in Co Donegal is an example. My itinerary on that cold winter's day had included meetings in Dublin and Billy was waiting at home in Laurencetown. The two of us travelled to the club which was finding the going tough and the challenge was to spread the gospel and highlight the significance of Gaelic games in what was a dominant soccer area.

Pearse's in Roscommon, just a few miles outside Ballinasloe, were experiencing difficulties with the construction of a car-park. What amazed me was the youthfulness of their committee. The treasurer was a young accountant who provided a very clear view of their financial situation. In County Leitrim, the Cloone club was based in a small village. But their facilities were top quality despite the challenges of a limited rural population.

The success and strides being made by many clubs in trying circumstances was a striking feature. Most of them were spearheaded by just a couple of hard-working officials. That's why these small clubs especially appealed to me.

Visitations to schools over the course of a week were also organised. On one occasion, there was a sheet of paper providing instructions about all the jobs which needed to be

A wide variety of correspondence was sent to Laurencetown during my Presidency. It's all in safe-keeping now in the Cardinal O'Fiaich Library.

Cumann Luith Chleas Gaeldael

St. Martin's Gaelic Football Club
Desertmartin
(DEVELOPMENT COMMITTEE)

23 Draperstown Rd,
Desertmartin,
<u>MAGHERAFELT</u>.
Co-Derry.

Padráig A Chára,

You may recollect some correspondence exchanged between us a few months ago regarding items of historical interest relating to St. Martin's G.F.C.

The matter in question goes back to the Derry Dinner in Maghera when the President referred to Desertmartin being the first Club in the country to apply for affiliation shortly after the G.A.A. was founded.

Following this relevation I wrote to Croke Park seeking further clarification, only to be informed that no record of that period existed. I then wrote to the President himself to find out where he got his information, and in his reply he explained that his speech was prepared in your house the previous night where subject matter on this particular issue was made available.

Acting on his advice I then wrote to you for information concerning the early history of the G.A.A. in this district, but for some reason nothing has arrived.

I am hoping to start in the near future to compile our Club history for publication in 1984 and it would be very nice to have all the details contained in it.

Perhaps you would kindly sift through any material you have that would be of interest to people in this district, old Press cuttings, extracts from Minute books, or any other source would be very much appreciated.

Knowing you will gladly co-operate with me in this venture I look forward to hearing from you in the near future.

Is Mise,
Le Meas, CAOIMHGHÍN Ó MURCHÚ.

Ba mhór ag

an Taoiseach agus ag Bean Mhic Ghearailt

Padraig Uasal Mac Floinn agus a Bhean

a bheith i láthair

ag Fáiltiú

i gCaisleán Átha Cliath,

Dé Máirt, 8 Bealtaine, 1984,

ag 8.00 p.m.,

tráth a bheidh

comóradh céid á dhéanamh

ag

Cumann Lúthchleas Gael

THE ROTARY CLUB, DUBLI
Founded 22nd February 1911 No.1 Club. Europe

Mr. Patrick Mac Flynn,
"The Laurels",
236 Banbridge Road,
Gilford,
Craigavon BT63 6DW.

March

Paddy

Dear Mr. Mac Flynn,

This is just to say how much your talk was en by all the members of our Rotary Club on Monday M 16th. I would hope that you may be able to speak again in the not too distant future.

Our President and all the members of this No Club send you their very best wishes for the futu

I am yours sincerely,

Henry Spring
Programme Convenor
25 Merrion Square
Dublin 2
Telephone: 767695/7638

CUMANN NAOMH PÁDRAIGH
CILL MHANTÁIN

c/o Gearoid O'Fearghail,
Chairman,
Marlton Road,
Wicklow.
Oct. 14, 1930.

An t-Uachtarain,
Padraig MacFlynn.

A Chara,
On behalf of Cumann Naomh Padraig, Cill Mhantain, I would like to take this opportunity of thanking you for visiting our new clubrooms to-day, and to say how delighted we were to meet you.

As you have seen from your visit, the club has not been idle in recent times and the members have been working very hard to provide much-needed facilities for G.A.A. activities in th town and county. Our new clubrooms are now practically completed and we urgently require finance to meet our commitments.

It is now almost two years since we applied for a G.A.A. loan of £10,000 and it is still not forthcoming although we have been promised that it will be along soon.

COULD WE PLEASE ASK YOU TO USE YOUR GOOD OFFICE AS PRESIDENT TO GET THE LOAN SANCTIONED AND PAID TO US AS QUICKLY AS POSSIBLE. WE HAVE ALSO APPLIED FOR A DEVELOPMENT GRANT AND WE WOULD APPRECIATE ANY HELP IN THIS RESPECT AS WELL.

Again, thanking you for giving us some of your valuable time.

Mise le meas,
Gearoid O'Fearghail,
Cathaoirleach.

The Taoiseach and Mrs. FitzGerald

request the pleasure of your company

at a Reception

in the State Apartments, Dublin Castle,

on Tuesday, 8 May, 1984,

at 8.00 p.m.

on the occasion of the

Centenary of the

Gaelic Athletic Association

S.V.P.
Room 325
Department of the Taoiseach
Tel: (01) 689333 Ext. 432

Informal

BALLINA STEPHENITES FOOTBALL CLUB

President—GERALD COURELL (096) 22375.
Chairman—JOHN KENNY (096) 21996.
Secretary—TOMMY KNIGHT (096) 22260.
Treasurers—P. J. Gillespie (096) 21829.
and LIAM BYRNE (096) 21055.

CLUBHOUSE,
BALLINA,
CO. MAYO.
'PHONE (096) 22449.

Moy Heights
Foxford Rd.
Ballina
(096) 21996

Accepted 10/1/1979

Go. Mr. Paddy Mc Flynn,

Uachtaran C.L.C.G.

Craigavon ,

Co. Armagh.

Padraich , Mo Chara ,

      I'm sure that you recall your election to the post of President Elect two years ago at the Ballina Congress and the moment after your election when you promised our Congress Chairman Mr. Terry Reilly in my presence that you would attend the Stephenites Annual Social in your first year in office .

      Well , ta an t-am ag teacht and our arrengements are practically finalised for the third Friday in January , which is Jan 18 th. As usual this will be in the Downhill Hotel and it normally attracts up wards of 200 followers . Of course with you in attendance we would anticipate much more and as well as boosting our Club the effects of a visit by you to our County would great help Mayo .

      At present our Club is involved in an £90,000 Extension to its Clubhouse and your visit would greatly help our plans .

      Shortly I will telephone you to encourage you to make visit . Go dti sin ,

      Mise , Sean O Coinnigh , (Cathaoirleach).
Sean O Coin

FOUNDED 1886.   ● COLOURS: GREEN AND RED.   ● GAELIC GAMES, ATHLETICS, SQUASH and SOCIAL CENTRE.

"Ros Goill",
Enagh, Milford,
Armagh.
Monday 26.1.81.

Paddy,

Having just read the Convention reports week-end I felt I had to write and ... late you on your clear statements against ...

You are in a position, through ... office, to do great good for the cause of peace ... the image of the G.A.A.

I offer you my encouragement ... support and urge you to continue to speak ... as an opportunity arises.

I trust Billy is still driving you ... and taking some of the burden. Give him ... ards and to yourself and Kathleen my ... wishes for the New Year.

Beannacht Leat,
Jack.

...CHT AN PHIARSAIGH
...ar fáilte roimh
...Mac Floinn

...AS AGALLAMH
...n Gresham, Baile Átha Cliath
...r a fhógrófar
...beartais na Fondúireachta
...uair a bhronnfar
...AN PHIARSAIGH
...IN, 10 SAMHAIN 1980
...g Oíche an Phiarsaigh —
...ht - Bronnadh Duaiseanna — ag 8 p.m.
...néid Gardner Íocht... Fón 01/854225 01/752231

BALLINA STEPHENITES FOOTBALL CLUB

President—GERALD COURELL (096) 22375.
Chairman—JOHN KENNY (096) 21996.
Secretary—TOMMY KNIGHT (096) 22260.
Treasurers—P. J. Gillespie (096) 21829.
and LIAM BYRNE (096) 21055.

CLUBHOUSE,
BALLINA,
CO. MAYO.
'PHONE (096) 22449.

Moy Heights
Foxford Rd.
Ballina
Co Mayo.
16-11-79.

Pádraic Mas Mac Floinn,
Uachtarán C.L.C.J.

Re Ballina Stephenites Annual Function

Pádraic A Chara ,

    Tá athás orainn a chloisteál ... mbeidh tú ábalta teact chucy an Sunack ... ... na Scríofaraig. Delighted to receive your ... the good news that you will be with us ... our Annual Function. We really look forward to your coming and I will be writing to you later with more precise arrangements. Let me assure you that there will be no problem about accumodation for you as yours. In a few weeks I will be forwarding you more detailed information re your ...

    Chara
    Sean O Coinnigh.

FOUNDED 1886.   ● COLOURS: GREEN AND RED.   ● GAELIC GAMES, ATHLETICS, SQUASH and SOCIAL CENTRE.

completed such as tidying up and cutting the grass. The club officers saw the visit of the President as a tremendous occasion and a milestone in the development of the GAA in their area.

Some research and preparations was needed prior to these visits. While I often spoke without notes, it was still important to weave a few details about the club and its history into a speech. The problems of this were highlighted to me at a function organised by the AIB when I thanked the Bank of Ireland. Needless to say, the AIB officials were unhappy.

Talking in public never presented a problem! The only pre-prepared speech was the one for Congress. Kathleen sub-edited the material, and always told me to get to the point. That kind of advice can be a humbling experience. [6]

But there were other things which became extremely trying. The H-Blocks added a lot of pressure and the continual meetings at national level could be cumbersome. Some of them were unproductive.

The Scór convention was a case in point because all the minor points of regulation were discussed. Scor was a brilliant concept for the GAA, but there were occasions when the organisation became too centred on rules and regulations. This spoiled the benefit.

The importance of Irish was something which I also tried to stress. My grasp of the language was reasonable, although there were occasions when group discussions with officials from the Gaelic League proved to be a challenge. It would be very difficult for a President of the GAA to survive without a strong grasp of the language.

Looking back now, though, my term as President was extremely enjoyable. It was great to have been able to serve the GAA in this role for those three years. Many of the people I met during that period remained lifelong friends. For that, I am very grateful indeed.

---

6 – Many of the speeches given by Paddy during his time as President remain in the family archives. Some are stored on an early personal computer purchased by him.

TAKING
A
STEP
BACK

The Ceannarus Building and planning Centenary Year

Two of the most important medium-term targets for my Presidency were the completion of the new Ceannarus GAA headquarters at Croke Park and plans for the Centenary Year of the Association in 1984.

It was important that the celebrations marking 100 years were significant. Discussions really began in 1979. Clubs were central to the plans with many producing histories of the GAA in their respective areas. Some of the books published were magnificent and were complimented by those produced at provincial level.

There were a wide range of functions held. As a past-President and someone who had a role in many of the organisations, I attended many of the events. The then Taoiseach, Garrett Fitzgerald hosted an event in St Patrick's Hall in Dublin Castle. Myself and Alf Murray were standing together at the event when suddenly Charlie Haughey came up to us and said "this is a poor show, if I had been Taoiseach we'd have done something decent."

Paddy Buggy was given a degree by Trinity College in recognition of the GAA's contribution to Irish life.

Perhaps the most notable and major decision was to hold the All-Ireland Hurling Final in Thurles. There was a degree of concern initially during my Presidency when Central Council decided to defer the issue of staging the final there. A number of questions had been presented highlighting a range of issues relating to hosting the game at Semple Stadium. The Tipperary County Board expressed dismay at this, but it was important for me to point out that no final decisions had been taken.

In the event, the final was switched to Thurles and proved to be a major success. On the night before myself and George Ryan, with whom I was staying that weekend, travelled into Thurles to sample the atmosphere. There was a great buzz around the town and they were still hard at work putting the finishing touches to the ground on the Saturday night before the game. That was a great occasion, although the match between Offaly and Cork proved disappointingly one-sided.

Another of the big developments of my Presidency was the opening of the new Canards building in Croke Park. It replaced the old Croke House which had hosted all the major GAA meetings for many decades and the new headquarters was spearheaded by Con Murphy during his Presidency.

Building work was progressing well by the time my term began. The total cost was in the region of £100,000, with each county being given a target for the amount that they needed to raise. However, there was great difficulty collecting the receipts.

At that time there were 26 staff based at Croke Park, so there was certainly a need for proper office accommodation. While there were aspects of the Canards building which

The opening of the Ceannarus Building provided modern office accommodation for a growing GAA.

Galway's Stephen Kinneavy in action against Dublin's Jim Roynane, during the 1983 All-Ireland Football Final

The old Croke Park was showing signs of decay during my Presidency and it was clear that a major redevelopment was required.

could have been improved upon, there is no doubt that it served a good purpose. It's amazing that it was only in place about 17 years before being replaced as part of the Croke Park re-development. [1]

Troubles with Croke Park

Liam Mulvihill often references the 1983 All-Ireland Football Final as the day on which the need for a Croke Park re-development began apparent. From this seed, he spearheaded the major scheme which has culminated in the magnificent stadium of today.

He warned that someone could have been seriously injured or killed at the rear of Hill 16 due to the wet conditions. But the problems associated with Croke Park as it was during this period also arose during my time as President.

The Cusack Stand, which had been constructed in 1937, was showing signs of deterioration and was generally giving trouble. The concrete was breaking away from the rusting steel reinforcements. The roof, made of asbestos, was another cause for concern.

---

1 – The Ceannarus building was completed in Croke Park following a major fundraising drive throughout Ireland through Ciste Gael and other initiatives.

As a result of these issues, myself and Liam initiated a survey not only of the Cusack Stand, but also the whole stadium. It was quite obvious that Croke Park required serious attention to bring it up to the standards demanded in the modern era.

The poor condition of the Cusack Stand brought an added urgency. As a result, the process of planning which was begun by Liam Mulvihill took on an added significance.

It was at Congress during this period that Liam first muted the idea of the possibility of moving to a greenfield site somewhere on the outskirts of Dublin. He believed that this would prove to be a cheaper option considering the difficulties with construction and development associated with Croke Park. However, the emotional and sentimental view in relation to Croke Park meant that the proposal never gained enough support.

In the last year of my Presidency, Liam had started visiting new stadiums in a variety of countries. Liam's desire was to see the latest standard of stadiums and how their plans could be brought to fruition within Croke Park. This also allowed him to discover how the experts were. This process then began in earnest when Paddy Buggy became President in 1982.

Of course, the efforts of Peter Quinn as President and the architect, Des McMahon[2], helped to make all of this a reality from 1993 onwards. Liam Mulvihill insisted on ensuring that everything was completed to the highest standard of design and building. John Sisk and Company carried out the work.

The fact that Peter Quinn was from a financial background professionally was a major help. The tremendous cost was a factor which caused a lot of apprehension among the ordinary GAA person. There was great opposition to the Corporate Boxes, with the usual complaints about the elite being given special treatment. However, it became very obvious that they were required to make the scheme financially viable.

Members of the GAA all over Ireland are now very proud of Croke Park. The standard of finishing, the wide range of events which are held, the GAA Museum and the spectacle on big match days is something that we could only have dreamed about as we surveyed the decaying old Cusack Stand all those years ago.

Why I wasn't at the 1993 All-Ireland Final

It was the third Sunday in September 1993. Derry had reached the All-Ireland Final for only the second time. But where was I? The bar man was from Donegal and when I asked him where the boss was he replied sternly "he's in Croke Park where every decent GAA man should be." I had got my come-uppance, although I didn't make him aware of why I was missing this All-Ireland. So, with the ice broken, we sat watching that famous match against Cork when the Sam Maguire came to the Oak Leaf county for the first time.

---

2 – Croke Park architect, Des McMahon is a native of Beragh, Co Tyrone and played for the Red Hands. He recounts a story of having spent a memorable night celebrating in Laverty's Bar with Paddy and former Down footballer, Leo Murphy.

Our holidays usually lasted around three weeks. Each Sunday evening my close friend, Billy Byrne, was on hand to take a call from me to get all the results and latest happenings from the big matches and the local games. Perhaps the only drawback of the holidays was the fact that I often missed these major games. But 1993 was different.

Above all times I was stuck in Paris. Being well aware of the fact that I wasn't going to make the match, I duly installed myself in a prime seat in a bar called Nancy O'Brien's. Amazingly, we were all speaking Irish and there we all were sitting watching the game.

This was a big mistake for me, especially considering my Derry connections and desire to be at what turned out to be an historic breakthrough for my native county. The dates of our holiday were changed at the last minute with the result that our flight was a day or so later than anticipated and planned.

An historic moment as Henry Downey lifts the Sam Maguire for Derry in 1993. Amazingly, I wasn't in Croke Park, but in Paris watching in a little Irish bar.

Now throughout my life I've always tried to take things as they come. During holidays, I always timed it that the holidays didn't clash with anything important. While watching the final from Paris was definitely something different, I still got very worked up and anxious about the game.

I was very disappointed initially, but the reception was very good on the TV and Johnny McGurk's great point near the finish showed that we were on the way to taking the title. Nevertheless, my sense of disappointment only increased when the final whistle sounded and I was so far away while my friends from Magherafelt and Derry were celebrating such an historic moment. I wasn't there the year that Derry won the All-Ireland.

This was a great achievement which, to be honest, I never expected to happen. To win an All-Ireland is something right out of the top drawer and sitting in the bar in Paris was in such a sharp contrast to being in Croke Park.

On my return home I did cash in and attended most of the Derry celebrations. They included the reception given by Magherafelt District Council a few weeks later which was, of course, significant after my experience with them on my election as President in 1979.

Speaking out against the GPA

Now I don't remember the reaction of those in the Gaelic Players Association (GPA) to my comments at the annual congress a few years ago, although it's doubtful whether they agreed with my very vocal opposition to their establishment and subsequent official incorporation into the GAA.[3]

In the 1960s I was one of those involved in trying to improve the treatment of the Down players during their golden era. I strongly believed then and continue to believe that players should be well treated, especially after a tough training session or match.

Players need to be looked after, but there's no doubt that this also set things on the road to greater professionalism particularly at the moment with the rise of the GPA. Unfortunately I think things are being overdone in the current era what with fleeces, gear and maybe two or three pairs of boots every year.

There is too much stress on players now and I never in the 1960s saw any players being badly treated and I had a lot of say because it was me paying the bills. Now the top inter-county stars expect immediate handouts all the time and then tickets if a final is reached. This is down to the trade-union type influence of the GPA of which I am certainly not a supporter.

First-hand reports in the newspaper tell of teams training at 6am and again in the evening and at weekends when there are no matches. I am amazed to see the amount of training teams are undergoing especially for amateurs. For someone who is holding down a job it must be extremely tough going and I have every sympathy for the commitment being shown amid these demands.

But the answer isn't more handouts. Rather, the Association will eventually have to seriously examine the level of training being completed at inter-county level and the bizarre and unmentionable new strategies like running up and down sand-dunes. It's something that we have to face up to because there's long and very hot debates about burnout, the close season in November and December. The biggest danger of burnout is the amount of training and not the number of matches with club, county and university.

As a past-President, it's good to sit back and observe away from the immediate pressures of the post.

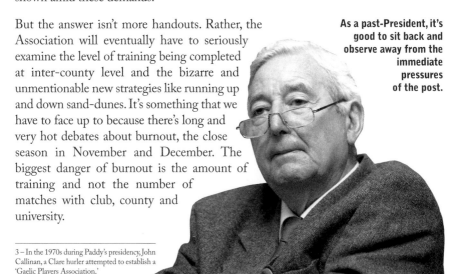

3 – In the 1970s during Paddy's presidency, John Callinan, a Clare hurler attempted to establish a 'Gaelic Players Association.'

Of course, gaelic football and hurling have become much more physical. A player will now run throughout the 60 or 70 minutes of a match, whereas in the old days the full-back marked the full-forward and didn't move unless the ball came into your area. But now the full-back is in the attack trying to score. The demands of the game are unreasonable and unfortunately this situation is going to be extremely hard to stop because winning is the sole object of each match. It's something which we see even at club level. Even small clubs which can't afford the expense are drafting in outside managers whose reputation is secure if they manage to win a title.

All of this is against the whole ethos of amateur sport which is about going out and enjoying a game of football or hurling. In contrast, teams are going out to win and if defeat is the result then it's a waste of time. It's particularly hard for the teams defeated in a provincial final or in the later stages of the All-Ireland. Take Mayo in 2012 as an example. They struggled through to the All-Ireland Final and the defeat meant that everything was for nought. It must be very tough psychology on the players.

There was a much more relaxed attitude when I was playing. Some games were won, some lost and it was far more enjoyable. Then, of course, there wasn't near the same pressure.

I was amazed in 2012 to be at a match and seeing a manager haranguing the players at the top of his voice, especially at half-time. This is most unfair because a player goes out to do their best. Sometimes nothing goes your way and there's nothing can be done. Then, it's terrible to be castigated by an irate manager.

The big question is where the next big change in tactics will come from and my hope is that we might see a return to the more historic catch and kick style. High fielding was one of the most eye-catching features and a joy to see. Now players aren't allowed to the space to make progress when they catch a high ball and I'm certainly not sure if the Australian-type mark would provide the answer.

Total responsibility for the way the game has evolved rests with the manager. No county board has any say on tactics, training or anything like that at the moment. It's all the responsibility of the manager. I'd be terribly worried that in certain counties the manager has become all important, dictating club fixtures and the welfare of players. He is not entitled to do that and it's a very sad situation.

There is far too much hand passing and the sight of seeing a full-back giving a pass to his goalkeeper is just ridiculous. We have to view the game as a spectacle and in sharp contrast to the intelligent football played by Down in the 1960s. A 60 minute game provided real entertainment.

Everyone with the interests of football at heart should pity the way the game has evolved during the intervening period. Teams are all in defence and then the modern way is

The Down team of 1991 finally made the breakthrough again for Ulster. Greg Blaney ranks highly in my estimation as one of the best footballers ever.

players carrying the ball up field through hand passing. You move forward when possession is gained and I'd say confidently that the majority of hand-passes are illegal. It's ridiculous to see a defender hand passing the ball back to the goalkeeper.

Martin Clarke of Down is an example of the way things could and should be in terms of the kick. His kick-passing was a joy to behold, the accuracy of his passes to a better-placed teammate. Improved kicking is something that we should be aiming for because the level of skill has definitely decreased.

Whether or not a more imaginative style can be encouraged is doubtful because the game is at the mercy of managers who can arrange a style to suit their team and the abilities of their players. Legislation through the rules is going to be problematic because policing something like the number of hand passes would be virtually impossible for a referee or official during a match.

New rules have often been introduced but haven't always been successful. A chief reason for this has been the astute strategies employed by the managers and the results are very mixed. For instance, the black card rule is extremely difficult to implement. A referee will be required to decide instantly whether a foul has been committed and what category the offence falls into and then what he has to do. This is an unfair imposition and threatens to leave referees, players and supporters confused.

There's too much analysis of the game which is coming up with the wrong results. Overall, the game is reasonably healthy with the exception, as I mentioned, of the over-use hand pass.

Michael Murphy captained Donegal to the All-Ireland in 2012. His goal in the final was sublime and one of the best I've seen.

Top players of the recent past

Everyone relishes the debate about who is the best player around at the moment or who was the best of a particular decade. For me, there's no doubt in my mind that Jim McKeever of my native Derry was the greatest of all and Greg Blaney of Down has been the outstanding footballer of the modern era.

He was a tremendous centre-forward, very much in the mould of Mick Higgins of Cavan from a previous time. What stood out for me with Greg Blaney was the way he could win possession and in a spilt decade get the rest of his forwards moving exactly where he wanted them.

Down's team of the 1990s was led by Greg Blaney and under his expert stewardship did very well to win two All-Irelands. They don't really compare, though, with the team of the 1960s which in my opinion is on a par with the great Kerry side of the 1970s and 1980s in the attractive style of football which they produced.

We have been fortunate here in Ulster to have witnessed some great teams and players during the past 25 years. The run of All-Ireland wins between 1991 and 1994 was brilliant, and then it was great to see Armagh coming in 2002 and then Tyrone in 2003, 2005 and 2008. Those teams played great football and, while they packed the defence, their tactic of counter-attacking at speed was extremely effective.

Now, of course, there's the case where full-backs and half-backs are scoring regularly, and even the goalkeepers are getting in on the act from frees. It's a vastly different from the past and in the modern view there have to be changes, primarily because managers are always striving to develop their teams and tactics.

It's obvious for example that Jim McGuinness has given the game great thought, working every possible scenario out within a game to great effect. He seems to be a very good man-manager and someone who has great respect for his players. That's extremely important and that ability to treat players fairly and evenly has been a quality possessed by all the great Ulster managers of the recent past like Mickey Harte and Joe Kernan as well. If a manager shows favouritism at all, then he's going to be in danger.

Of course, all of this is to the backdrop of failure resulting in dismissal from the post which is very unfair. Ultimately, what we have to realise is that the manager isn't playing. He prepares the team to the best of his ability, and yet he has to go in the ruthlessness of the situation when a team doesn't perform to the required standard. No matter how managers are sacked someone always takes the post again.

All of this produces some intriguing tussles at inter-county level. But I'd hazard a guess that few people will disagree with me about which match was the best I ever witnessed. Appropriately enough from a personal viewpoint, it's the meeting of Down and Derry in the 1994 Ulster Championship at Celtic Park because of the close affinity which I have for both counties.

On that occasion I was sitting in the broadcast box with Michael O and the game really was out of this world. Even at the time the winners were always going to win the All-Ireland. Derry were going for their second title and could have won only for Ciaran McCabe's goal which came at just the right time. Midfield was the key to that Derry team with Anthony Tohill and Brian McGilligan, who did most of the work.[4]

Their style was totally different from that of Jim McKeever who I would rank as the greatest ever. His gracefulness was perfectly captured in a painting by Brian Valleley which was present to Jim on the occasion of his retirement from St Mary's Teacher Training College. I went up especially to see it in Magherafelt and was very impressed.

The impact of unsettling rule changes

Each Congress brings about some new rule changes. While some have been positive for the game such as taking frees and sidelines from the hand, most have had the effect of proving unsettling on gaelic football.

Players are constantly having to adapt to some new suggestion. The black cards are the latest so-called innovation which have been introduced to try and stop persistent fouling. Why can gaelic football not be like hurling where the rules have remained more or less the same?

---

4 – The 1994 Ulster first round game between Down and Derry is widely regarded as the top match of the past two decades. It finished 1-14 to 1-12 for Down.

Caitriona Ruane, Northern Ireland Minister of Education with Tom Daly, Ulster Council GAA President and Ulster GAA Coaches, during a visit to Woodhall Kilrea, Co. Derry in 2009.

The biggest problem has been and continues to be the tackle. Our Parish Priest in Tullylish, Canon Trainor, trained St Colman's teams in the past and always maintained that there was a legitimate tackle in gaelic football. Skills such as the block or shadowing a player before knocking the ball out of their hand should be developed. At present, it's so disappointing to see a player with possession being unceremoniously pulled down. The prevalence of fouling is spoiling the game.

The saddest thing of all is to see a player catching a ball at midfield and then being surrounded by two or three players when he comes down and is penalised for over-holding. But the mark is a foreign notion and wouldn't be suited to the game.

Frees from the hands have speeded up the game in comparison to years ago when the ball was set down and valuable time was wasted waiting for the kick to be taken.

All of these changes are putting pressure on referees who have a multitude of decisions to make in spilt-seconds. Refereeing is a big issue and they are so scrutinised because every borderline decision is examined in minute detail. If a referee does have a bad game, then nothing shows his mistake up more vividly than television.

It is frustrating attending Congress annually listening to all these rule changes being discussed. The past Presidents generally do not get involved too centrally in the debate, although there would be interventions sometimes. Everyone gets up and says the same thing, which can be frustrating.

What worries me is that the majority of people attending matches are unaware of what exactly is going on.

How coaching has changed the face of football

Coaching was a dirty word for many years within the GAA. But a look at the newspapers today shows just how much things have been altered since the first coaching courses took place in the 1960s.

Daily I lift my newspaper and see advertisements placed by the Ulster Council and County Boards for a whole range of difference courses. Every week there are nine or ten sessions taking place. There could be 'shooting for scores' or 'how to tackle' and there's also the usual Foundation level and Level One qualifications. All of them are vitally important for the aspiring man or woman wanting to take a team.

Gone are the days when the trainer was the most important person for a county team and the success in reaching an Ulster Final or further resulted in the whole panel coming together for a training camp. I remember that there was great consternation caused when Joe Lennon began advocating the need for coaching nearly 50 years ago.

The belief that people would be paid for coaching in schools was totally out of the question. But one of the big factors was the realisation within the GAA that other sports were going into the schools introducing young people to their games. We were very badly behind as a result. With that came the challenge to get into the marketplace and compete because soccer and rugby already had paid coaches.

The belief that people would be paid for coaching in schools was totally out of the question. Now, of course, the amount of sessions being taken by full-time people means this whole area has changed immensely.

It would have been believed at the start that paid coaches would have been against the amateur ethos of the GAA. There was also a fear that it would introduce a foreign element into the Association. I remember Alf Murray launching a shocking attack on coaching at one of his speeches to Congress.

In addition to this, the changing face of schools was also an agent of change. Many teachers were no longer taking the time to organise football or hurling. Many of the lady teachers were perhaps reluctant, although I remember one school in Galway where a female teacher was out playing hurling and camogie with the pupils.

The change has been absolutely necessary and the schools look forward so much to the paid coaching coming on a weekly basis. In addition the county coaching officer will keep a check on how much coaching is being received by schools, and any alterations that might be needed.

It's the biggest new idea that I've seen within the GAA and now the wheel has turned full circle at the moment and everyone is coaching mad now. There are coaching officers and it gives me a certain satisfaction to see how Derry has been at the forefront of this growth. I was amused a couple of years ago when a coaching seminar was held in Down and the three people leading it were all from Derry.

Dr Eugene Young, Terence McWilliams and Tony Scullion have been doing great work in this area for a good number of years. They all came and shook hands with me, remarking on the great connection with the Oak Leaf county. The positive by-product is the number of people employed in coaching and I reckon there must be 100 working within the Ulster Council now.

The terminology in relation to coaching has changed so much. When I was teaching we were learning the boys how to play football and this work certainly wasn't called coaching even though that's what it was. I remember going as a sub-teacher to the Primate Dixon in Coalisland at one time and organising a small league on a Friday afternoon in a field beside the school. This was great for discipline because anyone who spoke out of turn during class was immediately warned that they could miss the football.

Coaching gives a great sense of achievement to the players and those taking the session. I used to relish seeing the enjoyment of some pupil who suddenly learned how to kick or catch the ball and then using their new skill in a game. They would be as pleased as punch!

But the big question is whether or not all this coaching makes a difference and if players are born or made. We have to believe that it does and I remember Eoin 'The Bomber' Liston starting out with Kerry as a very ordinary player. Mick O'Dwyer coaxed and developed him along.

James McCartan Jnr was a born footballer, even at U-12 and U-14 level in Tullylish. He had natural ability and it's usually quite easy to pick out both those with that inherent skill and the others who are struggling. It's with the later group that the coaching proves its worth.

Of course, the coaching has had an impact on how football and hurling are played. As a result, young players now have a much better idea of the basic skills rather than learning as they went along. There's the follow-on debate about the number of competitive games which should take place at U-12 or U-14 level.[5]

The problem is that the young players are naturally competitive while managers inevitably start thinking about league positions and so on. I think the idea of having no competition up to the age of 12 is worth pursuing in an attempt to instil in young players the need to enjoy their games rather than concentrating on a 'win at all costs' attitude.

As many young players as possible should be encouraged to participate. When I was taking Juvenile teams I arrived at the venue and immediately went to the other team

---

5 – Coaches are now employed on a full-time basis by the Ulster Council and the Co Boards. A range of specialist sessions are also held to educate those involved in coaching within clubs.

The Down team of the 1960s gather for a reunion in 2010, 50 years after their magnificent success.

officials to ensure that everyone on the field would be playing. Sometimes we'd be playing 17 or 18 a side. It's better than the constant call of "please sir can I go on now." If they got a kick at all, then their day was made. It's terrible that they should be denied the chance to play at such a young age.

Why hurling hasn't grown in Ulster

My hurling ability was never up to much, although there were a number of times when I did make some attempt to learn the skills. After a short while, I gave up and preferred to watch from the sidelines some of the greatest games and hurlers ever witnessed.

A few years ago, I was present when a statue was unveiled to Christy Ring in his home town of Cloyne. Just like at his funeral in 1979, the speech given by Jack Lynch was truly brilliant. I said to him "you put some work into that speech" and he said he just gave Bryan McMahon a call to put a few words together. Bryan McMahon was good at that stuff. "In the windswept hills of Tulla where the Claremen place their dead, three lonely trees stand sentinel above a hero's head." He also wrote a ballad on John Joe O'Reilly and I knew him well for many years. We used to meet in Dublin, always in book shops. He was great craic and very friendly and wrote some great material.

Christy Ring was regarded as the greatest hurler and I saw him play in the Railway Cup on a number of occasions. Paddy Buggy marked him and said he was like concrete because he was all muscle. The day after the match you'd be black and blue. He always went in for the ball.

Then there was the famous Tipperary full-back line Mick Roche, Carey and John Doyle 'Hell's Kitchen.' Doyle had a farm not far away from my friend, George Ryan. There's no doubt that the big Munster hurling matches were very physical and they expected and took the hits. There were no complaints. I went one time to Limerick to Tipperary and Cork and the place was jam-packed. Myself and Alf Murray went down and they are great occasions.

Hurling has changed very little when compared to football and perhaps the biggest evolution has been in the demise of the ground game. It's a wonderful site to have seen the best hurlers in place and I always retained a great interest.

Most hurling people would agree that it's a much better than football. The whole spectacle of a top hurling match is more impressive, the style is more direct. I took a friend of mine to a game on one occasion and he was astounded by the standard of the skills.

A hurling man is different from those involved in football. There is a tremendous camaraderie between all hurlers. I remember being in Limerick years ago and this man called me over to his table in an hotel. His pals were all fine hurling aficionados and met once a month to have a meal and play all the games over and over again.

George Ryan lives close to Latten-Cullen which is the home club of that great Tipperary star, Nicky English. George took me to a lake where there was a similar group who met monthly. If a top hurler dies his funeral is usually attended by current and former stars from throughout the country. Even the spectators are a breed apart in the way they mix even during the toughest game. There's no problems or trouble.

Sometimes I got far more enjoyment out of a hurling final, especially if there's no Ulster involvement in the football. I thought the Galway against Kilkenny final in 2012 was absolutely brilliant.

For all this, it's a disappointment that hurling didn't catch on in Ulster and the reason for this can be traced right back to the beginning of the 20th century. At that time, hurling was the dominant game here. There was a hurling team in Slaughtneill in 1915 which marched to the big day at the Carn which was addressed by Bulmore Hobson.

Derry won the Ulster title in 1903 when Inishowen had a great tradition. But for some reason the GAA revival in the 1930s didn't really provide the boost that might have been expected for hurling. Hurling wasn't mentioned and, while the reason isn't really know, it might have been something to do with the fact that BC Fay was a Cavan man and from a football background. Of course, the tradition remained in many pockets and it's interesting to look at the Derry team which won the Sam Maguire in 1993. That team contained a large number of talented hurlers, like Henry and Seamus Downey, Kieran McKeever, Brian McGilligan. If they had stuck to the hurling, their involvement would have filtered down to the clubs. After all, success breeds success.

One of the biggest problems we have here in Ulster is the absence of proper pitches. This is a major obstacle for young players who are trying to perfect their striking and is in sharp contrast to the billiard-table surfaces in the Golden Vale and the other top hurling areas.

The big thing is if hurling will ever change and I would be reasonably optimistic. Mid-Derry is now stronger than before and there have been great efforts made in Down with the non-Ards team. However, the hope that they would gradually develop hasn't worked. A lot of money was invested in the South Down team backed by Ballyvarley, Bellela and Laitroim. Eventually, it was envisaged that they would be of a sufficient   standard to play in a senior league against Ballycran, Ballygalget and Portaferry. But this turned out to be a bit of a fiasco because the players didn't have the same interest or commitment. A lot of people were against it due to the cost, but I tried to support the plan until I was persuaded that it had to be abandoned.[6]

Unfortunately, I don't think any of the other counties will ever reach the standard of Antrim, Down and Derry. Armagh were working very diligently for a while and making progress. However, that momentum seems to have been lost and part of the reason has to be the difficulty with dual players, especially when teams begin competing in league competitions.

Antrim have gone to great lengths to try and improve. But the travel for them is impossible. Two things which have prevented the development of hurling in Ulster are the grounds and apathy from County Boards. The grounds in the main strongholds are like bowling greens. They are perfectly kept and ideal for learning the skills.

Pitches in Ulster are generally football venues first and foremost. In addition, the County Boards are primarily involved in football. This is where all the money and interest goes.

Clubs commitments competing with inter-county scene

RECENT years have seen a big debate about the competing commitments of club or county football. The need to provide a regular programme of fixtures for club players is now viewed, and quite rightly so, as a primary requirement.

But the situation hasn't been helped by some county managers who over the past few years have decided to force the cancellation of club fixtures at weekends. This should not be allowed.

In some counties, like Down, the obstacle of counties preparing for big championship matches and clubs wanting their action to continue, has been overcome by what are called 'starred games.' It's positive that clubs have generally accepted this, and the policy has been maintained despite the occasional calls for further change.

---

5 – 6 - At the time of going to press, the Antrim under-21 hurlers reached the All-Ireland Final for the first time. This will be only the fourth occasion that a team from the county has played in one of the three main national deciders. The Minors reached the final in 1940, followed by the seniors in 1943 and 1989.

As a result, Down and other counties are able to continue with their games and ensure that the ordinary club player is getting action each weekend even when a county team is doing well. But there are problems, including when a club might only have one or two players on a county team and they are vital to their progress.

In Down this has been overcome by the top four and bottom four teams taking part in play-offs. But this, too, hasn't always been fair because a team might go through a long league campaign and win all their matches before finding that they have to compete all over again for the title. In lots of cases, the team which finishes top of the league doesn't end up winning it and that is the unfair part of things.

The big problem is, of course, the attitude of managers. Some of them are quite good at meeting the clubs, while others can be very dictatorial. This idea of county players not representing their own native area is a serious issue.

It remains to be seen whether a definitive solution can be identified or developed. I can't see a situation evolving something similar to rugby because that would entail professionalism. The average GAA club and county just couldn't afford the strong financial commitment to pay players.

The key difference between soccer and the GAA is that soccer clubs don't have facilities. Then, there's the up-keep needed to carry out maintenance and other works, along with rates, insurance and electricity which represent a constant drip on the finances. A massive effort is needed to raise that money.

A similar problem has developed in recent years in terms of the minor inter-county teams. If Down do well in the Ulster Minor championship, then adult and minor matches are called off a week before their next game. These young players are very fit and it's hard to see how they would be seriously affected by having to play a week before a county game.

The length of time before inter-county games is now a hot potato, although the All-Ireland Qualifiers are a bit of a rush. For Minors, I cannot see how they would be adversely affected. It's another example of the influence of managers and the managerial system has reached down to Minor level now.

There is always this fear of players being injured in club matches, yet they are as likely to receive a knock in training. I remember in the old days the county board picked the team and there was no talk of injuries at all or postponing club matches.

Any more inter-county matches than there is at present would be difficult to accommodate. We have the provincial championships, the All-Ireland Qualifiers, McKenna Cup, National League and then the Minor and U-21 grades. The next big move will be to tighten up the championship. In Ulster, there's only one game on a Sunday and to have a game in Ballybofey and another in Casement Park wouldn't affect

The decline of the Railway Cups, or inter-provincials to give them their official title, has been very disappointing.

the attendance in any way. I know that's an extreme example, but the championship stretching on isn't helping.

There is too much pressure on fixtures during the early months of the year. I haven't been a big fan of the change away from playing three rounds of the National League in the autumn. These games relieved that pressure and leave October and November as a barren spell, even though the club championships do fill the void to a certain extent.

Congress also debates the timing of the All-Ireland Finals and I think it must be the inherent conservatism within the GAA that prevents a change. The proposals are usually defeated without too much of a hearing and I think people have to agree that there would be an argument in favour of making that change.

Such a move would provide more time for club matches, leaving the whole of September, October and November for counties to complete their domestic championships.

The Railway Cups

One of my main GAA memories is that famous victory for Ulster in 1942 in the Railway Cup. The significance of that was clear at a time when few players from the province outside Cavan got the opportunity to play and win at Croke Park.

That's one of the reasons why I think it's an awful pity that the inter-provincials have failed to generate the same appeal as was the case during those halcyon days. On that famous day in 1942, Ulster emerged All-Ireland winners as it were. To win that title was tremendous. I also recall being in charge of the Ulster team during the early 1960s along with Mick Higgins of Cavan. Needless to say, he was the main man in organising things!

It's strange when you think back to that kind of interest that things have now dropped away to such an extent. However, the players do seem to be keen on representing their provinces. Paddy Heaney in the Irish News suggested that the competition be played on St Patrick's Day again as a curtain-raiser to the Club Finals and I think there would be merit in this.

But certainly the GAA has tried everything to breathe new life into the Inter-Provincials. They have gone foreign and it has taken place at provincial venues. Nothing has worked and the 2013 attendance of 2500 in Armagh for the football was pretty pathetic.

The Railway Cup final in the 1950s was the only opportunity which people had of seeing great players like Christy Ring. He was credited with helping to boost the attendances to the level which they enjoyed.

Of course, the difficulties being faced by the Inter-Provincials raise the question of whether competitions are organised for the players or based on attendances. We have to have some justification for competitions and interest and the numbers attending is crucial. While a large crowd isn't always necessary, if nobody goes to the game then why should the game be played.

I know well that some of the hurling competitions like the Lory Meagher and Nicky Rackard Cups don't attract sizeable crowds. It's different when you bring out the cream of the country's footballers and hurlers. Then, both they and the event in which they're participating deserve a reasonable interest.

Despite the concerns, though, I do believe that the Inter-Provincials will survive. My confidence is based on the fact that a strong number of people are in favour, and then the players have a big day.

The steep decline of the inter-provincials has been reflected by the equally impressive rise of the All-Ireland Club Championships and how these have brought the GAA right back to its roots in the 1880s and 1890s when clubs competed for the All-Ireland rather than counties.

A new dimension to this has been the All-Ireland Junior and Intermediate competitions. Allowing these to be played at Croke Park is great for clubs at those levels. About 40,000 attended the final in 1997 when Crossmaglen won the title.

The club championships began with clubs running championships within their own provinces. The popularity which these tournament games generated then sufficient interest to justify them becoming official. Of course, this was merely pushing an open door because there were so many of these unofficial competitions already taking place.

For a brief period in the early 1960s, I was involved in unofficially managing the Ulster team. This was the 1960 squad.

Our Rossa team from the 1930s and 1940s would definitely have fancied its chances if there had been an Ulster or All-Ireland Club at that time. We always did very well in tournaments all over Tyrone and Antrim, and that was after maybe playing a Derry League game earlier in the day. Those tournaments took in teams from all over Ulster and I remember playing Dundalk on the day that World War Two was declared.

Unfortunately, I haven't been able to get to as many of the All-Ireland Club Finals as I'd have liked. At my age you have to choose which games to attend because I'm not as fit as I was 50 years ago.

In Ulster, a club league has even been started to give players and officials from one county to meet teams of a similar standard from other counties. This has been facilitated by the ease of travel.

The separation between clubs and counties

We all know the routine of the door knocking on a cold winter's evening. Standing there will be two or three club men and women from a far-flung end of the province selling tickets for their latest fundraising initiative.

It is always a vivid illustration of the strength, commitment and loyalty which exists at grassroots level within the GAA. The amounts of money involved in running the association locally, providing equipment and fielding teams almost beggars belief. There are times when I have to take a deep breath when someone mentions that their club has 'just completed a big development and are only £100,000 in debt.'

Of course, the upkeep of these facilities for the long-term is a major issue and it comes in tandem with the requirement on clubs to support their individual county boards. My view is that there should be a greater onus on clubs to contribute financially to the long-term upkeep and sustainability of the many great GAA headquarters which have been constructed throughout the country, as well as the employment of coaches and the organisation of courses. The so-called centres of excellence have been made necessary for a variety of reasons, not least the understandable reluctance of clubs to let county teams train on their pitches, especially in the winter time.

Our club officials will undoubtedly object to such a suggestion. A couple of years ago Down began organising a draw which was made so attractive that clubs enthusiastically provided their support and it has been a great success.

The debate about how to engage clubs more effectively in the running of the county is particularly prevalent at the moment now that the GAA has become so organised. The full-time officials are working well and the county offices are a great point of contact for information and advice on filling forms and so on.

Members of the county board still view their individual clubs as number one. It's difficult to get the idea that the clubs are the county board and are running the GAA. Hopefully the fact that every club has a representative on county committees will in time lead to a more democratic association and a deeper understanding of the links between clubs and their county.

People will say that the opposite effect has happened. In Down, clubs do get an opportunity to air their views on issues like fixtures or any mistakes by the Competitions Control Committees. The system is fairly efficient at the moment, although there is no doubt that club football has suffered as a result of the greater emphasis on the county scene. Players are finding it increasingly difficult to combine the twin commitments, while the fear of injury means that their club suffers. Matt the Thresher played for the honour of the little village, but that type of distinction is gone.

The role of the Ulster Council

A visit to the Ulster Council headquarters in Armagh is a vivid illustration for me of how the GAA in the province has grown. It is far removed from the days when Gerry Arthurs ran the Association here almost single-handedly with a little help from people like myself.

Each week a series of courses are organised covering every conceivable aspect of GAA affairs. There is help for administrators at all levels, coaching courses and events specifically geared towards particular aspects of the games such as tackling or scoring.

Much of this growth has occurred under the guidance of the Ulster GAA Director and my good friend, Danny Murphy. The number of people employed at this level is amazing.

In days gone by, we were looked down upon, meetings were held in backstreets and there was active hostility from the authorities. But the GAA has now become respectable. It has proved its worth within society, and is a crucial part of so many communities.

I think we have now reached the situation where other organisations are looking at the GAA with a degree of envy. Afterall, a trip around any local area provides evidence of the immense work which has been and is being completed.

Other sports like soccer and rugby are hampered by their professionalism. The payment of players negates against investing in their sports at grassroots level. While they do present challenges to the GAA, our structures and physical development is superior.

It is amazing to reflect on the number of people employed within the GAA in Ulster. The recruitment into coaching of young players who have no job is a positive development.

Another major step forward has been in the organisation of the games. The hosting of the Dr McKenna Cup team during the pre-season in January has helped to increase its importance and boost revenue. The Ulster Club Leagues at Senior and Intermediate levels have also proved to be a welcome innovation. The meeting of teams from other counties has been an important benefit of this.

The big development at the moment is, of course, Casement Park and I still have the ticket for the original opening of the stadium in 1953.

That was a very significant development and which began as an effort to restore Corrigan Park. Then, Seamus McFerran, Ennis and Sean McGettigan began to run a weekly pool. The idea of Casement Park evolved. Sean Stinson and Seamus Clarke pushed the name of Casement Park. It was a great breakthrough because of the beautiful layout, the fine new stand and its location in the northern capital. The Ulster Council was very proud of this.

Now, the Casement Park development in Belfast will be a flagship not only of Ulster but also the whole association.[7]

In Ulster at the moment there are stadiums capable of holding around 15-20,000 supporters in each of the nine counties. Newry, Armagh, Omagh, Enniskillen, Celtic Park and Breffni Park are the main ones outside Clones and Casement. But less would have sufficed in all cases. It's a very big attendance if there are 10,000 people in Newry and lot of money has been invested for the venue to be filled just once every two years for an Ulster championship game.

---

7 – Casement Park is currently the focus of a major re-development planned for completion by 2016 which will it capable of hosting attendances of 40,000.

My only fear is in relation to the maintaining these venues in the next 10 or 20 years. The normal expenses of rates, electricity and grass cutting will be multiplied throughout every county. That was one of the reasons why I always encouraged clubs to reign in their ambitions. I cannot see Omagh, Armagh, Newry and Ballybofey being filled to capacity any more regularly.

Maybe we have had too much physical development. Things have changed and much more money is going developing the games. It's now time to ease off on the physical development and the same goes for clubs.

One area where physical development is welcome is in the provision of second or third pitches. The demand us so great at the moment that these are certainly required, what with the growth of ladies football and the large number of teams which have to be catered for in terms of training and matches. Ulster Council policy is now being geared towards this.

It's a long journey from South Derry, where the GAA's strength is, to Celtic Park and I think that venue would have been more suited to somewhere like Maghera. Owenbeg is also well away from the south of the county. Either Glen, Magherafelt or Ballinascreen could easily have been developed.

The other big departure has been the construction of GAA headquarters. It was something which I doubted initially, but this has worked well alongside the full-time secretaries. My only concern would be the burden that the upkeep of these facilities might present in the future. There will have to be rates paid, a caretaker employed and the grounds maintained to keep pace with the wide usage. All of this costs money.

As a past-Chairman of the Ulster Council, I retain a keen interest in our affairs and remain in regular contact with Danny Murphy. It's important that his staff have an affinity with the Association and its aims. Joan Cooney and the others in Croke Park a few years ago had a great knowledge of the issues and concerns of GAA members and I find the same level of expertise within the current Ulster Council employees.

There is a support structure for clubs at provincial and national level. Sometime ago, I visited the magnificent grounds of Eoghain Ruadh in Coleraine. They told me of the tremendous assistance which was received from the Ulster Council in terms of ensuring that legal documents were in order and accessing grants. To see the vibrancy of this club is great, because I remember Coleraine struggling to survive.

Their story of growth is one which is repeated all over Ulster. Long may it continue.

Paddy pictured with the late Seamus Heaney and George Shivers at Seamus Heaney's return to Bellaghy at a function in his honour in the mid 1990s

LIVING LIFE TO THE FULL

The MacFlynn Suite in Magherafelt

Almost 80 years ago in 1934, my brother Charlie and myself were in attendance at the first meeting of the Magherafelt O'Donovan Rossa club. It was a significant occasion, but none of us who were there could have envisaged our beloved Rossas have evolved and development.

Over the years, and right up until his death in 2000, Charlie retained a very keen and active interest in the club. My weekly visits home to Church Street were enlivened even more by hearing the latest happenings both on and off the field.

He was what you could describe as a 'bigoted Rossa man.' An interesting story centres on the now well-known District Judge, Liam McNally. He had been involved in the Rossas as well as being Charlie's solicitor. However, when Liam subsequently joined the Rainey Old Boys Rugby Club, Charlie decided to switch his legal allegiance. Leaving the Rossas was seen as being a heinous crime!

As well as being a talented player and official, in later years Charlie generously assisted the club financially and part of this contribution led to the development of the MacFlynn Suite. Charlie was often the first port of call when the club was struggling financially. He had a great interest in youth development and often purchased jerseys and medals.

The opening of this great facility took place in 2007. It was an occasion of great nostalgia for me, no least because Charlie wasn't alive to see it being opened. However, my brother Eddie and the rest of the family were all in attendance which was good.[1]

I was proud to have been there and to meet the surviving members of our 1936 Derry Minor team. As well as that, the chance to meet so many of the current members of the club - many of them sons and grandsons of my mates from the 1930s and 1940s, was very welcome indeed.

Everyone knew Charlie and I am referred to in Magherafelt as 'Charlie's brother' because everyone knew him. Unfortunately, there are no MacFlynn's in the town, with the result that it's only really the main officers in the club who realise my connection. But they have my £10 monthly contribution to Club Rossa.

Nevertheless, it's a great source of pride that the Rossas is currently such a vibrant club. The same can be said of many of the other clubs in South Derry who have grown so much since those tough early years.

My connections with other clubs in South Derry are also, thankfully, still strong. Slaughtneill and Bellaghy still regularly invite me back to functions on account of my role in helping to establish both clubs.

---

1 – The MacFlynn suite was opened in 2007 with the help of a sizeable donation from Charlie MacFlynn, who died in 2000 at the age of 82.

The past-Presidents gather for a photocall alongside the Liam McCarthy and Sam Maguire Cups. Pictured from left are Jack Boothman, Nickey Brennan, Joe McDonagh, Dr Mick Loftus, Sean Kelly, Christy Cooney, myself and Paddy Buggy.

Bosco O'Hagan presented me with a commemorative plate on one of my last visits to the Wolfe Tones. There is a very active Gaeltacht in Slaughtneill and a recent visit there co-incided with the presentation of certificates to local students. The clubs in South Derry like Slaughtneill, Swatragh, Magherafelt, Glen, Bellaghy have all great facilities. This list is by no means exhaustive.

Loup is probably the club with the greatest MacFlynn representation. This is ironic considering that it was the home area of my father, William J. The O'Kane's there are the related through their mother, Tess, a daughter of my uncle Barney. She married Roddy O'Kane and their son, Eugene, developed a very successful plumbing business. Another son was Sean O'Kane, the former Principal of St Pius in Magherafelt.

He was manager of a Derry Minor team which was playing Mayo. After the game the Mayo players were seen coming with pints of beer, something which Sean would never have permitted. If one of the Derry players had bought a pint, he would surely have poured it over them. Willie and Robbie Gribben - two of the famous Gribben brothers from Newbridge - also married two of the O'Kane sisters.

Meeting the Queen in Croke Park

MANY opportunities arose over the years to meet a variety of different signatories from all walks of life. In 2011, the latest of these was the Queen during her visit to Croke Park as part of a state trip to Ireland.

This, of course, was a highly significant event considering the relations between Ireland and England down through the centuries. It was in the weeks leading up to this that the tour of Croke Park became a reality. As a past President of the GAA, there was no doubt that I would receive an invitation to attend.

Whether or not to accept was an important decision and something which I gave much thought too. The simple fact of the matter was that our President, Mary McAleese, had invited the head of another state to come to Ireland. The GAA had then invited her to Croke Park and in my opinion it was only good manners to be there.

There was no other involvement in the visit of the Queen. Strangely, nobody ever uttered a word of criticism to me, although this was something which I had been anticipating. A lot of the northern delegates did not turn up and indeed took a dim view of the visit. Their views deserve respect considering the history, but staying away was not an option for me when I reflected on attending.

But my view was that this was now a different situation than if she had been visiting the north. In addition, Mary McAleese was an immense supporter of the GAA and I was keen not to let her down.

There was a large attendance of people in Croke Park on that occasion. Mary McAleese was a few steps behind the Queen and threw her arms around me and gave me a big hug in thanks for coming to Croke Park. She appreciated the fact of those from the north had made the effort to attend.[2]

It was extraordinary that one of the places to be visited by the Queen was Croke Park and I have no doubt that Mary McAleese had a large part to play in this.

Of course, while I made the decision to attend, I would have reached a different decision if the invitation had been to an event at somewhere like Hillsborough Castle. At Croke Park, a key factor was the fact that there was a guarantee of meeting the Queen.

That was a nice moment. I said to her "Your Majesty in seven years time, I will be expecting a letter and a cheque from you." She complimented me on my health at 93 and promised to make a note of my 100th birthday! The Duke of Edinburgh was much smaller than I had anticipated, in contrast to my expectation of a hefty big marine.

The event was held in the Hogan Stand and there was a certain amount of excitement and anticipation because it's not everyday that the chance arises to meet the Queen of England. Very few people get that chance, especially at somewhere like Hillsborough where she merely drives past. This was a chance in a million.

Of course, she wasn't the first head of state to visit Croke Park. The current Chinese President has been there prior to his election and the Prime Minister of Australia was at the 1993 All-Ireland Final – which unfortunately I missed.

---

2 – The Queen visited Croke Park as part of a tour of Ireland in 2011. She was invited by President Mary McAleese, who has remained a close friend of Paddy and visits him whenever possible.

Croke Park is an iconic stadium and the chance is there to showcase gaelic games in a way that was never really possible previously. During my Presidency, the chief rabbi was an annual attendee at the All-Ireland Finals, as well as the head of the Presbyterian Church.

That was always an important aspect of All-Ireland Finals as well as ensuring that they were properly catered for. There was also the task of avoiding any potential diplomatic incidents between ambassadors of countries which might be experiencing so. Liam Mulvihill used to have quite a task completing the seating arrangements. The ambassadors were always very keen to attend and see our top matches.

The GAA has become very good at spreading its wings and spreading the message of gaelic games. This was clear when Peter Robinson attended both the Dr McKenna Cup Final and also the Match for Michaela in late 2012. Martin McGuinness brought the First Minister over to me and introduced me to him. The whole night was very emotional and it was appropriate that someone like Peter Robinson was there to see exactly what the association means to people. Edwin Poots broke the mould and the fact that a DUP member was able to attend shows how much things have progressed. Obviously the next stage is for them to attend an Ulster Final, provided it's not played on a Sunday.

A lot of officials from the Northern Ireland Office attend major matches in Croke Park as has the Chief Constable of the PSNI, Matt Baggot. The good thing is that this isn't a very public thing any longer and that they are able to attend without fuss.

Staying grounded in Tullylish

A SOURCE of great pride for me during the past couple of decades has been the way in which the Tullylish club has gone from strength to strength. As their honorary president, my aim is to keep in touch with what's happening and attend as many meetings as possible.

Of course, the GAA was not always as strong in this local area. I remember attempting to initiate the formation of a team called Gilford Geraldines. However, there was great difficulty in obtaining a field and the team only last a couple of years. Each year the match between Gilford and Tullylish was inevitably a big local derby.

There was also a team known as St Patrick's Laurencetown which was formed in 1944 and was the main club when I arrived here in the early 1950s. The McCartans and Murphys were two main families involved. A lot of the people in the area had originally played for Ballyvarley or Banbridge until the formation of Laurencetown.

At that time there was a great connection with Lurgan and, despite being located in Co Down, many of the people supported Armagh.

The main challenge seemed centred on fielding a team and there appeared to be little desire to improve in other aspects of the association. It was during my first involvement with St Patrick's that I first came into contact with Billy Byrne, who became a lifelong friend.

Tullylish GAA Committee 2009 – Back row, left to right, M. McInearney, M. Millar, S. McDermott, S. Fegan, P. Drainey, J. McDermott, J. Conlon. Front row, left to right, G. Roberts, T. Rafferty, treasurer, P. McFlynn, president, S. McCartan, chairman, N. O'Dowd, secretary, E. Morgan, assistant secretary, K. Murphy, fixture secretary.

Eventually the two sections of the parish did amalgamate and it was decided to name it after Tullylish Parish in an attempt to entice players from all areas of the locality. That was an important decision because Laurencetown were proud of their achievements.

Then, it was in the late 1960s that I first became chairman of Tullylish. Canon John Trainor was someone who was very committed to the GAA and during the 1960s, the purchase of the current pitch was negotiated.

That was really when the club got on its feet. A small hall was constructed and then dressing-rooms and a second floor were constructed in the early 1970. Most of the work was done on a voluntary basis and I remember the work beginning on a Saturday morning. The initial plan was for just two dressing-rooms, but then the digger-driver said we'd be better making the whole site twice as big. So, a hall was constructed as well. Terence McCartan and Danny Purdy were two of the driving forces. Terence was the chairman and a great person for delegating and ensuring that work was completed. It was mainly through his effort that the hall and dressing-rooms were finished.

At that time, of course, there was only one team. However, a Minor team was started and my good friend, Mick Millar, was among those who helped start a reserve side. As in so many cases, the club really took off when the field was purchased.

The arrival of the McCartans from Glen really strengthened things and the Junior championship was won in 1968. Amazingly, one of the victories was over Gilford Geraldines who had been re-established.

But the biggest game was in the A-League In 1973 against Bryansford. Both teams were joint top of the main league, so this was a winner-takes-all meeting. Tullylish were also beaten in the championship. The main players were James and Dan McCartan and John Purdy and they won that A-League title. There is no doubt that both of them really gave their all when playing football for the club. In 1973, we were playing Newry Mitchells in the league and James was unable to field due to a sore back. However, when Tullylish were being beaten at half-time, James borrowed a pair of boots and came on for the second half to cause consternation. Newry were so busy watching him that they forgot about the other Tullylish players and we won the game.

James, Dan and John Purdy were among those from Donacloney which was within the Tullylish Parish. At one time I remember sending a car out to collect them for training and matches. It was something which certainly paid dividends in terms of strengthening the club.

Another big spell of development took place in the early 1990s and co-incided with Down's rise again at All-Ireland level. I became chairman in 1991 and a lot of work was done in improving and extending our facilities. Kevin Murphy was someone who was centrally involved.

At that time, my term as President had finished and I tried my best to help the club and develop the Juvenile set-up which has been very successful in the meantime. As the club advanced and began to field more teams, there was a need for additional space in terms of facilities. One thing that struck me was the commitment of the committee and others towards fundraising.

No matter who was chairman, I tried to offer them advice and support whenever possible. While my involvement was often limited by county board and central council commitments, I always retained a keen interest.

Apart from occasionally taking the team when the manager was absent, I never really got involved in the coaching end of things.

Winning a Down Scor title

ON-FIELD success has come occasionally for Tullylish. Now, while I am not one for blowing my own trumpet, one of the proudest moments arrived in Centenary Year in the GAA's Scor competition.

That year, 1984, saw us win the question time section and progress to the Ulster semi-final. Jimmy Curran, Colin McCusker and myself formed the team and I was particularly happy with being able to answer one question in the Ulster semi-final. The quizmaster was reading quotations from Eamon De Valera and recounted him asking what he was referring to when he said 'a terrible crime has been committed.' I was extremely happy to answer that the subject matter of the quotation was the murder of Kevin O'Higgins.

We had already won the first round in Ulster and were confident of reaching the provincial final. However, the question time could be a complicated event at that time because so much depended on the quiz master. Sometimes his questions suited us, as was the case in the Ulster first round. However, on the next occasion the quiz master seemed to concentrate on very obscure battles in Irish history which we hadn't heard off and proved all too difficult. No wonder, then, that we lost.

The same three of us participated in Scor on an annual basis. More success might well have come our way but for the fact that we always came up against the eminent Down historian, Shiela McAnulty. Her team were unbeatable, probably due to the fact that throughout the winter they met weekly to read and rehearse possible questions.

Our team was less diligent and we didn't train very much. The thing is, there was no substitute for preparations, especially when it came to questions like who had won the All-Ireland U-21 football title in 1976 or something similar.

Nevertheless, Scor was something which I enjoyed and the present practise of writing down the answers takes away from the suspense. The audience invariably prefers to see a team-member being put under pressure to answer. Now the system is very different.

To have won the Down title was a tremendous achievement which gave us all great satisfaction. The Tullylish club took part in Scor in what could be described as 'fits and starts.' The Monaghan family took part in the music and singing sections and Noel McEvoy in the recitation. There were many others, of course, as well who deserve great credit.

My involvement in Scor has continued and each year I attend the All-Ireland Final. This year's took place in Derry as part of the City of Culture celebrations and was very well run. The standard is always extremely high and the whole concept has been a tremendous addition to the GAA's activity.

Tony Williamson and a man called Derry Gowan from Fermoy in Co Cork were among those centrally involved in starting Scor in Down. The event began as an inter-county quiz and it gradually grew from that. Perhaps, though, another revamp now might be appropriate because the county, Ulster and All-Ireland Finals can be quite prolonged. During my time as President I suggested reducing the number of items to six.

Forging forward with Tullylish

THE retirement of players such as James and Dan McCartan and John Purdy led to the demise of the great Tullylish team which won the league and came so close in the championship in the early 1970s. But the club was now on a firmer footing and the arrival of a new generation of McCartans definitely helped.

James McCartan first started playing with us as a young boy and was an immediate addition. I also recall collecting him for training and matches and I remember on one occasion Paddy Buggy, who was President at the time, remarking on how good a footballer James was.

The U-12 team which James was on won the county title. They progressed through the ranks to represent the club at senior level. They held their own, without crossing the finish line as champions.

We have a rule in the club where anyone who wants a transfer is granted one whether they are entitled or not. The transfer request came from James to Burren and it became very complicated at a later stage. Tullylish, however, took no part in what happened subsequently and my outlook was that if a player wants to go it's better to grant the request because he's not going to make himself available in any case. The application had been received and the decision to grant the request was made.

Another good player from Tullylish was Joe Byrne who also represented Down and was on the team which reached the National League final in 1983.

A big advantage was our youth structure and a priority was as always to ensure that players from Gilford involved. There was a lot of hard work and effort put into coaching the skills and at the moment this appears to be paying off.

New and young men are now forging forward for Tullylish and I am watching their progress with great interest. The club is in good shape and has just purchased a new field which will soon be developed. Some of the club officials were reluctant to finish the deal due to the cost, but I was keen to encourage them because this land is absolutely vital to the club's continuing prosperity on the field. With so many teams at the moment in at youth and adult level and ladies, the additional space is imperative Put simply, we couldn't afford not to buy it.

Under the management of Mark Harte, the senior team is currently doing well in Division Two of the Down League.[3] As well as that, there is a reserve team and teams at the various youth agegroups from Minor down to U-8. There are also two ladies teams.

A significant achievement was in 2010 when the Intermediate title was won. That team was captained by John McAreavey[4] and a few months later he got married to Michaela Harte. Of course, she had been around the club a lot for a number of years at that time and I got to know her reasonably well.

3 – The Tullylish senior team are currently in contention for promotion. They are managed by former Tyrone Minor, U-21 and senior medalist, Mark Harte.

4 – John McAreavey captained Tullylish to their Intermediate title in 2010. A well-known photograph shows him lifting the trophy watched by his future wife and also Paddy.

It is impossible for me to add to all that has been said about her since her very tragic murder in 2011. She used to arrive with her future husband, John, to any functions which were held in the club. I found her to always be very amiable and friendly, and someone who spoke with everyone.

The two of us spoke in Irish and liked the language immensely. Michaela was a tremendous influence on the whole Tullylish club and team and the heart and soul of everyone here went out to John and the two families at her death. This was evidence in the very active part taken by so many within Tullylish at the funeral.

I have great respect for Mickey Harte and was particularly impressed a number of years ago when he addressed our annual dinner and never mentioned Tyrone or the Sam Maguire. His full focus was on the importance of the local club, the work that is being for the community within clubs and the help required. He remained on that theme and had obviously given the matter much thought.

In all my time involved with the GAA, I was never at such an emotional night as the Match for Michaela in Casement Park. To think that people were there from all over Ireland speaks volume. It was a great tribute to a very personable woman who was intent on becoming actively involved in the club.

Her brother Mark is now manager of the Tullylish team and their prospects for promotion are currently very good. My vision is that the club will continue to expand with a good committee and facilities which are available for all members. Maybe in a few years, we can establish ourselves again at senior level and perhaps win that long-awaited county title.

As someone who has been involved for a long number of years and have seen the difficulties, the rate of progress is extremely satisfying. It is now becoming an accepted part of the community and this was evidenced at the La Na nClub celebrations in 2009.

It won't be the lack of men which let us down, but the lack of ideas. An appropriate slogan for any and every club.

A regular duty for me at both the Tullylish and Down Conventions is to preside at the election of officers. As President, I always have the pleasant first task of re-electing myself. This inevitable generates some laughter among the delegates present.

George Tinnelly and TP Murphy preceded me as Down President. When TP died, a number of clubs proposed that I should replace them. The role does not involve an awful lot of work and technically speaking the post of President does not exist within the Official Group. I have followed the example of George and TP by attending the county meetings. My contributions are few and far between, although there are occasions when I might intervene or provide an opinion when asked.

A proud moment as I cut the ribbon to officially open the commemorative wall at the Tullylish clubrooms.

Living life to the full

Regular visitors to my home in Laurencetown keep me updated on the latest events both in the GAA world and elsewhere. They are too numerous to mention, but suffice to say that their friendship is very much appreciated.

Each year I have tried to attend a range of GAA activities. It was Derry's year in 2013 and the annual congress, All-Ireland Feile and Scor na Og were events which highlighted the progress which the GAA has made within the county and brought me much enjoyment and satisfaction.

This was also emphasised when at their special 125th anniversary event in May. Many of those who have been involved in the association over the years were in attendance and expressed their views on the major events and matches which have enlivened all our lives during this period.

I have been fortunate that the re-development of Croke Park has facilitated my continued attendance at the All-Ireland football and hurling finals. There is a great sense of enjoyment and excitement in the build-up to these showpiece occasions. The changes with the 1930s and 1940s when I began attending are almost unbelievable.

In Down, too, my interest in how the GAA continues to develop is very keen. The work of so many people has transformed the organisation of gaelic games and culture and the numbers of young people participating is testament to the efforts of our volunteers within the association.

There can be no doubt that the GAA will continue to grow and developed in the future, just as it has done since my first involvement in the Magherafelt of the early 1930s.

The GAA has provided me with many happy moments and friendships which I will always remember. From Church Street to Laurencetown and all the milestones in between, it really has been a life lived to the full.

EPILOGUE

Paddy MacFlynn
An appreciation by former GAA Director General, Liam O Maoilmhichíl
Paddy and I

I was a member of the Central Council from 1971 and I knew Paddy from meeting him at Congresses over the years, but with his election as President-elect in 1978, I got to know him very well. He attended the official opening of our Club Park in Kenagh in that year and got to know all the members of my family. From an early stage, I noticed that he had a marvellous recall of facts, stories and places and he was able to rhyme off the names of all my nine brothers and sisters and recognised each one of them individually.

Paddy and I had a lot in common in that we were both Primary school teachers, we shared an interest in novels and books on Irish local history and we both had a strong commitment to Irish language and literature. When I first met Paddy's wife, Kathleen, I discovered that she also had a great interest in education and literature, but she opted out of the GAA and the Irish language debates. Kathleen and Paddy made an ideal couple in that he was extremely talkative and approachable, while she was more reserved and reticent, but she was a master of the apt phrase to end a discussion and her broad range of knowledge was astounding. I learned from Kathleen that the family and locals knew him as Pat, but Kathleen always referred to him by surname only if she was annoyed about something! Anyhow, I continued to use the name Paddy in all my dealings with him.

As far as I know, Paddy was the first GAA President to have a driver available to him and Billy Byrne was an exceptional person with an extraordinary degree of loyalty and of commitment to making a success of Paddy's term as President. He never complained about the length of a journey or of the lateness of the night and he always remained in the background during the proceedings. However, on the way home in the car, Billy came into his own as he gave a critique of the whole night's events. Billy's own style of speaking was brief and to the point and he had an abhorrence of long-winded speeches; if Paddy erred in that regard, he could anticipate a tongue-lashing on the way home.

I often marvelled at how critical Kathleen and Billy were of Paddy's speeches at times, but Paddy enjoyed the feed-back and was prepared to take any amount of criticism in good humour. This was a priceless gift for a GAA President, as he has to listen to a lot of complaints of one sort or another about the games and the events surrounding them. Paddy had the extra pressure of being President at a time of extraordinary bitterness and divisiveness among the Nationalist and the GAA community arising from the H Block hunger-strikes and the tensions and violence that were a part of life in the North at that time.

To revert to our early meetings, the position of Ard-Stiurthóir was advertised in early

1979 and I applied at the last minute for the position. I was called to Croke Park for an interview and the first person I saw when I entered the interview room was Paddy. He was accompanied by Con Murphy and three external people and Paddy's role was obviously to observe, as he didn't ask me any questions. Also, despite my friendship with him, he has never divulged anything to me about the deliberations of the appointments committee.

In April of 1979, I was appointed as Ard-Stiurthóir and I took up the position formally on 1 June of that year, but I was working closely with Paddy from the start of his Presidency. From now on, our relationship was going to be a very close one, as it always is between a President and a Director General. A highlight of the start of our working together was the visit of the Pope to Ireland, and we both had a very prominent position for the Papal Mass in the Phoenix Park.

Working Relationship

From the beginning, we struck up an excellent working relationship and enjoyed the various problems and issues that came our way, as we had a habit of teasing out all the issues very thoroughly and of coming to a joint decision. Despite the age gap between us, I never felt that Paddy tried to be in control but he was prepared to listen to all sides of an argument and he invariably looked for a consensus. As Paddy was the first President-elect and had worked with Con Murphy for a year, Con was inclined to give advice to him on a wide range of issues and Paddy invariably listened and came to a decision eventually on the basis of our joint discussion. It wasn't unknown for Con to get on to me if he failed to convince Paddy of something, as he was a member of the Management Committee and Central Council for a year after the end of his own term as President, but we generally stood by our decision.

For me, it was ideal to be taking over as Director General with such a kind, considerate and knowledgeable person, who at this stage had served the Association with such distinction in his native county of Derry and in his adopted county of Down. Even though I was careful by nature, I would have been a little more hot-headed than Paddy and he taught me to take my time in coming to a decision, which served me well in later years. If there were a major issue on which the media were baying for a comment, Paddy used to advise leaving them until the following day, as there would be no shortage of other people prepared to comment, and by the time the issue was addressed on the following day the story was dead and forgotten.

A measure of how kind and friendly Paddy was with everyone is that he made it his business to speak to anyone and everyone who came into contact with him and all the staff of the office loved him. My secretary in the first few years was Máire Ní Dhrisceoil from Cork and both she and her successor, Siobhán Ní Chuana were and are great friends of both of us. Máire went home to Cork to Cill na Martra and raised a fine family, one of whom is Noel O Leary the Cork footballer. Joan, who is also from Cill na Martra, took over from Máire and was my Rúnaí Pearsanta for the remainder of my term working in Croke Park. She is still working in Croke Park and is admired by all.

The other major impact Paddy had on me was in regard to knowing people and how he treated them. He had an unbelievable collection of friends from every county and from overseas and he had the gift of being able to know them all personally and of knowing their spouses and family members. No matter what issue was being discussed or how fraught and animated the debate, Paddy treated everyone with respect and with dignity. On a few occasions, he was badly treated at public meetings during his Presidency and I wanted to take the matter up at the Management Committee or Central Council, but he vehemently opposed me and said that the people involved had damaged themselves more than they had hurt him.

While Paddy came to Croke Park about three times a week, I also paid numerous visits to him at The Laurels and got to know every one of the Ulster counties very well as a result. He enjoyed setting off on a trip to show me places I hadn't visited and to give me a lesson on the history of the area. One trip, however was special for him and that was the visit to Magherafelt to his home place and to speak with his family members. He also loved introducing me to Mugsy Keenan and various other people who were childhood friends and acquaintances.

Canon Treanor was the Parish Priest in Tullylish at this time and he travelled frequently with Paddy and Billy to the big games in particular. Paddy put great trust in the Canon, in particular in regard to the playing rules of Gaelic Football and in regard to all aspects of refereeing. I discovered from my visits to the Laurels that the Canon put an equal amount of faith in Kathleen as an adviser in regard to various aspects of parish affairs. As a result the relationship was equally beneficial to the GAA and to the parish.!

I mentioned Alf Murray earlier and another former President that Paddy really admired was Hugh Byrne of Wicklow. In those days there were receptions for the four teams and officials on the morning after the final, and Hugh invited Paddy and myself to his home in Rathcoyle to relax on the Monday evening after the reception. We went for a long bracing walk accompanied by Hugh and his dogs and we came back home to tuck into a beautiful meal prepared by his wife, Rose. We enjoyed this so much that we repeated it for all three years of Paddy's Presidency.

Help in my role as Director General

As I have already indicated, Paddy was a very tolerant and experienced administrator and I valued greatly being able to tap into his wealth of knowledge, which was always given in a non-critical and very generous fashion. He was able to provide contacts who would advise me in the event that he hadn't the personal information or expertise required. At the outset of our term, we agreed that I would be responsible for the administration of the Association through the work of the head office in Croke Park and the Provincial and County Secretaries, while he would be the public face of the organisation, and would attend functions all over the country.

All the Presidents prior to Paddy were part-time and attended to their GAA role mostly at night and at week-ends, but Paddy retired from teaching and made his role a full-time one. With the help of Billy Byrne he was able to go to events at County and at Club level that Presidents before him could not do to the same extent. This travel was a great boon to me, as Paddy was such a good listener and a very astute observer and he was able to advise me in a non-confrontational way of issues that were being raised at the grass roots that needed to be addressed. The most important impact of his visits, however, was that he gave a great boost to the people who were working at Club level and his well chosen words of praise gave encouragement to many a Club official to redouble their efforts on behalf of their Club : thereby increasing the strength of the whole Association.

Paddy was a very meticulous note taker and he was a great one for recording all meetings in his own schoolmaster's handwriting. As a chairperson, he was businesslike and very patient in giving everyone an opportunity to speak, while he had a good ability to summarise a debate.

While Paddy wasn't critical of people in public, he was a great one to sum up a person and he gave me very good advice on numerous occasions about people I was dealing with at that time. Down to the present, I am still in receipt of advice from him and I value it as much now as in the period of his Presidency.

Significance of his Presidency

As I referred to already, Paddy was the first President to devote himself full time to the role, and the protocol he established of visiting schools, attending Club and County functions and of visiting officials in their homes has stood the test of time and is still being followed at the present time. Paddy was the ideal man to build on and enhance the relationships with the major Association sponsors, which had mostly been established during Con Murphy's term as President. Paddy was so well informed and prepared to speak on any topic that he was in his element in meetings with Frank O Rourke and Jim Whitty of Bank of Ireland, who were the then sponsors of the All Stars; with Jerry Mc Auliffe and Pat O Mahony of AIB Bank, who were the sponsors of the Club of the Year Awards; and with John O Connell and Jim Whelan of Coca Cola, who were the sponsors of Féile na nGael. The Banks did cause one major embarrassment to Paddy when he was speaking at a gala function of one of our major sponsors and proceeded to thank the other Bank twice in the course of his speech!

In GAA terms, Paddy's hero and most important mentor was the late Alf Murray, who had made a major impact on the Association as President in the 1960's and who lived just down the road from him in Lurgan. Paddy said to me at the start of his Presidency that he would be very pleased if he was considered to have done half as good a job as Alf-this was a mark of how highly he rated him, but Paddy went on to make his own very considerable contribution. Alf, however, gave much valued advice to Paddy and to myself, during these years.

Undoubtedly, the major contribution that Paddy made was that he steered the Association safely through the stormy period of the Hunger Strikes, when feelings were running very high in the North among people who felt that the GAA should show more sympathy towards the strikers, while most of the membership in the rest of the country favoured a measured and a limited role. This left the leadership of the Association in an impossible situation, which wasn't made any easier by the lack of response from Westminster to attempts to intervene behind the scenes. This period was an awfully difficult time for a person from the North, and it was a lot more difficult for Paddy, because he was such a public and a well known person. In addition to the H Block crisis, there was ongoing tension caused by the occupation of GAA property by the British Army, in particular Crossmaglen, and this also had to be handled very sensitively.

It will always be to Paddy's credit that the GAA remained united during this traumatic period, and it wouldn't have been possible but for the presence of a Northern person of such stature as President and the great patience he showed in dealing with those who put him under severe pressure to back a more interventionist stance. At this period, Paddy's friendships were sorely needed and he was able to call on the right people to control the influence of certain people within and outside the Association.

I believe it was the influence of Alf Murray that caused Paddy to give such wholehearted support to various schemes aimed at increasing the involvement in Hurling throughout the country, while he saw Féile na nGael as an ideal vehicle to help encourage more young participants to concentrate on improving their skill levels at the game. Another former President, Séamus O Riain had founded Féile na nGael and Séamus was always ready to lend his support to the Féile activities.

Paddy also gave great support to the Irish language during his period as President and he never failed to make his annual pilgrimage to the Donegal Gaeltacht despite the demands of his presidency.

Despite his kind and friendly manner, Paddy could lose his temper on an odd occasion, and he was able to give a strong tongue lashing when required. Invariably, he would ask me afterwards if he had gone too far in his condemnation, and if I answered in the affirmative, he would be full of remorse. However, this happened most infrequently and he never enjoyed it.

Our Latter Friendship

When Paddy's period as President came to an end, he was very careful not to interfere in the day to day running of the Association, but he was always available to give advice or practical help, if called upon. He loved his visits to Croke Park for meetings of the former Presidents or for the major games and it was always a pleasure to meet him on these occasions. If a glass of red wine was available-preferably a Fleurie- the humour was all the better and the stories flowed. As I mentioned already, Paddy was a voracious reader and he enjoyed supplying me with cuttings from local papers about GAA affairs and he would have his pile of books to hand to show me what he had read recently or what he would next be undertaking. When we met, he liked nothing better than to discuss family and other acquaintances and the meetings could go on for hours.

Kathleen's sudden illness and death was a huge blow to him as they were a really united couple and she was forever driving him to do something new. She was a perfect foil for him and her passing was a huge loss to him and to all who knew her. While she took no direct involvement in the GAA, she was very well acquainted with the happenings of the day and Paddy always listened carefully to what she had to say.

The other great blow of recent years was the sudden death of Billy Byrne, as Billy was a great friend and ally of Paddy and of Kathleen. He was a fixture in the Mac Flynn household and was always ready and willing to give help if required. The time and energy that Billy gave to helping make Paddy's presidency so successful was a perfect example of the amateurism and the voluntary ethos of the GAA in action.

Despite the losses referred to, Paddy kept up the interest in the GAA and in all its affairs, and while illness began to take its toll, it didn't prevent him from getting to the major events up to a matter of weeks ago . The last time I met him outside the North was a couple of months ago when he insisted on attending the funeral of the former President, Paddy Buggy, because he held him in very high regard. For that outing he was driven by Seán Og Mc Ateer, but Kevin Murphy and Mickey Keenan also took him to various parts of the country. He often talked about his surprise at the lengths to which people were prepared to go to help him, but I said it was a tribute to him and to his caring personality.

When I retired from my job in 2008, I had more time to visit him and took him out for lunch on a number of occasions. On my first visit after my retirement we went to a local restaurant for lunch and the red wine was of such a high quality that Paddy really appreciated it, but Alfie didn't see the fun in it when he had to put Pat back into bed in the middle of the night. From then on I was warned to give no more than one glass of wine with his lunch!

During the most recent stay in Lurgan hospital, the meitheal of people prepared to help at the Laurels was extraordinary and affairs were controlled by Margaret as if the Master himself were in control.

Críoch

Fear iontach uasal, macánta isea Pádraig Mac Floinn agus bhí an t-ádh orm gur tháinig mé trasna air agus go raibh mé cairdiúil leis thar tréimhse de cúig bhliain agus triocha (ag an bpointe seo). Is léir i gcónaí go mbíonn suim aige i ndaoine, go mbaineann sé ard-taitneamh as bheith ag éisteacht le scéalta agus ag scéalaíocht agus gur duine lách, flaithiúil é a théann go mór i bhfeidhm ar aon duine a chuireann aithne air don chéad uair.

Nuair a théann tú siar ar an saol a bhí ag Pádraig, is féidir a rá go raibh saothar iontach rathúil mar mhúinteoir bunscoile, mar pheileadóir den scoth, mar oifigeach den Choiste Chontae i nDoire agus i gContae an Dúin, mar bhainisteoir ar an teach tábhairne,mar Uachtarán ar an gCumann Lúthchleas Gael, agus mar gníomhaí deonach ina pharóiste áitiúil agus ina chumann áitiúil den CLG aige, agus thairis san ar fad, ba fear céile grámhar, dúthrachtach, dílis é dá bhean céile, Kathleen.

Tá áthas orm gur tugadh an deis dom na smaointe fánacha seo a chur ar fail don bheathaisnéis seo ar dhuine de na fir is léannta agus is flaithiúla atá ina chónaí sa timpeallacht seo.

BIBLIOGRAPHY

Interviews with Paddy MacFlynn between October 2012-August 2013.

The Paddy MacFlynn papers and correspondence
in the Cardinal O'Fiach Library and Archive, Armagh.

Scrapbooks kept by Paddy MacFlynn covering his time as President of
the GAA, 1979-1982.

Photographs in the MacFlynn family archive, courtesy of Rory
MacFlynn and Paddy MacFlynn.

Old photographs of Magherafelt courtesy of Muriel Bell, Magherafelt.

GAA photographs courtesy of Sportsfile.

The Magherafelt GAA History, published 1988.

Photographs in the Cardinal O'Fiaich Library and Archive.

Main front cover photograph courtesy of GAA Museum, Croke Park.

Tullylish GAA photographs courtesy of Tommy Morgan,
Tullylish GAA club.

Photographs of Magherafelt GAA courtesy of Enda Quinn,
Magherafelt GAA club.

Derry 1947 National League winning team,
courtesy of Chris McCann.

The Evolution of the GAA in Ulster. Edited by Donal McAnallen,
David Hasson and Roddy Hegarty, 2009.

The Ulster GAA Story 1884-1984 by Con Short.

Front cover images:
Paddy MacFlynn's official portrait as President (above)
Telegram to Paddy MacFlynn requesting silence at Croke Park following death of Kevin Lynch.
Presentation to the Offaly captain after 1981 All-Ireland senior hurling final.

Back cover images
MacFlynn's Bar, Church Street, Magherafelt.
The Tullylish GAA club crest.

ABOUT THE AUTHOR

Alan Rodgers is a native of Beragh in the heart of County Tyrone and
has been involved with the GAA since getting into football and
handball at primary school. Later he was instrumental in starting
hurling within the Red Knights club. He served as club Secretary from
1999-2002 and is presently a member of the club Executive. A
journalist by profession this is his fourth book. Alan began his career in
Church Street, Magherafelt, the birthplace of Paddy MacFlynn.

BY THE SAME AUTHOR

Down from the Cross - A GAA Journey - 2006
Forever Young on the Fields of Moy - A 100 year history of Moy Tir Na nOg - 2008
Real Horses and Replicas - Stories from Mid-Tyrone -2011